£2-50

Robert Farquharson,

THE SENSE OF
THE PRESENCE OF GOD

THE
SENSE OF THE
PRESENCE OF GOD

Gifford Lectures, 1961-2

by

JOHN BAILLIE

OXFORD UNIVERSITY PRESS

LONDON   TORONTO

1962

Oxford University Press, Amen House, London E.C.4

GLASGOW NEW YORK TORONTO MELBOURNE WELLINGTON
BOMBAY CALCUTTA MADRAS KARACHI LAHORE DACCA
CAPE TOWN SALISBURY NAIROBI IBADAN ACCRA
KUALA LUMPUR HONG KONG

Printed in Great Britain by
Morrison and Gibb Limited
London and Edinburgh

CONTENTS

v

Foreword

Among the many deep regrets experienced by his friends on hearing of the death of Principal John Baillie on September 29, 1960, was the disappointment that he would not now deliver his Gifford Lectures in the academic session 1961–62. We knew that he had been preparing them for some considerable time; he had read excerpts from his provisional material to the Edinburgh Theological Club; and every indication pointed to the series being both distinguished and exciting. When, therefore, Professor Torrance and I, at the invitation of the Gifford Committee of Edinburgh University and by the kind permission of Mrs Baillie, Dr Baillie's widow, read the manuscript through, we were more than delighted to be able to report that it was in completed form both for the purposes of the lecture series and for publication. Even the summaries to be presented to the Press for each lecture had been meticulously written out. Indeed, so thoroughly was the manuscript revised that no editing whatsoever has proved to be necessary. The Gifford Committee, under the Convenership of the Principal of the University, Sir Edward V. Appleton, G.B.E., K.C.B., LL.D., F.R.S., decided to accord the prepared lectures the status of Gifford Lectures and in this way to recognize their worthiness to stand within that eminent tradition. For those who are already acquainted with Dr Baillie's writings, those lectures will have a particular interest. They show how to the very end of his life he actively maintained his concern with contemporary problems, and how clearly he continued to state the great certainties of the faith in the context of a changing intellectual environment. There could scarcely be a finer conclusion to a life of such academic brilliance, theological literary achievement and profound Christian devotion.

JOHN MCINTYRE

Edinburgh, 1961

Acknowledgements

The quotations from the following works are included by kind permission of the publishers mentioned:

Karl Barth, *Church Dogmatics*: T. & T. Clark, Edinburgh;
Gilbert Murray, *Essays and Addresses*: George Allen and Unwin Ltd., London;
P. H. Nowell-Smith, *Ethics*: Penguin Books Ltd., London;
Reinhold Niebuhr, *The Nature and Destiny of Man*: James Nisbet and Co. Ltd., London; Charles Scribner's Sons, New York;
W. G. Pollard, *Chance and Providence*: Faber & Faber Ltd., London; Charles Scribner's Sons, New York.

The Author's widow and the Publishers would like to express their gratitude to Professor T. F. Torrance and to Professor John McIntyre for reading through this series of lectures initially, and for giving them the assurance that the lectures were suitably prepared for publication. And they are particularly indebted to Dr McIntyre for his great kindness in seeing them through the press, and for the work involved in reading the proofs.

CHAPTER I

Knowledge and Certitude

§ 1

The candidate sat staring at the sheet of questions placed before him by the examiner, but not writing anything. 'What ails you?' asked the examiner. 'The questions are too difficult,' replied the candidate; 'I cannot answer them.' 'Well,' said the examiner, 'put down what you know.'

Hearing this told, it occurred to me that perhaps I also ought to put down what I know, but the attempt made me realize afresh how limited my knowledge is, nor did I find it by any means easy to define these limits. Hence arose the following reflections.

Many of the questions put to me, and not least those I am accustomed to put to myself, I just cannot answer at all, and many others I can answer with only a low degree of assurance. But it would seem that to know is to be quite sure. You would laugh if I said 'I know he is a Frenchman, but I am not quite sure', or 'I know there was a frost last night, but I'm not certain'. Knowledge, then, implies certitude, complete assurance. On the other hand, this does not exclude the possibility of probable knowledge in the sense of knowledge *of probabilities*. There is no contradiction in saying that I can be certain of a probability or a likelihood; for instance, that of the next thousand babies born in this city some are likely to be boys and some girls; or that if I plant my vegetable garden at the usual time this year, some at least of the seeds are likely to germinate; or that of the next hundred men I ask a question, some are likely to be more strictly truthful in their answer than others. Furthermore, however, I should hold that such knowledge of the probable behaviour of things implies some certain knowledge, however limited, of the things themselves.

If this were not so, we would have to say that the natural sciences do not yield any knowledge of nature, and so to exclude them from the realm of knowledge altogether (as indeed Plato wanted to do for a somewhat different reason); for it is generally agreed that a high degree of probability is the most that can be claimed for any scientific result. Again, to say that knowledge implies certainty does not mean there are not different degrees or levels of knowledge, for there is clearly a difference between knowing something less well and knowing it better. If you ask me whether I know John Smith and the town he lives in, I may answer: 'Yes, I know both, but I know neither very well.' What is implied is only that if I have no certitude at all in regard to either, I cannot be said to have any knowledge of them.

I have spoken both of certitude and of certainty, and perhaps it is well to follow Cardinal Newman in maintaining, as far as may be, a distinction in usage between the two words, applying the former to the state of mind of the knowing subject and the latter to the propositions he enunciates.[1] Yet, if we do this, we must remember that neither word has any meaning except with reference to the knowing subject. Certitude would mean such an assurance as leaves no room for doubt in the inquiring mind, while certainty would mean the character accruing to a proposition through its being supported by such evidence as makes it impossible for the inquiring mind to doubt it. The realities with which the inquiring mind is confronted are themselves neither certain nor uncertain; they simply are.

Plato did us a great service in insisting on the difference between assured knowledge and mere opinion, and this service remains even when we are unable to agree with him as to the relative incidence of the two. Yet I fear I still introduce many of my utterances with the words 'I know that' or 'I am sure that', when I have no real right to do so. Plato's Greek word *doxa*, which I here render as opinion, really means seeming, being cognate with the expression 'It seems to me that'; and

[1] *A Grammar of Assent* (1870), chap. VI. 2.

there is a multitude of sentences which I have full right to introduce with that phrase but which fall far short of assured knowledge. It is my duty as well as my necessity to form opinions. But to opine is not to know.

Some indeed have said that all pretended human knowledge is mere opinion, that there is nothing of which any of us has a right to be sure. It was even said of one such that 'the consciousness of a single certainty would have lain as an intolerable burden upon his mind'. Such a view was, as we know, widely canvassed in a late period of Greek thought, not least in Plato's own Academy after his death. To be consistent, of course, all that such sceptics could affirm would be, not that there is no certainty, but that it is not certain whether or not there is; and the best of them were sufficiently clear-minded and self-critical to realize this. The same view is still frequently reaffirmed, as by Professor Ayer in his *Language, Truth and Logic*, where he writes that 'There are no objects whose existence is indubitable'[1] and that 'It is only tautologies that are certain'.[2] But since these statements are clearly not tautologies the writer has no right to be certain of them, and perhaps should not affirm them with such dogmatic assurance as he appears to do.

We recall also that the most representative philosopher of modern times, Immanuel Kant, declared that the purpose of his greatest work was 'to abolish knowledge', and not only so, but to do this 'in order to make room for *Glaube*'.[3] Now this word is German for belief, and Plato's word which I have rendered as opinion (*doxa*) has likewise often been rendered as belief. Was Kant's purpose, then, the anti-Platonic one of renouncing knowledge in order to rest content with mere opinion? By no means; and the confusion is to be explained in the following way. Kant was here speaking of our apprehension, not of the things of sense, but of things beyond sense. He was not unwilling to allow that our apprehension of the things of sense could be spoken of as knowledge. Plato (as we have said) had denied this, holding that of the things of sense we could only

[1] Op. cit., 2nd ed. (1946), p. 121.   [2] Ibid., p. 93.
[3] *Kritik der reinen Vernunft*, Preface to 2nd ed.

have opinion; but he claimed that we could have assured knowledge of the super-sensible realm, and he pointed out a way by which he thought this could be attained. Something of this way had been followed by Kant's predecessors in the medieval period and after it, chiefly under the name of natural theology, but Kant himself denied that this way was viable. He therefore said that we have no knowledge of super-sensible realities, but only belief. Yet the belief he had in mind was not mere opinion but *faith;* and the confusion is partly caused by the fact that the German *Glaube* covers both our English words belief and faith. Now this concept of the kind of belief which is faith is something that came into Western thought long after Plato's time, presenting the problem in an entirely new light. It represents the specifically Christian view of the way in which super-sensible realities are apprehended. It is the correlate of the Christian idea of revelation, though for Kant himself its meaning had been greatly curtailed through the influence of the rationalism of the Enlightenment.

It is, however, a mistake to set faith, as Kant did, in contrast to knowledge. To do this is to mingle two different terminologies, the Greek and the Christian (or we might even include a third, that of modern empiricism) in a most confusing way. In the Bible there is no such simple contrast between faith and knowledge. The Biblical contrast is rather between faith and *sight.* 'Faith is . . . the evidence of things unseen.'[1] 'We walk by faith, not by sight.'[2] Tennyson speaks like Kant when he writes that

> We have but faith, we cannot know;
> For knowledge is of things we see.[3]

But while from the Christian point of view Tennyson is right in holding the unseen world to be apprehended by faith, he is wrong in denying the name of knowledge to such apprehension. In the New Testament[4] to know God and to have faith in him

---

[1] Heb. 11.1.   [2] 2 Cor. 5. 7.   [3] *In Memoriam*, Prologue.

[4] 'This knowledge (whether ἐπίγνωσις or γνῶσις) scarcely differs in substance from faith, except that it emphasizes *the element of knowing* which is contained in the very structure of faith.'—R. Bultmann, *The Theology of the New Testament*, Eng. trans., Vol. II, p. 128.

are often hardly more than two ways of saying the same thing. And yet this knowledge that is faith is not the best kind of knowledge. The concept of faith always contains both the idea of knowing and the idea of not knowing fully.

§ 2

No Christian, then, can say that he knows nothing. What he must say is that such knowledge as he has is severely restricted both in extent and in kind. None of us can claim to have been granted more than certain slender divinings of truth, which is otherwise surrounded by clouds and thick darkness. 'Now I know in part', writes St Paul. Nor was it only that his knowledge was small in extent, but what he had of it was also dim. 'Now we see as in a mirror, as in a riddle', he says in the same verse.[1] And when the New Testament gives to our present knowledge the name of faith, this is part of the meaning. The Apostle is as little satisfied with the quality as with the quantity of his knowledge. He longs for a clearer apprehension which, using the same visual figure, he calls 'seeing face to face', and one of the things he claims to know by his present faith-knowledge is that the better kind of knowledge, in which faith is transcended, will hereafter be his. He has faith that one day he will be granted something better than faith.

We must also remember that there is a difference between knowing, and knowing that we know; or, what is the same thing, a difference between knowing that we know (or do not know) and merely thinking or opining that we know (or do not know). If there were no such difference, my endeavour to set down what I know would have been far less difficult than I actually found it to be. It seems to require strenuous mental effort on my part to distinguish my real from my putative knowledge—and hardly less to distinguish my real from my putative ignorance. There might not indeed be any such difference, were I what the psychologists call a completely integrated personality or what the theologians call sinless, but in fact the

---

[1] I Cor. 13. 12.

part of me which recognizes truth is not always identical with the part of me which acknowledges my recognition of it. That is why, in any tally I make of things I assuredly know, I shall be likely to include some things that should have been left out; and also, and equally, likely to leave out some things that should have been put in. To follow a makeshift terminology which I have used elsewhere,[1] I should say that there are doubtless some things which 'in the bottom of my heart' I know full well to be true, but whose truth I have never fully acknowledged 'with the top of my mind'. Perhaps therefore we all know both more and less than we think we know. This comes partly from intellectual indolence, but partly also from a failure in intellectual honesty; for there are some things we so much want to be true that we stifle our doubts concerning them, and other things the acknowledgement of which would make such unwelcome demands on us, or entail so inconvenient a readjustment both of our professed outlook and of our habitual conduct, that we succeed in suppressing or 'repressing' what would otherwise be a fully assured conviction of their truth. Neither the gnostic not the agnostic is always fully honest with himself.

There can thus be no indefectibility in my tally of the things I know. All human thinking is defectible. I may indeed believe that there is an indefectible authority on which I can lay hold, but I still remain defectible in my way of laying hold upon it. Whatever is of divine revelation must be infallible as it issues from God, but we can make no such claim for it either as it is transmitted to us or as it is received by us; for the human element always enters both into the transmission and into the reception. Or even if we believe with the Roman Catholic that the transmission is no less infallible than the original emission, the reception by us at least remains fallible. *Omne quod recipitur*, says Aquinas, *recipitur per modum recipientis*—which is always a fallible mode. Moreover, even if the ground appear solid enough beneath our feet once we have accepted our authority as infallible, so that Newman could say that after he

[1] *Our Knowledge of God* (1939), chap. II. § 5.

had been received into the Roman Church in 1845 he never again 'had one doubt',[1] yet that initial step of accepting the authority, of choosing this from among the several authorities in the world that claim infallibility for themselves, must be taken on our own responsibility. We should hope indeed that in exercising this responsibility and making this choice we were aided by divine grace, but we should not claim the plenary guidance of the Spirit of God, plenary inspiration, not to say infallibility, for our exercise of it. Newman is quite clear about this. The credentials of the Roman claim, he says, must be examined by the ordinary rules of evidence before the claim is admitted. We must

confess that there is no ultimate test of truth besides the testimony borne to truth by the mind itself, and that this phenomenon, perplexing as we may find it, is a normal and inevitable characteristic of the mental constitution of a being like man on a stage such as the world.[2]

Moreover, if our reliance is on Holy Scripture instead of on the Church, the same considerations apply. Its teaching, says Archbishop William Temple, is

so inextricably human and divine in one that no single sentence can be quoted as having the authority of an authentic utterance of the All-Holy God.[3]

And

The Christian will believe that he has an infallible authority in the mind of Christ; but he has no infallible means of ascertaining its application to given circumstances.[4]

And the fallible elements in its transmission are such that

there is no single deed or saying of which we can be perfectly sure that He said or did precisely this or that.[5]

§ 3

But, it will be asked, does this mean that after all there is no such thing as certitude and therefore no such thing as

---

[1] *Apologia pro Vita Sua*, chap V.   [2] *A Grammar of Assent*, chap. IX. § 1.
[3] *Nature, Man and God* (1934), p. 350.   [4] Ibid., p. 353.
[5] William Temple in *Revelation*, ed. Baillie and Martin (1937), p. 114.

knowledge? If it meant this, then indeed we should have to say with George Meredith,

> Ah, what a dusty answer gets the soul
> When hot for certainties in this our life.[1]

But I shall contend that it does not mean this. The most it means is that, while all authentic experience has some certitude in it and is, as it were, transfused with certitude, it is never possible to distil this certitude in its complete purity into the particular theoretical affirmations we make. We are convinced we are in touch with reality, we do know something assuredly, but when we try to express in theoretical terms what we know and are sure of, we never have the same assurance that we have got our answer quite right. We know we are thinking something that is certainly true, but there is always the risk of error in our way of thinking it. As the late Lord (then Mr A. J.) Balfour wrote in 1894,

Though the fact is apt to be hidden from us by the unshrinking definitions with which alike in science and in theology it is our practice to register attained results, it would . . . be a serious mistake to suppose that any complete correspondence between belief and reality was secured by the linguistic precision and the logical impeccability of the propositions by which beliefs themselves are communicated and recorded.[2]

Consider first the case of the natural sciences. None of their results can be regarded as final in the form in which it is at any time envisaged and formulated. They are all corrigible and in fact subjected to constant correction; and it is or should be the very pride of natural science that this is so. Yet in each result something of indubitable truth is contained. There are of course many instances of the outright reversal of scientific conclusions, but even in these instances something of true apprehension was present in the approach to the conclusion, though the conclusion itself was wrongly drawn. What usually happens, however, is rather in the nature of a revision—it may be only a deepening—of the original insight. The scientist

---

[1] *Modern Love*, XLVIII.   [2] *The Foundations of Belief*, p. 271.

knows that he is seeing something, has hit on something, but always there may be something he has not yet hit upon which may greatly modify his understanding of what he has already hit upon. If no element of certain knowledge entered into the probabilities of science, science could not be progressive. But we are certain that it does make progress, that its later conclusions, however far they may be from the final truth, are at least nearer it than those which they have superseded. The Copernican cosmology may in its turn be departed from no less than the Ptolemaic, but it is *certain* that it makes an advance upon the Ptolemaic.

Consider again our moral convictions. These are governed, as Kant rightly said, by a sense of unconditional obligation, which is to say that there is about them something of absolute certainty. Yet it is notoriously difficult, and much more difficult than Kant supposed, to distil this sense of obligation into specific moral rules or commands for which the same unconditionality can be claimed. Kant insisted that it was our unconditional duty always to speak what we believe to be the truth, but most of us would wish to qualify this by the mention of a number of conditions such as would apply in certain cases. We are indeed under absolute obligation in respect of truthspeaking, but our efforts to codify this obligation are always to some extent provisional. The obligation itself is absolute, but the particular duty to which we are obliged is manywise relative. As has been well said:

The *ought* is unconditional. If I ought to do X, I ought do it without qualification or reserve. Any qualification falls on the side of the content of duty, not on the side of the obligation.[1]

Then there are our religious convictions. Here, if anywhere, we find that certitude is claimed. The Christian has full assurance of being in authentic touch with the unseen. He has been visited by God's revelation of himself, of his mind and will in Jesus Christ our Lord, and divine revelation can be no other than infallible. What it proclaims is absolute truth, subject to

[1] W. G. de Burgh, *From Morality to Religion* (1938), p. 53.

no qualification or revision, 'irreformable'. On the other hand we have said that the Christian can never perfectly capture into his own thinking this infallible revelation, this absolute truth. He tries by means of the most suitable concepts his mind can frame, and the best language he can command, to grasp what it portends, but in this he never achieves anything like complete success, so that his theological formulations are always 'reformable', subject to correction, revision and development. Yet it is precisely and only because he has been visited by infallible divine revelation that such correction, revision and development are possible; and as these processes are carried forward, they are controlled and guided by this revelation, and ought to be controlled and guided by nothing else. This means that all his thinking has been invaded, and continues to be pervaded, by an infallibility, an absoluteness, and therefore a certainty, which he nevertheless remains unable to hold securely in his own very human grasp or, to vary the figure, to domesticate into the household of his own very human mind.

And this, according to Kierkegaard and those theologians who have come under his influence, is why theology must always be 'dialectical'. God, they say, addresses himself to us in revelation; and we, if we face towards him and respond to this address, receive this revelation in faith. But when we try to *think* just what it is that has been revealed to us, we have to proceed by means of human concepts, abstract concepts each of which takes away (*abstrahit*) something from the concrete reality which has been revealed. Each such concept therefore grasps no more than one aspect of the truth which it regards in isolation from the rest; and thus misleads at the same time as it enlightens. This situation can be rectified only by allowing each concept to correct the others. When the revealed content is subjected to human reflection, it is, as it were, diffracted by our thought in several different directions, each leading to a result which is invalid until complemented by all the rest. Yet this process of complementation can never be completed without the appearance of those antinomies which must always continue to characterize finite reflection on the infinite. From a truly dialectical theology the element of paradox can never be eliminated. This has been illustrated as follows:

The attempt to put our experience of God into theological statements is something like the attempt to draw a map of the world on a flat surface, the page of an atlas. It is impossible to do this without a certain degree of falsification, because the surface of the earth is a spherical surface whose pattern cannot be reproduced accurately upon a plane. And yet the map must be drawn for convenience' sake. Therefore an atlas meets the problem by giving us two different maps of the world which can be compared with each other. The one is contained in two circles representing two hemispheres. The other is contained in an oblong (Mercator's projection). Each is a map of the whole world, and they contradict each other to some extent at every point. Yet they are both needed, and taken together they correct each other. They would be either misleading or mystifying to anyone who did not know that they represent the surface of a sphere. But they can serve their useful purpose for anyone who understands that they are intended to represent in handy portable form the pattern covering the surface of this round earth which he knows in actual experience.[1]

Especially in the writings of Professor Paul Tillich I find many excellent statements of the point I have been trying to make. In one of his essays, for example, he is defending the Christian conviction that the ultimate ordering of our destiny is not in the hands of a demonic fate, but in the hands of God who stands above fate:

Without this certainty, which is the inmost kernel of Christianity, we should be thrown back to the Greek situation, and should have to begin to traverse the whole fateful path of philosophy over again. But this eternal truth, this logos *does pulsate through all our thinking*; There can be no act of thought without the secret presupposition of its unconditional truth. But this unconditional truth is not in our possession. It is the hidden criterion of every truth that we believe we possess. There is an element of venture or of risk in every statement of the truth. Yet we can take this risk in the certainty that

---

[1] D. M. Baillie, *God Was in Christ* (1948), p. 109.

this is the only way in which truth can reveal itself to finite and historical beings.[1]

With this we may compare what Dr Karl Barth has to say when, speaking of such knowledge as we have of God and his Word, he speaks of its inevitable *Welthaftigkeit*, which I can only translate as 'involvement in the world':

God alone conceives of Himself, even in His (revealed) Word. Our concept of Him and His Word can be no more than a pointer to the limits of our conceiving. . . . Above all God's speech is and remains God's mystery in respect of its involvement in the world. . . . When God speaks to man, this happening is never so marked off from the general run of what happens that it could not easily be interpreted as being a part of it. . . . The veil is thick. We do not possess the Word of God otherwise than in the mystery of its world-involvement. But that means that we always have it in a form which as such is *not* the Word of God, and as such does not even betray the fact that it is the form which encloses God's Word. . . . Its form is not a suitable but an unsuitable medium for God's presentation of Himself. It does not correspond to the content but rather contradicts it. It does not unveil it but rather veils it. The 'world-involvement' of the Word of God does not mean merely that it meets us in the dress of creaturely reality; for we must say also that, because this creaturely reality is that of fallen man, it meets us in a form which is not that of a pure nature. . . . Hence our knowledge of God's Word is not mediated to us by a reason that has somehow remained pure and can consequently see through the creaturely reality to God's mystery, but is always mediated to us by our fallen reason.[2]

It is for such reasons that, instead of claiming certainty or finality for our particular thoughts about God and the unseen world, I must content myself with claiming that certainty 'pulsates through all our thinking' or that our experience in this realm is everywhere 'transfused with certainty'.

[1] *The Protestant Era* (Chicago 1948, London 1950), chap. I. iv; italics mine. Karl Jaspers has much to say in the same vein. His position is thus summarized by David E. Roberts, *Existentialism and Religious Belief* (1957), p. 250: 'Being-itself, although it transcends every finite mode, is nevertheless *encountered in the midst of finitude*' (italics mine).
[2] *Kirchliche Dogmatik*, I. i, p. 171 f.

§ 4

But the difference between these two claims calls for further elucidation, and I should wish to elucidate it by distinguishing between two kinds of knowledge—knowledge of truth and knowledge of reality. As we have seen, there are those who claim that we have no knowledge, because no certainty, of either kind. I have already quoted Professor Ayer as saying that only tautologies are certain and that there are no objects whose existence is indubitable. Professor Tillich appears to agree. 'Knowledge of reality', he writes, 'has never the certitude of complete evidence. . . . Every knowledge of reality by the human mind has the character of higher or lower probability.' There are, he says, two types of knowledge which yield complete certitude, our knowledge of the propositions of logic and mathematics (Professor Ayer's 'tautologies'), and our apprehension of immediate sense-data concerning which he writes, 'He who sees a green colour sees a green colour and is certain about it. He cannot be certain whether the thing which seems to him green is really green. He may be under a deception. But he cannot doubt that he sees green.'[1] Neither of these knowledges, however, is knowledge of reality. It should at once be added, however, that Professor Tillich saves himself from this apparent scepticism by claiming that there is a certitude of faith, which is of another kind. But to this faith he will not allow the name of knowledge—any more than Kant would have done.

Let us first consider whether it is really true that there are no objects (within which category we can for our present purpose include other subjects) whose existence is indubitable. It is well known that in an essay entitled 'A Defence of Common Sense' published in 1925[2] Professor G. E. Moore protested strongly against such a view, repeating and developing this protest in a number of subsequent papers. He claimed complete certainty for such affirmations as that he himself was a bodily existent, that this body of his had existed for many

---

[1] *Dynamics of Faith* (1957), p. 33 f.
[2] In *Contemporary British Philosophy*, ed. Muirhead, Vol. II.

years, that there are and have been other living bodies not
unlike his own, and that these, like his own, have been the
bodies of persons who in their turn enjoyed a like certitude
regarding other existents. Here, then, is roundly challenged
the view that the direct and only indubitable objects of our
knowledge are sense-data (noises, patches of colour etc.) and
not anything 'out there' (*exsistens*). Bertrand Russell had
argued that even so simple an affirmation as 'I am sitting, as
I write this, in a chair before a table' requires 'much careful
consideration before we can be sure that we have stated it in
a form which is wholly true'.[1] But Professor Moore insisted
that this confuses the meaning of the affirmation, which is quite
clear and of whose truth it is possible to be quite certain, with
the philosophical analysis of that meaning, which may be very
hard to come by.

The view that our direct and indubitable knowledge is only
of sensations or so-called sense-data, and not of existent objects,
has been further and most interestingly challenged in a recent
little book by Dr E. L. Mascall. It has been assumed by Locke
and Berkeley, and has continued to be assumed by the contemporary logical empiricists, that the perceptive element in
sense-experience consists simply of sensations, of the registration
of sensible particulars like colours, sounds and tactual resistances,
and that from these latter the intellect then deduces, by way of
inference from effect to cause, the existence of extra-mental
existents.[2] Against this Dr Mascall contends that, 'while there
is no perception without sensation, the sensible particular or
sense-datum is not the terminus of perception, not the *objectum
quod* . . . but the *objectum quo*, through which the intellect grasps,
in a direct but mediate activity, the intelligible extra-mental
reality, which is the real thing'.[3] He thus sums up his position:

First, that although perception normally takes place through the
medium of sensation, its essence is not sense-awareness but

[1] *The Problems of Philosophy* (1912), p. 11.
[2] 'A material thing is a logical construction out of sense data.' So C. D. Broad
summarizes Bertrand Russell's position. See *British Philosophy in the Mid-Century*
(1957), ed. C. A. Mace, p. 59.
[3] *Words and Images* (1957), p. 33 f.

phenomena as an *objectum quo* through which it passes to the apprehension of the *objectum quod* which is the intelligible trans-sensible being. Hence, in the second place, the intelligible object is not something whose existence is *deduced from* that of the sensible phenomena, as Locke thought, nor is it something mentally *constructed out of* the sensible phenomena, as many modern empiricists have held, but something *grasped through them*. Thirdly, in order to penetrate beneath the sensible phenomena to the real intelligible things that support them, we need, not an attitude of detachment, ratiocination and attention to the phenomenal surface of things, useful as this is for certain purposes, but an attitude of involvement, contemplation and penetration into their intelligible depths.[1]

So also Professor Macmurray protests against the assumption 'that what is given in immediate sense-experience is a sense-datum, not a physical object',[2] and insists that we have certain and indubitable knowledge of particular extra-mental existents. If I say that I know John Smith and also the village in which he lives, these statements, unless I am lying, are certainly true in the sense in which I mean them.[3]

I find it difficult to escape from these conclusions, but meanwhile let us consider more carefully the distinction I have drawn between the two kinds of knowledge, knowledge of truth and knowledge of reality. There is indeed an exalted use of the word 'truth', doubtless of Hebrew origin, which makes it equivalent to reality. I find it stated as a main Biblical usage in Cruden's *Concordance* that 'Truth is put for reality'. So we read 'I am the way, the truth and the life'.[4] But when I here speak of knowledge of truth, I mean knowledge of truths, that is, of propositions. Sometimes I say 'I know X', but sometimes I say 'I know that X is Y'. This is the distinction between knowledge by acquaintance and knowledge by description to which Lord Russell directed our attention in a famous essay published in 1911: part of his contention (and I am not here concerned with the further logical problem which is perhaps the main concern of the essay) being that the former is logically prior to the latter, because our ability to make affirmations

---

[1] Ibid., p. 70 f.   [2] *The Self as Agent* (1957), p. 112.
[3] Compare for example, ibid., p. 101 f., p. 129.   [4] John 14. 6.

about anything presupposes our acquaintance with it—or, to put it a little differently, that I cannot enunciate truths about anything unless I am already directly confronted with the thing itself. 'The relation between subject and object which I call acquaintance', he writes, 'is simply the converse of the relation of subject and object which constitutes presentation. That is, to say that S is acquainted with O is essentially the same thing as to say that O is presented to S.'[1] What is disappointing, however, is that Lord Russell still insists that, apart from 'universals', our acquaintance is only with sense-data and not with real objects or with other subjects. 'We have acquaintance with sense-data, with many universals, and possibly with ourselves, but not with physical objects or other minds.'[2]

The validity of the distinction (however it may be applied in detail) has frequently been denied, especially by philosophers of the idealist tradition who contend that our only knowledge is of ideas in our minds. 'All knowledge', according to G. F. Stout, 'is of propositions, and of other things only as forming constituents of propositions.'[3]

I do not at all doubt that what is here called acquaintance actually exists. Without it there can be no knowledge, for if we were not acquainted with some things, we could not know anything. . . . But it cannot, I think, properly be called knowledge. . . . How indeed can we know anything, if it is supposed that we know absolutely nothing about it?[4]

To this I should reply that we cannot indeed know anything without at the same time at least thinking we know something about it, because in the very moment that we are confronted with any reality, so becoming acquainted with it, our minds start to frame certain propositions regarding it, but that it is nevertheless the reality itself, rather than the propositions,

---

[1] *Proceedings of the Aristotelian Society 1910-11;* reprinted in *Mysticism and Logic* (1918), pp. 209 ff.
[2] Ibid., p. 231.
[3] *Studies in Philosophy and Psychology* (1930), p. 369.
[4] Ibid., p. 392.

which is the prime and direct object of our knowledge. Stout argues as follows:

On Mr Russell's view, acquaintance is not acquaintance with characters or attributes, but with the subject as something distinct from all that can be truly asserted of it in judgements. This is a position which I cannot accept. The subject, taken apart from all its characters and attributes, can only be known, if it can be known at all, as that to which the characters or attributes belong. In other words, it can be known only by description. If we persist in asking what it is in itself and yet refuse to take as an answer any statement of its attributes, we can only say with Locke that it is a 'somewhat, we know what'.[1]

Now it has always appeared to me particularly paradoxical to say, as Stout here does and as others have done, that what they nevertheless allow us to call our 'acquaintance' with persons 'cannot properly be called knowledge.' Nothing could be more contrary to the accepted usage of the term. We habitually speak of our knowledge of persons as being much more fundamental than the knowledge of propositions which may be enunciated concerning them; as when I say, 'No, I have not the pleasure of knowing John Smith, but I know a good deal about him', or again when I say, 'Yes, I know him, but I do not know him very well. I hope soon to get to know him better'—in the latter case recognizing that there are various degrees in our knowledge of persons. To my mind knowledge of persons is the very type and pattern of what we mean by knowledge. Of no other existents is our knowledge so intimate or so direct. 'When we distinguish between persons and material things', writes Professor Macmurray, 'the characteristics we attribute to things are a selection from the characteristics we attribute to a person.'[2] And again, 'We use the term "know" in (the) primary sense when we say that we know our friends and are known by them.'[3]

Certainly this is the kind of knowledge of which the New Testament speaks and which it so often designates as faith. 'Ye have known God, or rather have been known by him.'[4]

[1] Ibid., p. 392   [2] Op. cit., p. 117.   [3] Op. cit., p. 129.   [4] Gal. 4. 9.

Characteristically and primarily faith is faith in God, confidence in him rather than the uttering of judgements concerning him. What Christians do when they say the Creed is to confess their faith in the three Persons of the Godhead, whom then and only then they proceed to identify by 'descriptive' phrases such as 'Maker of heaven and earth', 'Who was conceived by the Holy Ghost. . . .' Archbishop Temple wrote, 'I do not believe in any creed, but I use creeds to express, to conserve, and to deepen my belief in God.'[1]

Instead therefore of saying that we have no knowledge of realities but only of the judgements we make about these realities, we must say that our knowledge of the realities themselves—whether these be the external world or our fellow men or God—is primary, and our knowledge of truths concerning them secondary. The point, then, that I am most concerned to make is that, however difficult we may find it to ascribe certainty to these truths, we may nevertheless enjoy the certitude of having authentic acquaintance with the realities they fallibly seek to describe.[2] It is in this way that our experience is everywhere transfused with a certitude which pulsates through all our thinking, and whose pervading presence can on occasion make even of our most speculative theorizings something better than mere fantasy and baseless fabric.

[1] *Nature, Man and God* (1934), p. 322.
[2] According to J. M. Keynes (*Two Memoirs*, 1949) 'Moore had a dream once in which he could not distinguish propositions from tables'.

CHAPTER II

The Really Real

§ 5

When I ask myself what manner of things I know, my first thought will perhaps be of the innumerable things I have observed in the external world by means of my bodily senses. Plato, as we have said, would have denied to these the name of knowledge. In my speaking of them he would not have allowed me to say 'I know that . . .', but only 'It seems to me that . . .'. Knowledge is knowledge of reality, and to him the world perceived by sense was not reality but only seeming, only appearance. Later idealists have agreed with him. But I cannot agree with him, for I believe the world of things seen to be real. On the other hand, I believe it to be, not ultimate, but only proximate reality; or, to put it more accurately, created as distinct from uncreated reality. The mess into which our modern idealists have so often landed themselves has come from their discarding the idea of creation which Christianity had introduced into Western thought, and their consequent reduction of the fundamental Christian distinction between the created and the uncreated to the pagan (both Greek and Indian) distinction between the apparent and the real. Furthermore, Plato was equally unwilling to allow the name of knowledge to the depositions of the historians, since all they did was to call up the memory of past appearances. Here too I should have to disagree, but at the same time to say that the historical stream of events is not ultimate reality.

But though Plato thus denied the name of knowledge to our sense-experience, he did not deny it to the findings reached by science. Science is simply the Latin translation of Plato's own word for knowledge, *epistēmē*; and where we speak of the different sciences, Plato spoke of the different knowledges,

epistēmai. He was able to distinguish thus sharply between
ordinary sense apprehension and the conclusions of the
scientists, calling the latter knowledge but the former only
opinion, because he believed that science was concerned only
with the essences of things, and that these essences were not
accessible to sense, but were 'apart'[1] from sense, eternal and
alone real, belonging not to the phenomenal but to the
noumenal world. Of course there could be no science had
there not first been sense-experience, yet Plato's science relied
far less on such a starting-point, that is, was altogether less
empirical (which is Greek for experiential), than our modern
science, being more inclined to rely on deductions made from
the essences of things, once these had been brought to light.
The real difference between ancient and modern science is
that the latter takes the witness of sense-experience much more
seriously, giving it a place in real knowledge; while on the
other hand the influence of the Christian tradition leads us to
deny that the realm into which it introduces us is that of
ultimate, which is to say uncreated, reality.

§ 6

But it is knowledge of ultimate reality that we most desire to
have, and certitude in this region of our thinking that is most
precious to us. No other discovery that we could ever make
could for a moment compare in its importance for us with the
finding of a clue to the meaning of the universal drama in
which each of us has been assigned his tiny part. In the absence
of any such clue I cannot know either what I myself am or
what I ought to be doing, since the part can be understood
only in the light of the whole. As one looks back over the whole
history of our race, one must realize that this was at all times
and in all places the most deep-seated of human interests. But
never more so than it is today. The real rivalries of our time
are those between what we have come to call the different
'philosophies of life' but which are at the same time philosophies

---

[1] See Aristotle, *Metaphysica*, 1078b.

of the universal nature of things—*Weltanschauungen* at the same time as they are *Lebensanschauungen*; whether that of Christianity, or of Marxist materialism, or of atheistic existentialism, or of some renascent paganism, or of something else. We have of course many lesser and more restricted interests to keep us going, and some of these are absorbing enough and can and ought to be happily pursued in relative detachment from our master concern. Those who think themselves still unable to answer what is the first question, not only of our Scottish catechism, but of the catechism of every philosophy of life, 'What is the chief end of man?' do not really sit all day in bored idleness. All such have found some proximate end or ends which it seems worth while to pursue. Yet is not this because in and through their appreciation of these proximate ends something of the chief end has been revealed to them? One may clearly know that it is his duty to help his neighbour in distress and yet deny that he knows anything about the ultimate purpose of human life. Another may find profound satisfaction in music or some other art, while making a similar denial. Yet if human existence as a whole does possess meaning or significance, these more restricted ends must in some way be derivatives from it, or at least be subsumed under it; and if they are, then it is some revelation of that meaning and significance, however unacknowledged by men 'with the top of their minds', that points them to the duty or creates the satisfaction in question.

I myself have in my time cultivated many subsidiary interests, however inexpertly. I have had much happiness from watching and helping things grow in my garden, from getting to know the flora of the countryside, from travelling in many lands, from the study (and sometimes the collection) of old porcelain and old prints, and most of all from my reading of poetry and *belles lettres*. These interests have to me been in a real sense ends in themselves, worth pursuing for their own sake. Yet I believe that if life had held no deeper interest for me, each of these others would have quickly palled, turning to sand and grit in my mouth. Ends in themselves they no doubt were, but I do not think I could have endured the thought that any of them was an ultimate and sufficient end. Not only so, but I believe also that my pursuit of each was at all times redeemed from a triviality, such as would otherwise have tarnished my pleasure in it, by a barely conscious awareness that it was somehow pervaded by a relevance to man's ultimate concern; while any deliberate denial of such relevance, had I been tempted to make it, would certainly have disturbed me deeply. Thus like Wordsworth, if hardly with the same romantic overtones, 'I have felt . . . a sense of something far more deeply interfused'.[1]

There is an essay of Dr Gilbert Murray's dating from 1917 which struck me, when I first read it shortly after that date, as saying something which was very close to my own experience. It is entitled *Literature as Revelation,* and here are a few sentences of it:

There are among lovers of literature . . . some who like it for all sorts of other reasons, and some who demand of it nothing less than a kind of revelation. Most people of culture, I believe, belong to the first class. They like literature because they like to be amused, or because the technique of expression interests them. . . . Or they like to study the varieties of human nature as shown in books, and to amass the curious information that is to be found there. . . . And the other class—to which I certainly belonged all through my youth and perhaps on the whole still belong—does not really much like the process of reading, but reads because it wants to get somewhere, to discover something, to find a light which will somehow illumine for them either some question of the moment or the great riddles of existence; and, considering their disappointments, it is remarkable, and perhaps not altogether discreditable, how often they cling to this hope far into the region of grey hairs or worse than grey hairs.[2]

§ 7

These words, however, hardly prepare us for what Dr Murray next goes on to say:

[1] *Tintern Abbey,* lines 93-95.
[2] *Essays and Addresses* (1921), p. 126 f.

I will confess my own private belief, which I do not wish anyone
to share, that of all the books and all the famous sayings that have
come as a revelation to human beings, not one is strictly true or
has any chance of being true. . . . They are cries of distress, calls of
encouragement, signals flashing in the darkness; they seem to be
statements in the indicative mood, but they are really in the
imperative, or the optative . . . They never are concerned with
direct scientific fact or even with that part of experience which
is capable of being expressed in exact statement. They are concerned
not with that part of our voyage which is already down in the
Admiralty charts. They are concerned with the part which is
uncharted; the part that is beyond the mist. . . . They are all in
the nature of the guess that goes before scientific knowledge; the
impassioned counsel of one who feels strongly but cannot, in the
nature of things, prove his case . . . Their weakness is that they
are never exactly true, because they are never based on exact
knowledge.[1]

That such light as we have on our ultimate human concern,
and our divinings concerning the meaning of life, are not of
the same kind as scientific knowledge, that they are not 'concerned with direct scientific fact', and that they cannot be
'proved' by the methods of natural science, we should of
course have to agree; and of that more anon. But what does
Dr Murray mean by saying that they are not 'strictly true'?
Is he saying only what we ourselves have been insisting upon,
that not one of the concepts in which we seek to imprison the
realities of which we are aware is ever fully adequate to the
realities themselves? When he writes that they cannot be expressed in *exact* statement, something like this would indeed
seem to be Dr Murray's meaning. But no, our statements are,
properly regarded, not statements of truth at all, nor statements of any kind, but merely cries of distress, summonses to
courage, confessions (as we read on another page) as to the
things we most desire and long to know, though we do not
know them and apparently never can. They are in fact what
the logical positivists began, in the decade following the first
appearance of Dr Murray's essay, to call 'merely emotive
utterances'. They are not, if all Dr Murray says about them is

[1] Ibid.

true, even guesses at truth in any significant sense. If they have anything to do with truth and falsity at all, it is only because, being utterances in the optative or imperative moods, they indicate what we would like to be true. Dr Murray does indeed describe them as 'in the nature of the guess that goes before scientific knowledge', but this adds nothing but confusion to the rest of his account of them. Such a scientific guess or hypothesis (a) is worthless unless it has been suggested by something in the observed facts, (b) is put forward in the belief that it *may* turn out to be true, (c) is capable of verification, of proof or disproof, and (d) should not be affected in its verification by any thought of what the scientist wishes to be true.

There are, however, many others among us, empiricists and positivists of several different schools, who, without any such vagueness or confusedness of statement, declare that we have no knowledge of reality other than what is verifiable by natural science or by the sense-observation on which such science founds.[1] This declaration cannot, of course, itself be verified by natural science; it is something extra or something presupposed. When men speak thus they are speaking as philosophers or as logicians, and the burden of their contention is that no statement can be accepted as enlightening us concerning the nature of the real world, or of any part or aspect of it, which cannot be proved true by reference to what we observe through our bodily senses. Aesthetic, ethical and religious affirmations cannot be so proved, and hence they are dismissed as merely subjective and emotional preferences. Of course, if they cannot be so proved, it follows by the same logic that they cannot be so disproved—and both these statements seem to me inexpugnable. Some, like Rousseau's Savoyard Vicar, have indeed found consolation in taking one of them without the other. They believe, let us say, in the immortality of the human soul, and they rejoice to think that no evidence *against* immortality can ever conceivably be found. Never, never will anybody be

---

[1] Compare L. Wittgenstein, *Tractatus Logico-Philosophicus* (1922): 'The totality of true propositions is the total natural science' (4.1); 'The right method of philosophy would be this: To say nothing except what can be said, i.e the propositions of natural science' (6.53).

able to affirm with any show of reason that souls are *not* immortal. But in taking to themselves this particular comfort, they are really playing into the hands of their positivist critics, whose most characteristic challenge is that none has a right to any conviction unless he is able to define some possible evidence which, if it should emerge, he would accept in disproof of it, so obliging him to surrender it. Their real recourse is not in refusing this challenge, but in submitting that the evidence on which they rely, and the failure of which would indeed oblige them to surrender their belief, is of another kind than that furnished by the bodily senses; and in defending their reliance on it by the submission that, since our bodily senses clearly do not inform us that there is no other kind of evidence than theirs, the empiricist cannot affirm this negative proposition without contradicting his own premises. Yet, as was wisely said many years ago—again by Lord Balfour:

Who would pay the slightest attention to naturalism if it did not force itself into the retinue of science, assume her livery, and claim, as a kind of poor relation, in some sort to represent her authority and to speak with her voice? Of itself it is nothing. It neither ministers to the needs of mankind, nor does it satisfy their reason. And if, in spite of this, its influence has increased, is increasing, and as yet shows no signs of diminution, if more and more the educated and the half-educated are acquiescing in its pretensions and, however reluctantly, submitting to its domination, this is, at least in part, because they have not learned to distinguish between the practical and inevitable claims which experience has on their allegiance, and the speculative but quite illusory title by which the empirical school have endeavoured to associate naturalism and science in a kind of joint supremacy over the thoughts and consciences of mankind.[1]

§ 8

To say that we have no knowledge save what can be empirically established on the evidence of our bodily senses is either to say that we have no knowledge of any reality that is not corporeal in nature, or else to say that our only knowledge of

[1] A. J. Balfour, *The Foundations of Belief* (1895), p. 135 f.

non-corporeal reality is such as can be logically inferred from our observation of the corporeal.

The latter view, as we know, was followed by many earlier empiricists from St Thomas Aquinas downwards, who held that the existence of other centres of consciousness than our own, namely, our fellow men and God, could be validly so inferred. This was a dreary enough belief, because the only argument that could be used to establish these other existences was one of analogy, which can yield only a probable result, and it was as distressing to the lover to be told that he could not be quite sure of the existence of his beloved as it was to the devout worshipper to be invited to rest content with a merely probable God. Moreover, even these probabilities were soon to come under suspicion. They were for the most part frankly dependent upon the prior admission of at least one non-inferential apprehension of a non-corporeal reality, namely the lover or worshipper himself, who was allowed to have a direct awareness of his own being by means of what could only be called an 'inner sense'; the argument for the existence of other minds being that since there exist other bodies closely resembling our own (major premise), and since our own body is inhabited by a mind (minor premise), it is probable that these other bodies are similarly inhabited. But when the psychologists began to point out that such self-consciousness as we have is socially-conditioned, that the awareness both of the *ego* and of the *alter* is embedded in the consciousness of the relation between them, the familiar argument from analogy seemed to break down; while it was at the same time breaking down under the weight of the other psychological consideration that we know the corporeal world from the beginning as a 'shared world', so that it could not be apprehended as real prior to our apprehension of our fellow men as real. We shall return to these points later, when we come to consider the folly of speaking as if each of us could retrace the course of his experience to a point when, as a bare knower, his mind a *tabula rasa*, he opened his eyes and ears and other senses to a world consisting only of shapes and colours and sounds and smells.

But our empiricists today prefer themore radically empiricist view, holding that we have no direct knowledge of any self-hood of our own other than our bodily selfhood, and therefore also, because the supposed argument from analogy thus loses its minor premise, no possibility of validly inferring any other non-corporeal existent. This really means that the modern empiricist must be, and usually avowedly is, a behaviourist in his psychology, a subjectivist in his ethics and aesthetics, and an agnostic in his attitude to religion. It leads, when consistently carried out, to an admittedly very strange result. Since all reality is corporeal, the knower is as corporeal as the things he knows. But how can body know body? Only if knowledge is itself body. Knowledge then is of the nature of electricity, and electronic machines can be so constructed as to yield it. It is, however, interesting to observe Professor Ayer's perplexity in having to choose, as his positivist premises force him to do, between a last-ditch defence of the analogical argument and the adoption of this behaviourist interpretation in spite of what he calls 'the air of paradox' which characterizes it and prevents him from being 'wholly confident that it is true'.[1]

Of course when one tries, as I have done, to compress the history of empiricism into two short paragraphs, one is laying violently simplifying hands on what is really a very complicated story, since there have been and still are many who represent positions subtly intermediate between these I have mentioned; but what I have said may perhaps serve my immediate purpose.

§ 9

Is it true that I have no knowledge save what can be verified by the methods proper to natural science? When the question is asked I am tempted to reply that, on the contrary, none of the things I most securely know can be verified in this way. As to the current findings of the natural scientists themselves,

---

[1] See *Language, Truth and Logic*, 2nd ed., pp. 19-20 and 129 f.

of the physicists, chemists and biologists, I have, I think, as much confidence in them as have most of my contemporaries. I cannot believe that the general picture they yield can ever be entirely overthrown. Yet obviously this picture may have to be drastically revised as scientific thought proceeds, and we know not what or how many details of it may not have to be completely expurged. As is generally admitted, a high degree of probability is the most that can be claimed for any scientific result. This does not trouble me and should not trouble anyone. Science does not need to apologize for its inability to offer us certainties; that, we have said, should rather be its boast, as signalizing its prospects of further advance. Yet I must at least confess to the certitude that it has advanced and is advancing, which can only mean that some true knowledge of reality pervades its results and that the sum of such knowledge increases as time goes on.

Yet the strange fact is that I have more confidence in what common sense and pre-scientific experience tell me about my natural environment than in any of the things I have learned from science. What science does is to make plain to me the real nature and implications of what I already knew, but the explanations never have the same quality of certitude as pervades the original knowledge. Furthermore, there are some things which I believe myself to know about nature concerning which natural science has not a word to say to me, and to that I shall perhaps have occasion to return.

But the certitudes I have principally in mind at the moment are of another kind. I have, for example, a greater degree of assurance of the honesty and loyalty of some of my friends than I have of the validity of any scientific doctrine, and still more secure is my conviction that honesty and loyalty are things *required* of us all. There is nothing of which I am more assured than that I must not exploit my fellow man in the interest of my own selfish gain, but must seek his good no less than my own and, if need be, at the cost of my own. There is nothing of which I am more assured than that Hitler was wrong in attempting to exterminate the Jews. These are convictions in the defence of which I hope I should be prepared to lay down my life, and in defence of which many of my young friends did lay down their lives. But nobody has ever laid down his life in defence of an empirically-verified scientific doctrine. That is not to say that science has not had its martyrs, for it also has had its 'noble army' of such. But it was not in defence of their scientific conclusions that they died; it was in defence of liberty of thought, freedom of research and the right of free speech; and the reality of these rights and liberties is certainly not itself scientifically verifiable, but can be established only by a mode of apprehension quite other than that on which science rests.

It may perhaps be suggested that the reason why men are prepared to die in defence of their moral and religious convictions is not that these are accompanied by a greater measure of assurance but only that, as bearing directly upon the very foundations of their lives, they are of more vital importance to them than any doctrine of natural science could be. In the essay from which quotation has already been made, Dr Gilbert Murray says:

A good Moslem believes in Mohammed far more passionately than anyone believes in the multiplication table. This is just because in the case of the multiplication table he *knows* and has done with it; in the case of Mohammed he does not *know* and makes up for his lack of knowledge by passionate feeling.[1]

That, however, is simply bad psychology. No doubt the multiplication table is not a suitable example to illustrate what Dr Murray means to say, since it neither is scientifically verifiable nor claims to give us any factual knowledge, being merely a mnemonic compilation of analytical propositions of the type 'two and two are four'; but it is at least nonsense to suggest that the things men most passionately believe are the things of which they are least sure. It looks indeed like a contradiction in terms. But perhaps all that is meant is that, while indeed the Mohammedan is certain in his conviction about the

[1] Op. cit., p. 136.

Prophet, Dr Murray himself is certain that the conviction is a mistaken one.

It will be advanced by some that such moral convictions as I have instanced do not, however they may be justified, yield us any knowledge of objective reality, but represent only our own subjective preferences. This doctrine was first put forward by the more extreme of the ancient Sophists who, as Plato informs us, endeavoured to persuade the young men of Athens that such convictions were in no way grounded in the nature of things (*physis*) but were human artifacts (*technē*) resting only on convention (*nomos*); but it has been widely resuscitated by contemporary philosophers. I shall presently be quoting from several of these, but at the moment I shall content myself with instancing only a little book written by Bertrand Russell in 1925—which I select because of the clarity of its statement:

We are ourselves the ultimate and irrefutable arbiters of value . . . It is we who create value.[1]

All moral rules must be tested by examining whether they tend to realize ends that we desire. I say ends that we desire, not ends that we *ought* to desire. What we 'ought' to desire is merely what someone else wishes us to desire—parents, schoolmasters, policemen and judges.[2]

Outside human desires there is no moral standard.[3]

This is put forward as a theory of ethics. What theories of ethics have offered us from the dialogues of Plato and the *Ethics* of Aristotle onwards has been an analysis, explication and systematization of our moral consciousness. But is Lord Russell here really analysing our moral consciousness? Rather is he flouting it. He is deflating it by denying that it is consciousness of anything external to itself. His ethical theory is thus parallel to a solipsist theory of our consciousness of our natural environment which would reduce the great globe itself and all which it inherit to such stuff as dreams are made on. But I cannot believe that what Lord Russell here wrote was based on a fair examination even of his own moral consciousness, which has led him to be valiant in the defence of

[1] *What I Believe*, p. 24 f.   [2] Ibid., p. 37 f.   [3] Ibid., p. 40.

many excellent moral causes, if also of some doubtful ones. If I were really to believe that his honesty or his concern for the welfare of others is nothing but a personal predilection, I should not trust him farther than I could see him. In fact I do trust his moral integrity, but I do so in spite of what he says about it. Yet I should be very much afraid that such views as he propounds would conduce in the end to a disastrous weakening of moral standards. Or are they perhaps too absurd to be taken so seriously as to have practical effect, just as theories of the unreality of the physical world are too absurd to disturb our practical relations with it? And has Lord Russell perhaps changed his mind? Certainly, and to my great relief, there are passages in his latest writings that read very differently, and to some of these I shall have occasion to refer at a later point.

At all events, when I set myself to analyse my moral consciousness, I cannot doubt that it sets up to be a consciousness of standards that are not of my own making, of ends not of my own choosing, of commandments not of my own issuing. The whole dignity of man, the whole much-boasted 'value of human personality', resides in man's awareness of being thus under obligation to something greater than himself. His dignity does not reside in what he actually does or actually desires—God help it if it did! It resides in his awareness of what he *owes*. And if the native hue of this awareness were to become so 'sicklied o'er by the pale cast of thought' as to be altogether dissipated, should we not all feel and know that (if I may so mingle my poetic allusions) 'there has passed away a glory from the earth'? Would there not, if this reduction were made, be a definite leakage of value?

If there would, then that gives me all that I wish at the moment to contend for. I do not at present wish to contend that men ever act honestly or unselfishly—or even that they ever pursue their scientific inquiries disinterestedly!—but only that they know they should. My affirmation at this point is only, if you like, that in the course of human evolution the ideas of absolute honesty, utter unselfishness and pure disinterestedness have appeared in men's minds, and that their appearance

represents the highest values that have so far emerged. It is
only with ideal values or standards that ethics deals. How
valiant it was of Kant to combine his contention that, as
creatures who know we ought to obey the moral law disinterestedly, we are citizens of the 'Kingdom of Ends', with the confession that there is no certain case of anybody's having so
obeyed it.[1] Here I have often been tempted to frame a sort of
ontological argument, contending that the appearance in our
human consciousness of the idea of a constraint laid upon us
from without is itself sufficient evidence of the truth of that
idea; and it has been thought by some that a parallel ontological argument is all the assurance we have of the objectivity
of the physical world or of the real existence of other selves.
I must trust my experience, my sense-experience, my social
experience and my moral experience, believing that I am not
merely dreaming it all.

§ 10

I have been asking what are the things of which I am most
fully assured, but it may be well to ask the same question in a
somewhat different form. Where do I find myself in most unmistakable contact with reality? But just as there are degrees
of assurance, so there are degrees of reality. Some things are
more real than others, as we have already acknowledged by
talking of *ultimate* reality and distinguishing it from realities
that are not ultimate. The word 'reality', being derived from
a Latin word which means 'thing' or 'object', literally means
thinghood or objectivity, but it would have been better and
simpler if, like the Greeks, we had relied for the expression of
this meaning on the forms and derivatives of the verb 'to be'.
For when we say 'reality', we mean simply being or that which
is; and Aristotle's way of saying ultimate reality is *to ontōs on*—
essential *esse*, that which is-ly is. It is implied in this way of
speaking that reality or being that is not ultimate has in it also
some unreality or non-being. This table is, but there is also

[1] *Grundlegung zur Metaphysik der Sitten* (1785), Sect. II.

that in it which is not. I myself am, but there is that in me which is not. We may quote Dr Tillich:

Certainly we belong to being—its power is in us—otherwise we would not be. But we are also separated from it; we do not possess it fully. Our power of being is limited. We are a mixture of being and non-being. This is precisely what is meant when we say that we are finite.[1]

The test of reality (which is the same as to say of being or of objectivity) is the resistance it offers to the otherwise uninhibited course of my own thinking, desiring and acting. Reality is what I 'come up against', what takes me by surprise, the other-than-myself which pulls me up and obliges me to reckon with it and adjust myself to it because it will not consent simply to adjust itself to me. Reality *presents* itself to me, and that means that it always meets me in the *present*, never in the past or in the future. The past has been real and the future may one day be real, but neither *is* real—or at least is not real as such. The remembered past and the anticipated future may indeed profoundly affect my present experience, but it is only as so doing that they enter into what is for me the real world at all. These are truths which have been very fully developed by many writers of recent years, principally under the influence of Kierkegaard, very notably by Dr Martin Buber—but nowhere more elaborately than by the late Eberhard Grisebach in a book which, though published in 1928, has never found an English translator and has been sadly neglected in the English-speaking world. It is entitled *Gegenwart*, which could be Englished either as 'Presence' or as 'The present'; but an overtone from the word's etymology still lingers in the German ear and in Grisebach's use of it, its literal meaning being 'that which waits over against us'.

Where then do I find a reality that is present to me in this way, pulling me up short? No doubt I find it in the physical world, as in the stone that so obligingly offered resistance to Dr Johnson's boot, enabling him, as he believed, to refute

[1] *Biblical Religion and the Search for Ultimate Reality* (1955), p. 11.

Bishop Berkeley. Yet so long as I am permitted to act as if I were sole lord of the physical world, so long as I can regard myself, like Alexander Selkirk, as 'monarch of all I survey, Whose right there is none to dispute', I can within limits make that world a fairly comfortable place for myself. Within these limits it will allow itself to be bent to my will, and exploited in my own private interest. It may also be remarked incidentally, that if a scientist should remind me that I here come up against the 'cast-iron laws of nature', I can find another (or the same) scientist to assure me that these laws are in some sort of my own casting, and that the very reason why I do so cast them is to enable me to exploit the nature to which I make bold to attribute them. As one has put it, 'Science is a ruse of the human mind to conquer the world'. But however that may be, and though the world of nature does undoubtedly offer me resistance, yet the truly significant collision comes when I meet another lord of nature claiming the same right as my own. If only he and I could have different worlds to conquer, different alls to survey, things would go smoothly enough, but that we are claimants to the same world, two competing centres of the same circle—there's the rub. Did he permit me to treat him merely as part of the world I know and use, making him subservient to my own interests as I make natural objects to be, no further trouble would arise. I would then still be the sole centre, and he within the circumference of my dominion; but this he will not do, and thus I am pulled up short in an altogether new way. I may hitherto have found it possible to doubt whether I had encountered any truly objective reality at all; but if, for instance, my immediate dominion has been (as is more likely with such people as ourselves), not Juan Fernandez, but perhaps only a single bed-sitting room, and if I find I have now to share it with another fellow creature whose temperament is, as we say, incompatible with my own, then I am unmistakably 'up against' reality at last! Hence it is, in words that are now so familiar, that 'others are the real world' and 'all real life is meeting'.[1] Or in M.

---

[1] Martin Buber, *Ich und Du* (1923), p. 18.

Sartre's bitter words, *L'enfer c'est les autres*—'Hell is other people'.[1]

Nor is it only that the world of natural objects, real as it is on its own level, offers to my will a much less stubborn resistance than that offered by my encounter with my fellow men, but also, as I have already contended, that it is doubtful whether its reality could be apprehended by me at all, if it were not apprehended as being not merely my own world but a world common to myself and my fellows. This means that my sense of the reality of the physical world is in some sort a derivative from my sense of the reality of other selves. 'The world is what I share with others', writes Dr Martin Heidegger; and again, 'all existence is co-existence (*Alles Dasein ist Mitsein*).'[2] Or, as Professor W. E. Hocking had already written in 1912, 'I do not first know my physical world as a world of *objects*, and then as a world of *shared* objects: it is through a prior recognition of the presence of other mind that my physical experience acquires objectivity at all. The objectivity of nature is its community.'[3]

According to Grisebach reality is presence; but it is not without significance that we do not normally speak of the presence of physical objects. We do not say 'a lawn-mower was present in the garden' or 'I was acutely aware of the presence of a table in the room'. Again, according to Dr Buber, 'all real life is meeting' (*Begegnung*), but we do not speak of meeting a table (or say, *Ich habe einen Tisch begegnet*). M. Gabriel Marcel makes the same point, distinguishing between 'what we call an *object* and what we call a *presence*';[4] and he further reflects interestingly upon the significance of the preposition 'with', contending that it properly indicates an 'intersubjective relationship', not a relationship between subject and object.[5] A chair may be *beside* me in the room, but I should

---

[1] *Huis Clos*, ad fin.　　　　　　　　　[2] *Sein und Zeit* (1927), p. 117.
[3] *The Meaning of God in Human Experience* (1912), p. 288 f. I have already quoted some of the above passages in my book *Our Knowledge of God* (1939), § 17. Compare also John Macmurray, *The Self as Agent* (1957), p. 145: ' The resistance to the Self through which the Self can exist as agent must be the resistance of another Self.'
[4] *Reflection and Mystery* (1950), p. 204 f.　　　　[5] Ibid., p. 177.

not say that a chair was with me, still less perhaps that I was *with* a chair. It is only persons that I can be with. Later on we shall have to examine further this concept of presence.[1]

§ 11

Nevertheless I may do my best to ignore the claim my neighbour makes on me, as I fear I often do. I may act towards him as if he were merely a part of the world of which I dispose and not another disposer of it; merely within the circle of my own dominion and not another centre of it. I may treat him not as a person but as a thing, or, as Kant would say, not as an end in himself but as a means to my own ends. If I am sufficiently astute, I appear to 'get away with it', but so far as I do this, I am evading the reality and the presence with which I should otherwise be effectively confronted in my encounter with him. For that reality does not lie merely in the *existence* of my neighbour as an object among other objects in the world, but in the *right* he embodies as over against my own otherwise unlimited desires. This right is obviously not of his own making. No man can confer rights upon himself. If he tried to do so, they would be bogus rights which I should not dream of acknowledging. Nor again is it a question of merely respecting my neighbour's desires. Why should I do so if he has no *right* to have desires, or to have just these desires? My concern must not be merely for his desires, but for what is right in his desires; not merely for his desires but for his *good*; not merely for what is desired *by* him but for what, because it is good in itself, is good *for* him. Hence if 'others are the real world', it is because they embody for me, in my encounter with them, something greater than themselves, an intrinsic right and a universal good. My relations with my fellows have the significance of reality for me only because and in so far as they mediate to me this greater reality; so that we might quote:

[1] We may recall also that in Martin Heidegger's terminology a person may be *gegenwärtig*, whereas a chair can only be *vorhanden*.

I could not love thee, dear, so much,
Lov'd I not honour more.[1]

To all those who have not entirely surrendered their hold upon religious truth, this greater reality is God. All peoples in all ages have known this to be true, however dimly. As has been said: 'All human societies care for righteousness among their members, and all human societies before this present century seem to have found a source and sanction for this righteousness in their gods.'[2] In Christian thought the two great commandments, enjoining the love of God and the love of the neighbour, are related to one another in precisely this way. The way to God passes through my relation to my neighbour, and the way to my neighbour passes through my relation to God.

If a man say, I love God, and hateth his brother, he is a liar; for he that loveth not his brother whom he hath seen, how can he love God whom he hath not seen?[3]

Inasmuch as ye have done it unto one of the least of these my brethren, ye have done it unto me. . . . Inasmuch as ye did it not to one of the least of these, ye did it not to me.[4]

I have indeed often been struck by the larger measure of agreement there is in this matter between Christians and the acutest of contemporary atheistic thinkers. They seem to agree in their analysis, though drawing from it precisely opposite conclusions. For instance, Dr Emil Brunner writes that 'Man has spirit only in that he is addressed by God. . . . Therefore the human self is nothing that exists in its own right; no property of man, but a relation to a divine Thou. . . . The essential being of man . . . is identical with his relation to God.'[5] Nicolas Berdyaev writes that 'Man without God is no longer man.'[6] But here is M. Sartre:

[1] Richard Lovelace, *To Lucasta, on Going to the Wars.*
[2] H. A. Hodges, *The Pattern of Atonement* (1955), p. 62 f.
[3] 1 John 4. 20.
[4] Matt. 25. 40, 45.
[5] *God and Man*, Eng. trans., pp. 155-7.
[6] *The End of our Time* (1933) p. 54; written in 1919.

Dostoievsky said 'If God did not exist, all would be permitted.' That is existentialism's starting-point.[1]

There is no human nature, because there is no God to have a conception of it.[2]

The existentialist finds it very troublesome (*génant*) that God does not exist, because with Him disappears all possibility of finding values in an intelligible world; nor can there be any *a priori* good, because there is no infinite or perfect consciousness of it; nor is it anywhere written that good exists, that we ought to be honest and not tell lies; for we are precisely on a plane where nothing exists but men.[3]

Men, that is to say, who embody no values but invent their own; for M. Sartre goes on:

I am very much vexed (*fâché*) that this should be so, but if I have suppressed God the Father, there must be somebody to invent values.[4]

We found Lord Russell speaking very similarly. 'It is we who create value',[5] he said; and though a man may still call himself a man, yet he is no more than a physical mechanism; 'his thoughts and his bodily movements follow the same laws that describe the movements of stars and atoms.'[6]

The position for which I myself have been contending finds further support in an early work by Dr Karl Heim, entitled *Glaubensgewissheit* ('The Certitude of Faith'). The author begins by laying it down that all a philosophy of faith can do is to offer a theoretical analysis of the faith which is in the possession of the simplest man who in face of the buffetings of fate can say with the psalmist, 'Nevertheless I am continually with thee.'[7] Only by faith, he claims, can we reach certitude of anything beyond immediate and present sense-data. But faith is essentially trust, and we can trust our fellows only because, and in so far as, we believe them to be motivated, not by self-regarding desire, but by the recognition of an absolute obligation to which they are subject. We trust them, therefore, only as

[1] *L'Existentialisme est un Humanisme*, p. 36.   [2] Ibid., p. 22.   [3] Ibid., p. 35.
[4] Ibid., p. 89.   [5] *What I Believe*, p. 25.   [6] Ibid., p. 9.
[7] *Glaubensgewissheit, Eine Untersuchung über die Lebensfrage der Religion*, 3rd ed. (Leipzig 1923), pp. iii, 54.

they embody in themselves something greater than themselves. Thus,

Every relationship of trust between two men has its root in a faith which extends far beyond their relation to one another, the faith that there exists an obligation valid for all subjects, all places and all times, constraining them to a certain disposition of will independently of their own pleasure.[1]

Moreover, unless we believe that this obligation proceeds from a source that can supply him with some power to fulfil it, we can never fully trust a fellow mortal.[2] Even when it is our friend whom we trust, our trust is ultimately in the ground of all being.

What I have contended, then, is that where I find myself in most assured contact with reality is in the relation with God that is mediated to me through my relation with my fellows, and in the relation with my fellows that is mediated to me through my relation with God. Here I take leave once again to quote Dr Tillich:

But what is 'really real' among all the things and events that offer themselves as reality? That which resists me so that I cannot pretend its non-being. The really real is what limits me. There are two powers in the whole of our experience which do not admit any attempt to remove them, the unconditional and 'the other', i.e. the other human being. They are united in their resistance against me, in their manifestation as the really real. The unconditional could be an illusion if it did not appear through the unconditional demand of the other *person* to acknowledge him as a person. And conversely, 'the other', if he did not demand an *unconditional* acknowledgement of his personal dignity, could be used as a tool for my purposes; as a consequence he would lose his power of resistance and his ultimate reality. The unity of the personal and the unconditional,

---

[1] Ibid., p. 27.
[2] Ibid., p. 30. The following is also relevant: 'The other is infinitely distant from me, more distant than the farthest stars. I can wander through all the ways of space that are geometrically possible, traverse land and sea and fly in the upper air, without coming one pace nearer to where the other dwells. Nevertheless the other is infinitely near to me, nearer than the room in which I sit. I cannot, if I have once become aware of it, escape his mysterious "presence", as I can escape from the room.' (p. 121).

or of the ethical and the religious, is the manifestation of the really real, for it resists absolutely any attempt to be dissolved into subjectivity.[1]

Here 'the really real' is, of course, Aristotle's *to ontōs on*. The physical world, Dr Tillich would say, is real enough for us, but its reality is conditioned for us by its context in our apprehension of something more real than itself. 'And I beheld', confessed St Augustine, 'the other things below Thee, and I perceived that they neither altogether are, nor altogether are not; for they are, since they are from Thee; but are not, because they are not what Thou art.'[2]

---

[1] *Religiose Verwirklichung* (1929), p. 56: Eng. trans. in *The Protestant Era*, p. 215 f. This translation is really a very free version of the original, but it has the author's approval, and I have thought it better to use it. There is a footnote in the original in which the author expresses his indebtedness to Grisebach's book.
[2] *Confessions*, VII. 11.

CHAPTER III

The Range of Our Experience

§ 12

In reading the works of naturalist philosophers from Lucretius downwards, I constantly feel that I am being invited to form a mental picture of the human race waking to self-consciousness on this planet and finding itself alone in a bleakly alien universe whose ways and concerns, whatever they may be, bear no relation to its own.

> I, a stranger and afraid
> In a world I never made.[1]

Sometimes I have to shake myself to realize that this is a purely fanciful picture, a piece of modern mythology, but of course it is no more. Not thus did our race come to its first awareness, and not thus has any human individual come to his. The further back we penetrate towards anything that can be called primitive, the clearer does it become that early man conceived himself to be confronted with a situation of an altogether different kind. He felt himself to be at one with nature, and with a nature that was full of divine and sacral significance. All we know even of palaeolithic man indicates that for him reality was a single whole, embracing the natural, the human and the divine in a mutual inter-relatedness of the most intimate kind. For it is in fact not only a later, but very much a *fin de siècle* picture that the naturalists encourage us to contemplate. Our more accustomed picture was not reached by foisting later constructs on to this, but rather this itself was reached by a process of reduction. Of this reductive process I wish now to speak, and I shall call those who indulge in it *reductive naturalists*, because I wish to distinguish those who

[1] A. E. Housman, *Last Poems*, xii.

contend merely that all our experience can be viewed as part of nature from those who contend that there is no other legitimate way of viewing it, thus interpreting the whole of it in the light of that aspect of it which is lowest in valuational significance.

It was (as has already been indicated in an earlier chapter) the Greek Sophists and Atomists who first attempted such a reduction, and the whole philosophic labour of Socrates and Plato was devoted to resisting their teaching, which the latter thus describes—the noun 'art' (*technē*), which appears in this passage, being used in the sense contained in our adjective 'artificial' (*technikos*) or in our word 'artifact', that is, man-made:

They say that the greatest and fairest things are the work of nature and chance, and the lesser things the work of art which, taking over from nature the great basic things, proceeds itself to fashion and frame the lesser things, which they thus term artificial. . . . I can make the matter clearer still. They say that fire and water and earth and air are all of nature and of chance, not of art; and that the bodies that come next in order of being, the sun and moon and stars and our own earth, are the products of these entirely inanimate elements, being made to revolve by the chance action of some kind of force; and that in this way the whole universe and all it contains, including the animals and the plants, have come into being—not by the action of mind, or of any God, nor by art, but, as I have said, by nature and by chance. Art, they say, was developed afterwards and out of these. It is human and of human origin, and has produced for our entertainment a number of things which have very little truth in them but are imaginative constructions such as music and painting and their companion arts produce. . . . They say also that the gods exist by art, not by nature, but by law and custom which differ in different places. They even assert that one thing is good by nature, and quite another thing by law, there being from the point of view of nature no such thing as justice. And all this, my friends, from sages, poets and orators— and addressed to young people.[1]

Moreover, such a picture of the human situation is as late an emergent in the life-story of the individual as it has been in

[1] *Laws* X, 889-90.

the history of the race. Not in such utter nakedness does any child begin its self-conscious life; that nakedness, where it exists, being again the result of a much later process of stripping. Most of us, I suspect, would have to say Amen to at least the first lines of Wordsworth's Ode:

> There was a time when meadow, grove and stream,
> The earth, and every common sight,
> To me did seem
> Apparell'd in celestial light.

The reality with which we first remember finding ourselves faced was no alien or unfriendly one, but a reality rich in meaning, in beauty and in promise, warm in human interest, and at the same time most solemn in its demands.

Now I suppose that such an account of our original awareness of things will be readily accepted by the reductive naturalists, and perhaps even discounted as too obvious to justify my adducing it. Yet I doubt whether either they or the public who read their books have yet rid their minds completely of the influences deriving from their eighteenth-century predecessors who strove so hard to represent mankind's spiritual outlook as something foisted on to a more primitive 'state of nature', however completely they may have now abandoned the idea that it was, in the words of one eighteenth-century writer, but 'a politick trick to awe the credulous vulgar'. For it should follow from the rejection of such a doctrine that, instead of the defence of the spiritual outlook having to start from a prior naturalist one, the argument should be the other way about. I did not start from a barely naturalist outlook; and if I have ever been tempted to adopt such, it was as the result of a highly sophisticated process of thinking which required its own defence. It would therefore be an entirely artificial exercise on my part, were I to begin my defence of what I believe from a prior position of unbelief, trying to find room for God within a situation, or by the enlargement of a situation, in which he did not yet exist. It is on the denial, not on the affirmation, of the divine, that the burden of argument rests, both for our race as a whole and for every individual within it.[1]

No doubt many of the reductionists will be ready enough to take up that burden, and on those terms. It is therefore important to consider the lines which their argument is likely to follow. They must admit that when, before scientific inquiry begins, I look out upon the world about me, it presents itself to me as something very different from what they themselves now believe it really to be. When like the psalmist I 'consider the heavens' and look up at the sun in the noonday sky, the impression it makes on me is both a single impression and yet a very complex one. It is likely to include in an implicit way the judgements that the sun is round and white and very bright; but also the judgements that it is beautiful and sublime; and further the judgements that it is a great work of God, and a gift graciously designed by him for the benefit, not only of myself, but of the whole human race, and indeed of all that has life and breath. All these judgements are for me, as they, or something closely related to them, have been for the generality of mankind, indissolubly united in the wholeness of a single concrete experience. In the language of the psychologists, they form a *Gestalt*, a configuration of constituent elements which have not been put together synthetically, though our minds may by a process of abstraction separate them out analytically. When I turn natural scientist, what I do is to abstract from this *Gestalt* those judgements which can be expressed in quantitative terms, and, by more particularized attention and the artificial creation of experimental conditions, to develop them in temporary isolation from the other judgements contained in the *Gestalt*. Needless to say, such a process is entirely legitimate, being indispensably necessary for the admirable purposes which natural science has at heart. But like so many other justifiable and necessary things, it has its own manifest and very great dangers, and notably the danger

[1] Speaking of our sense of contingency, or of our dependence upon a power greater than ourselves, Ian Crombie declares that 'One is not *persuaded* to believe one is contingent; rather one feels that it is only by persuasion that one could ever believe anything else'—*The Socratic*, Number Five, p. 14.

to which the late Professor Whitehead once directed our attention when he remarked that a man may know all about the laws of light and yet, perhaps just because he has learned so much about them, 'miss the radiance of the sunset and the glory of the morning sky'. What reductive naturalism has done is to succumb to these dangers. It champions the doctrine that those elements of my total experience of the sun which science abstracts from it are the only elements yielding veridical knowledge of what the sun really is; or more generally, that my real human situation is constituted only by what physical science can tell me about it.

I have illustrated my point from our vision of the sun, but in further illustration of it I would quote the following passage from that profoundly perceptive Victorian author George Macdonald:

What, I ask, is the truth of water? Is it that it is formed of hydrogen and oxygen? . . . Is it for the sake of the fact that hydrogen and oxygen combined form water, that the precious thing exists? Is oxygen-and-hydrogen the divine idea of water? Or has God put the two together only that man might separate them and find them out? . . . The water itself, that dances, and sings, and slakes the wonderful thirst—symbol and picture of that draught for which the woman of Samaria made her prayer to Jesus—this lovely thing itself, whose very wetness is a delight to every inch of the human body in its embrace . . . this water is itself its own truth, and is therein a truth of God. Let him who would know the love of the maker become sorely athirst, and drink of the brook by the way— then lift up his heart—not at that moment to the maker of oxygen and hydrogen, but to the inventor and mediator of thirst and water, that man may foresee a little of what his soul may find in God. . . . As well may a man think to describe the joy of drinking by giving thirst and water for its analysis, as imagine he has revealed anything about water by resolving it into its scientific elements. Let a man go to the hillside and let the brook sing to him till he loves it, and he will find himself far nearer the fountain of truth than the triumphal car of the chemist will ever lead the shouting crew of his half-comprehending followers. He will draw from the brook the water of joyous tears 'and worship him that made heaven, and earth, and the sea, and the fountains of water.'

The truth *of a thing*, then, is the blossom of it, the thing it is made for, the topmost stone set on with rejoicing; truth in a man's imagination is the power to recognize this truth of a thing; and wherever, in anything that God has made, in the glory of it, be it sky or flower or human face, we see the glory of God, there a true imagination is beholding a truth of God.[1]

But let me now return to my first example. I said that the sun impresses me not only as round and bright, but also as beautiful and sublime. But it is contended that the latter two adjectives add nothing to the *description* of the sun. Taking the example of a hilltop view which is judged to be 'extensive and sublime', Mr Nowell-Smith says that:

The adjective 'sublime' does not form part of the description of the view. . . . The question whether the view was extensive or not is a question of empirical fact. But the sublimity of the view is not part of its contents. . . . I shall refer to words of the same family as 'sublime' as Aptness-words . . . because they are words that indicate that an object has certain properties which are apt to arouse a certain emotion or range of emotions.[2]

To this I can only say that if Mr Nowell-Smith chooses to define the word 'descriptive' as applying only to those features of the view which are simply apprehended by our senses, he is of course at liberty to do this. My own concern is sufficiently satisfied by his admission that in addition to these the view has 'certain other properties' of a very different kind. Needless to say, also, whether or not the view is sublime is not a question of 'empirical fact', if the *empeiria* or experience he has in mind is mere sensory experience. But I shall be contending that not all our experience is sensory experience.

It will be remembered that one of the world's earliest scientists, Anaxagoras, found himself in serious trouble with the general public because he said that the sun was only a mass of blazing metal about the size of the Peloponnese. That greatly shocked the good Athenians, who had him up for impiety; and though the eloquence of Pericles secured his acquittal he was forced to retire from Athens as science's first martyr. It

---

[1] *Unspoken Sermons*, Third Series (1889), pp. 67-69.
[2] *Ethics* (1954), pp. 70-72.

is very significant that a century later Plato is still found protesting against the impiety of Anaxagoras's conclusion.[1] One
is reminded of Blake's couplet:

> If the sun and moon should doubt,
> They'd immediately go out.[2]

But the incident excellently illustrates the complex nature of
the issue as between natural piety, scientific discovery and a
reductive naturalism. As a scientist Anaxagoras was more
nearly right about the sun than anybody had ever been before,
but the Athenians 'felt in their bones' that what he affirmed
could not be the whole truth about it, and therefore they were
led to deny the truth even of his scientific affirmation—a state
of affairs that was constantly to repeat itself in much later
times. The Athenians, even including Plato in his own more
sophisticated way, believed the sun to be itself a god. Christianity has destroyed that belief, correcting it into the very different
one that the sun is God's gift and the work of his hands; not
itself divine but (as we might say) sacramental of the divine
presence. Thus the scientific and the Christian affirmations,
instead of conflicting, mutually help each other's case; but
Christian piety is as opposed as was pagan piety to the naturalist
affirmation that Anaxagoras and his kind were telling us *all
there is to know* about the sun.

Christianity, then, has taught us to regard as inanimate
objects very many things which the Greeks, including Plato
and Aristotle, regarded like other pagans as *zoa*, living subjects. Yet our human situation is far from being exhaustively
constituted by our relation to this inanimate environment,
since it is determined no less by our relations with one another
and with the living God. It is not only with objects that I have
to reckon every moment of every day, but also with other
subjects. These two components of my situation are indeed, as I
have already contended, most closely interconnected, my
apprehension of the world of objects being from the beginning
a shared apprehension, while conversely there is not one of my

[1] *Laws* X, 886, 889.   [2] *Auguries of Innocence.*

relations with other subjects that is not mediated to me by our common relation to the world of objects. Nevertheless Christian thought has made this distinction between *persons* and *things* quite fundamental to its case, while our reductionists, in order to make good their own very different case, could not rest content with naturalizing our experience of *things* but have attempted equally to naturalize our *personal* relationships. Man, we are told, is a natural product, and that is the whole truth about him. Except perhaps for one strange fact, namely, that he habitually *thinks* himself to be something more? But no; for according to Lord Russell, 'what we call our "thoughts" seem to depend upon the organization of tracks in the brain in the same sort of way in which journeys depend upon roads and railways. The energy used in thinking seems to have a chemical origin';[1] so that 'undoubtedly we are part of nature, which has produced our desires, our hopes and fears, in accordance with laws which the physicist is beginning to discover.'[2] Our thinking that we are more than things is thus only another thing. (But then so equally must be Lord Russell's thinking, when he makes these assertions! As has been well said, 'The only creature that can prove anything cannot prove its own insignificance without depriving the proof of its proof-value. Any radical depreciation of man involves an equally radical depreciation of the scientific thinking which supplies the supposed evidence.'[3])

Nor is it only our moral, social and sacral values that are thus forced to retreat from their traditional status in reality to a merely subjective status in the mind of man. The line cannot be drawn thus simply between Kant's 'starry heavens above' and his 'moral law within'. As has been seen, our experience of beauty, our aesthetic values, must certainly share the same fate. Perhaps also our experience of light and colour, of sound and taste and smell? Is it that, when I perceive the noonday sun as a round white object, the roundness is really there, independently of my perceiving it, whereas the white-

[1] *What I Believe*, p. 12.
[2] Ibid., p. 23.
[3] T. E. Jessop in *The Christian Understanding of Man* (Church, Community and State Series), 1938, p. 37.

ness is there only for my perceiving mind?[1] This also was taught by the Greek naturalists. The real world, wrote Lucretius in giving us the fullest account of their teaching that now remains to us, is a fortuitous concourse of atoms 'bereft of colour, sundered altogether from cold and warmth and fiery heat, and carried along barren of sound and devoid of taste, nor do they give off any heat of their own'.[2] Such a dichotomy draws the line between objective reality and subjective appearance very low down, but it has been found notoriously difficult to maintain. Bishop Berkeley's contention that *if* light and colour and sound are only in my sense and mind, so also are form and size and weight, is not easily answered. On this point, therefore, the naturalists are divided amongst themselves, not all agreeing with Lucretius. Where they are at one is in declaring our aesthetic experience to be, no less than our moral experience, purely subjective in origin, yielding no intimations of reality. When I have judged a landscape beautiful, I have always supposed myself to mean that it was beautiful in itself, independently of my thinking it so;[3] but now I am told that what I mean, or ought to mean, is that I can make anything I like beautiful by merely liking it; since 'it is we who create value, and our desires which confer value',[4] these desires

---

[1] 'The world that people had thought themselves living in—a world rich with colour and sound, redolent with fragrance, filled with gladness, love and beauty, speaking everywhere of purposive harmony and creative ideals—was crowded now into minute corners in the brains of scattered organic beings. The really important world outside was a world hard, cold, colourless, silent and dead; a world of quantity, a world of mathematically computable motions in mechanical regularity'—Said of the picture of the world resulting from Newtonian mechanics by E. A. Burtt in *The Metaphysical Foundations of Modern Physical Science*, p. 236; as quoted by E. L. Mascall, *Words and Images* (1957), p. 32.

[2] *De Rerum Natura*, II, lines 842 ff. Lucretius is, of course, here repeating Epicurus, who was in turn repeating Leucippus and Democritus, the latter of whom wrote: 'In common usage (νόμῳ) sweet, in common usage bitter, in common usage hot, in common usage cold, in common usage coloured: in reality only atoms and empty space' (Sextus Empiricus, *Adv. Math.*, VII, *135*).

[3] Compare John Macmurray, *The Self as Agent* (1957), p. 200, 'Scientific knowledge is more subjective than artistic knowledge'; and A. D. Ritchie, *Studies in the History and Methods of the Sciences* (1958), p. 212, 'There is no justification for the common view that aesthetic judgement is more specially subjective than any other kind of judgement'.

[4] Russell, *What I Believe*, p. 25.

having themselves been produced by the operation of atomic 'laws which the physicist is beginning to discover'.

It would thus seem that all along the line the reality of which the reductive naturalists speak is different, as night from day, from the reality with which I believe myself to be in daily and momentary encounter. I have claimed that the burden of proof rests, in the first instance, not on me but on them who are the real innovators. Yet I must not understand this as relieving me of all further responsibility in defending the tradition against such innovation. It is a commonplace among historians that no dogma has ever been either defined or as such defended until an opposing heresy had already raised its head, but the appearance of heresy has always been regarded as obliging those who abide by the tradition to produce reasons for the faith that is in them, making explicit what had hitherto been only latently contained in their minds—the interior logic of their own existing convictions. 'Salt', defined the schoolboy, 'is what makes my porridge taste nasty when they don't put it in.' I had hitherto hardly been aware of the salt that rendered palatable my existing outlook on reality, but when the naturalists leave it out, I certainly find the resulting dish nasty and insipid enough. It is therefore incumbent on me to find a better definition of salt than the schoolboy's, and a better reason for restoring it than simply that I am unhappy without it.[1]

§ 13

We have seen that the experience we enjoy when we look at the sun is a single whole, for all the diverse elements of which it is compact. We have now to expand this into a statement of the utmost generality and say that in the same way our total experience of reality presents itself to us as a single experience, each diverse strand of which is intimately related to, and inextricably intermingled with, all the others. The world we

[1] In this section I have, with the kind consent of the publishers, drawn largely on what I said in my William Ainslie Memorial Lecture on *The Human Situation*, which was published by Messrs Longmans, Green and Company in 1950 and has been long out of print.

know is known by us as one world. 'The philosopher', writes Professor Macmurray, 'does not need to prove that reality is a whole, though he sometimes tries to do so. Indeed it cannot be proved. But that is because, unless it were given in immediate experience, philosophy would never arise.'[1]

At a later stage we bring our powers of rational analysis to bear on our experience, and to do this we have to concentrate our attention at any one time on a single strand or aspect of it forming abstract mental concepts which, just because they are abstract, enable us to regard it in convenient temporary isolation from the rest. These concepts we then use to draw inferences from the fundamental knowledge we already have, and to extend and improve that knowledge in such a way that we now understand the temporarily abstracted aspect better than we understood it before. Clearly, however, such abstractive analysis cannot begin unless we already have some knowledge of the reality we are analysing. Scientific conclusions, writes Professor Macmurray, 'signify something only because they interpret our immediate knowledge of the world.'[2] 'If there were no immediate knowledge there could be no reflection, because there would be nothing to reflect upon.'[3] And he formulates it as a general principle that '*All thought presupposes knowledge*. It is not possible to think about something that you do not already know.'[4] Thought is here identified with reflection, that is, with the secondary activity of the mind in which it bends back (Latin, *re-flectere*) upon its own primary operations; and I believe correctly so identified. Thought implies a ratiocinative process which makes use of the apparatus of inference. But it must not be supposed that what is here called 'immediate knowledge' is merely sensation, the reception by the organism of sense-data. It too is a product of intelligence, though not yet of reflection. It is the work of *nous*; but of the *nous aisthētikos*, not of the nous *apodeiktikos* (or, in the Latin equivalents of these Greek philosophic terms, of the *ratio intuitiva*, not of the *ratio discursiva*). When such knowledge is said to

---

[1] *Interpreting the Universe* (1933), p. 27.   [2] Ibid., p. 17.   [3] Ibid., p. 13.
[4] Ibid., p. 15, the italics being Professor Macmurray's.

be immediate, what is meant is that it is not mediated by any process of inference. It is, as was agreed in our first chapter, a direct knowledge of the real, extra-mental world. It is indeed mediated by sense-data, but its relation to these is not one of logical entailment. In Dr Mascall's phrase, already quoted, it is 'grasped through them', but not inferred from them.

§ 14

Nearly all contemporary philosophers profess to be empiricists, and to be an empiricist is to believe that all our veridical knowledge derives from our experience and can be checked by reference to it. But the *empeiria* or experience many of them have in mind is our experience of the corporeal world as revealed to us by our bodily senses, and these assume that this is the only experience, and consequently the only knowledge, we possess of trans-subjective reality, whether it be *Umwelt* or *Mitwelt*. The spectacular success of modern physical science in enabling us not only to understand the world of nature but also to manipulate and control it to our own advantage, has undoubtedly had much to do with the prevalence of this assumption. It is, however, an assumption that we must strenuously oppose. Our lives would indeed be poor and savourless if we had no awareness, in which we could repose the least degree of trust, of anything in reality save what we can see and hear and touch and taste and smell. My contention will indeed be that we have even what can properly be called *sense* experience of other things than these. The human spirit, I shall say, develops certain subtler senses or sensitivities which go beyond the bodily senses. Newman, in arguing for what he called 'the illative sense', referred to our familiar employment of the word in such phrases as good sense, common sense and a sense of beauty.[1] Any number of examples could, however, be added. We variously speak of a sense of humour, a sense of honour, a sense of propriety, a sense of proportion, a sense of (literary) style; and likewise of a sense of duty, a 'sensitive' conscience, a

[1] *A Grammar of Assent*, chap. IX, ad init.

sense of the holy or of the divine, a sense of the presence of God. These are all refined or sublimate developments of our experience, and it is needless to say that they all presuppose for their possibility the experience gained through the bodily senses. Nevertheless they carry us far beyond such experience, making us sensitive to aspects of reality of which these, taken by themselves, could not conceivably inform us. They enable us to perceive something not otherwise perceptible; to *perceive* it, I say, and not merely to conceive it as a concept to which we are led by argument.[1]

It may indeed be contended that, though this extended use of the word 'sense' is firmly established in ordinary speech, it is more convenient to confine the word in philosophical discourse to the corporeal senses, and not, for example, to speak too glibly of a 'moral sense', as did Shaftesbury and his followers in the early eighteenth century. But we need not here do battle about words, though I propose to abide by my own, my concern being only that these other awarenesses should be recognized as so far analogous to the corporeal senses as to enable us to perceive something not otherwise perceptible. This point was cogently made by the late John Laird with reference to another such awareness which I did not mention above, namely that awareness of our own being which philosophers had often spoken of as an 'inner sense'.

Introspection . . . is not literally an 'internal sense', but as Locke says, 'though it be not sense, yet it is very like it', for it is *observation* of those mental events which we call passions, resolves and cogitations—an inspection of their *being*, not an inference concerning them.[2]

Those who have thus insisted on the perceptual character of our non-corporeal awarenesses have commonly been labelled

---

[1] 'There might be such a thing as *religious experience*, and I believe there is. And I mean by the word "experience" something cognitive, not just an emotion, though doubtless emotion accompanies it. I mean a mode of awareness, a unique one, not reducible to any other. . . . If we *must* classify it under one of the familiar heads, I would rather call it "a sense" myself, *a sense of the divine;* for it does have this in common with the ordinary senses, that it is an original source of *data*. . . . '
—Professor H. H. Price in *The Socratic*, Number Five (1952), p. 43.

[2] In *Contemporary British Philosophy* (ed. Muirhead), Vol. I, p. 227.

intuitionists. This is in itself a suitable enough name, since intuition and perception are two Latin words which in this usage are virtually identical in meaning. Both mean 'observation'—the term used by Laird in the passage quoted, and they were employed indifferently by Latin-speaking philosophers to translate the Greek *aisthēsis*—so that the *nous aisthētikos* could be either *ratio perceptiva* or *ratio intuitiva*. But in later times there has been a tendency to speak of an intuition as an apprehension of a truth or proposition rather than of an aspect of reality, and from this usage I should wish to dissociate myself. Nor should I wish to bind myself to any of the particular formulations even of those 'intuitionists' who have not shared this tendency, such as Jacobi, Fries, Rudolf Otto or certain representatives of the Moral Sense School above referred to. I am convinced, however, that these were all trying to say something which urgently needs to be said, however defective was often their way of saying it.

In his Pelican volume on Ethics, already referred to, Mr Nowell-Smith selects as examples of contemporary intuitionism (which he roundly condemns) the ethical theories of Professor G. E. Moore, Sir David Ross and Professor Pritchard. What is common to them all, he says, is the contention that in the exercise of our moral consciousness we are being aware, in a way that is analogous to sense-perception, of aspects or properties of reality other than those of which we are aware in sense-perception itself. According to these,

We do not literally see these properties with our eyes; but the faculty concerned is called 'non-sensuous intuition', 'awareness', 'apprehension', 'recognition', 'acquaintance', words which all strongly suggest an analogy with sight or touch.[1]

Against such views Mr Nowell-Smith argues as follows:

If we are to justify the analogy between moral properties and empirical properties, which is implied by the use of objective terminology, we must show that there is a contrast in moral matters between 'is right' and 'seems right', which corresponds to the contrast between 'is red' and 'seems red'. . . . But this is exactly

---

[1] p. 34 f.

what the intuitionist cannot do; for in making direct awareness the test of real ethical properties he eliminates the whole point of the objective-subjective contrast.[1]

The double language only has point if we allow that the observer himself is the best judge of looks but not of what a thing really is. And this enables us to admit ourselves consistently wrong in empirical cases. If a man finds his judgements about colour differ consistently from those of others, he will admit himself to be colour-blind. . . . If each man had to judge the real colour of an object by his individual sense of colour, the very distinction between 'is red' and 'looks red' would have broken down and we should have no use for redness as a real property at all. For, where real properties are concerned, general agreement is admitted, even by a dissentient, to be the criterion for the property.[2]

Further, people disagree about what is good and right in a way

that could not possibly occur in the case of objective empirical properties. . . . The parallel case would be that in which a number of scientists failed to agree about the reading of a scale or a meter or about the colour of an object. . . . If this sort of disagreement were of frequent occurrence, the property in question could not be treated as a 'real' or 'objective' property at all.[3]

Now this whole argument seems to me to be manywise fallacious. To begin with, we should not dream of claiming that individual moral (or aesthetic or religious) judgements are not subject to error. When an individual observer says 'This is right', the chances of his being mistaken are even greater than when he says 'This is red'; the reason being (as we shall afterwards have further occasion to note) that there is more likelihood of his going astray in the subtler and more delicate regions of his experience than in the grosser ones. On the other hand it is as true of such physical properties as colour, as it is of ethical properties like rightness or goodness, that we are in the end wholly dependent for our knowledge of them upon the judgement of individuals. Alike in both cases the *single* individual's judgement is seriously shaken if he finds that he is alone in making it. He then says: 'This seems to me to be right,

[1] p. 56.   [2] p. 56 f.   [3] p. 58.

but since most of those whose good judgement I would otherwise trust judge it to be wrong, it may be that it is not really
right after all.' Yet the situation remains unsatisfactory for him
until or unless, having been stimulated by these contrary
judgements, he has had another look at the matter for himself
and is now able to see things otherwise than he had formerly
seen them. Of course, if there were *no* degree of consensus as
to what is right and what is wrong, we might well come to feel
that our moral judgements were no more than individual
seeming, but Mr Nowell-Smith himself writes in another connexion that 'The more we study moral codes, the more we
find that they do not differ on major points of principle'.[1]
Moreover, when he argues that the double language of 'seems
so' and 'is so', which must be able to be used when objectivity
is claimed for our judgements, entails the possibility of admission by the individual that he is 'consistently wrong', as in the
case when a man is forced to admit that he is colour-blind; I
should remark, first, that this is a case of constitutional
abnormality, in fact a pathological case; and second, that
abnormal psychology is by no means unfamiliar with pathological cases in which the patient is, and may even come to be
persuaded that he is, consistently aberrant in his moral perceptions. Thus our apprehension of what Mr Nowell-Smith,
following Professor Moore, calls non-natural properties is on
all fours with our apprehension of natural properties in respect
of all those features which Mr Nowell-Smith himself considers
necessary to our regarding it as yielding a knowledge of trans-
subjective reality. Hence we cannot be forced in respect of the
former apprehension, any more than of the latter, into the
situation once cleverly caricatured,

> When suave politeness, tempering bigot zeal,
> Corrected *I believe* to *One does feel*.[2]

'General agreement', writes Mr Nowell-Smith, 'is not a test
of truth; but it is a necessary condition of the use of objective
language.'[3] The measure of truth in this dictum appears to be
as follows. Universal agreement is usually attainable, apart

---

[1] P. 18.　　　[2] Ronald Knox, *Absolute and Abitofhell.*　　　[3] Op. cit., p. 55.

from constitutional or pathological abnormalities such as colour-blindness, for judgements of ordinary sense-perception like 'This rose is red'. *L'homme moyen sensuel* is here at no disadvantage compared with the most sensitive minds. But when we pass to the higher regions of our experience, to what we have called our subtler and more delicate awarenesses, we do not expect universal agreement. Not all will agree that chastity is good, or that the songs of Shakespeare are beautiful, or that God is gracious. On the other hand, however, some considerable measure of agreement, though it is still not 'a test of truth' is normally a necessary condition of the security of individual judgement. If I *alone* found chastity good or Shakespeare's songs beautiful or God gracious, I should find my conviction almost impossible to sustain and would indeed be driven to say 'seems to me' rather than 'is'; just as would happen if I alone saw the rose as red. Not even in our apparently firmest convictions can we dispense with the 'great cloud of witnesses.'[1]

Thus no sound reason has been given us why we should depart from our accustomed use of 'objective language' when discoursing of those acts of apprehension that go beyond ordinary sense-perception; or why we should depart from our accustomed belief that here also certain things are being *perceived* by us. It is not really reason or logic, but an initial naturalistic bias, that makes the reductive empiricists desire these innovations. Because they have already decided that there is no objective reality but matter in motion, they are forced to believe that our ethical judgements are merely statements concerning our own subjective desires and intentions. 'To say that something is good', writes Mr. Nowell-Smith, '. . . is not to make a statement about it or to describe it, but to express a desire for it or an attitude towards it, to express approval of it, to grade it, to praise it, to commend it, and so on.'[2] 'A moral belief', writes Professor Braithwaite in his well-known lecture on *An Empiricist's View of the Nature of Religious Belief*, 'is an intention to behave in a certain way: a religious belief is an intention to behave in a certain way (a moral belief)

---

[1] Heb. 12. 1.   [2] p. 95.

together with the entertainment of certain stories associated with the intention in the mind of the believer.'[1] Such a reading of the nature of our moral judgements could not, however, possibly arise from a direct examination of these judgements themselves, which certainly purport to say something very different. It is just not true that when I acknowledge something to be good, I mean that I desire it; for very often, unfortunately, I do not desire it. It is just not true that my moral beliefs are intentions to behave in a certain way: for very often, unfortunately, my intended behaviour runs contrary to my belief. Usually, indeed, it is admitted by the reductive naturalists that their theory of the nature of moral judgements does violence to their apparent meaning and to the meaning attached to them by those who make them. Lord Russell, for example, begins a recent treatment of ethics as follows:

Ethics differs from science in the fact that its fundamental data are feelings and emotions, not percepts. . . . An ethical judgement does not state a fact; it states, *though often in a disguised form,* some hope or fear, some desire or aversion, some love or hate. It *should be* enunciated in the optative or imperative mood, not in the indicative.[2]

---

[1] Op. cit. (1955), p. 32. Already in 1927, in a small volume entitled *The State of Religious Belief,* Professor Braithwaite had adopted this view. The book concludes with the following words about our religious experiences: 'To deny their metaphysical efficacy is not to deny their emotional and ethical importance. Indeed the opposite is rather the case, and because they can tell us nothing about the meaning of the universe, we expect more from them in themselves. Because life has no meaning, it does not follow that it has no value; nor that it is not those things in it which were wrongly supposed to explain it that are the most important.' (p. 74 f.)

[2] *Human Society in Ethics and Politics* (1955), p. 3. It appears, however, that (in this particular publication) Lord Russell is reluctant to believe that the indicative form is *merely* a disguise, and that there is nothing in ethics that is not subjective (p. 92). He is even prepared to consider the view 'that we know by ethical intuition one or more propositions about the kind of acts that we ought, or ought not to perform.' 'There is', he says, 'no *logical* objection to this theory, and I am not prepared to reject it decisively' (p. 93). In the end, however, he departs from it, and tries instead to find some ethical statements which are rightly enunciated in the indicative and of which truth or falsity may therefore rightly be predicated (p. 98). But those which he finds are not ethical statements in the proper sense at all. They are, or purport to be, statements of psychological fact; and although he speaks of ethics as 'containing them', he insists that 'its basis is still one of emotion and feeling' (p. 100). His search for a genuinely ethical statement that is not purely subjective therefore fails. Why then does he not have a further look at the 'intuitionist' theory, which he has not yet decisively rejected?

Here the phrases which I have taken the liberty of italicizing show clearly enough that what the moral agent believes himself to be doing when he makes a moral judgement is not what Lord Russell says he is doing. Can it then be anything but a preconceived naturalistic bias that prevents Lord Russell from taking this whole region of our experience at its face value?

CHAPTER IV

The Epistemological Status of Faith

§ 15

What we do when we 'reason things out' is to try to bring to the light of full consciousness the real nature and interior grounds of such knowledge as we already have, and thus to add further knowledge to it. This effort is a very arduous one and can never achieve complete success. Even in the case of my simplest and most elementary pieces or acts of knowledge, it is not quite easy to 'reason out' how I have come by them. I have no difficulty at all in distinguishing the real world from the world of my dreams, but when I am asked how I do this, I am more than likely to give a wrong answer; and indeed philosophers and psychologists have long argued about it. Or when, crouching in the water-meadow, I see the trees through the reeds, and am asked just how and why I know the trees to be longer than the reeds, though they appear much smaller, it requires careful thought to get the answer quite right. Moreover, I am to the end much surer of the knowledge I am analysing than of the added knowledge that comes from my analysis of it. Knowledge gained by later inference can never have the same certitude as that contained in direct experience.

When, however, we pass to the subtler regions of our experience, this becomes far more evident. I know that a certain landscape or painting or building or poem or musical melody is beautiful, but if I am asked to say why it is beautiful, or wherein its beauty consists, I do my best to answer but I shall in this case despair of ever getting my answer quite right, and certainly I shall never be so sure of the correctness and adequacy of my analytical theory as I am of my original judgement. Or again if, in an act of comparison, I judge Shakespeare's blank verse to be better than Tennyson's (or Martin Tupper's), I may do my best to say why, but I shall be far from staking the justice of my preference on the success of my later explication of its implicit grounds. Still again, my knowledge that it is my duty to help my neighbour who is in need is attended by far greater certitude than is the ethical theory I construct to explain why this should be so. Even John Stuart Mill was much more assured where his duty lay in this matter than of the correctness of his hedonistic explanation of it. And to consider one more instance, when I say about some new acquaintance 'I trust that man', and am asked to say why, I may in this case find it almost impossible to give any answer, and certainly my confidence in the man will be greater than in the adequacy of any tentative explanation of it I may venture to offer. This, incidentally, is one of Newman's examples of the illative sense —'the intuitive perception of character possessed by certain men, while others are destitute of it'.[1]

Even our most direct perception of reality, corporeal or otherwise, is indeed far from infallible. We have already allowed that it is not easy to attach certitude to any single such perception. Nevertheless we have claimed that each field of our percipient experience is transfused with certitude. If there is not certitude here, there is none anywhere. Starting from such knowledge as is thus already in our possession, we proceed to draw inferences from it, but the inferred knowledge cannot have the same quality of certitude; and the more elaborate the chain of inferences required to reach it, the less assurance we have in respect of it. There may always be an error in our logic, a neglected alternative perhaps, and the further our speculation goes, the greater is the possibility of such error. All in all, therefore, the seat of human wisdom will always remain with our intuited rather than with our inferred knowledge of our human situation.

§ 16

This brings us to the much discussed question of verification. When this word is spoken, we think first of its use by the natural

[1] *A Grammar of Assent*, chap. VIII. § 3.

scientists. These proceed by forming hypotheses which go beyond our immediate experience in attempting to systematize and explain it. They say, 'Let us suppose this or this to be true of the things we experience.' They then test the truth of the supposal by returning to their experience of these things and seeing whether it accords with it, correlating different parts of it in a way of which they had not previously been aware; and to this end they frequently arrange for themselves special little complexes of experiences in a carefully planned pattern and sequence—they call them experiments, but that is only another form of the same word. If the supposal in question turns out to be in accord with these experiences and really to correlate them, it is said to be verified. Among the many hypotheses for which verification is thus claimed are, for instance, that the air is a mixture of two different gases, that water is a compound of two different gases, that the earth revolves round the sun, and that the human race is genealogically related to the apes.

Those who are anxious to persuade us that we should accept nothing as true unless it can be verified usually mean that it must be verified in this particular way. To begin with, however, we must remember that pre-scientific common sense has its own much simpler variant and anticipation of this scientific procedure. If I look out of my window in Edinburgh in the month of January and 'see' a tulip in bloom in my garden, I certainly do not at once accept this apparent perception as veridical, but I go out into my garden to look again more closely, and I may then see the supposed tulip as only a fragment of Christmas bunting which has been discarded and caught in the wind. You may call that a case of experimental verification, and you may also say, if you like, that when I first saw the object, I merely 'supposed' it to be a tulip and that I was therefore putting forward what was in essence a scientific hypothesis. 'There is nothing perverse or paradoxical', writes Professor Ayer, 'about the view that all the "truths" of science and common sense are hypotheses.'[1]

[1] *Language, Truth and Logic*, 2nd ed., p. 72.

In all this, however, we are still dealing with our knowledge of the corporeal world, but what the empiricists are accustomed to claim is that no knowledge can be accepted as true unless it is capable of verification with reference to *the same region of experience* as that with which natural science deals, namely, that gained through the bodily senses. 'Every factual proposition', Professor Ayer next tells us, in distinguishing these from what he calls merely emotive utterances, 'must refer to sense experience.'[1] But against this I would submit that, whereas indeed our ethical, aesthetic and religious knowledge is capable of verification and should constantly be subjected to such, this must be carried out by a return, not to our experience of corporeal reality, but, as the case may be, to our ethical, aesthetic or religious experience itself. The demand we should make of our judgements in these fields is, as Professor Niebuhr has said, that they should be 'verifiable on their own level'.[2] If, for example, I listen to a new piece of music and am inclined to judge it beautiful, how do I proceed to 'verify' this judgement? Obviously by returning to the experience, by hearing the piece over and over again, by living with it. I can and do indeed bring such knowledge of musical theory as I possess to bear upon my judgement, and in this way I may be stimulated to some revision, perhaps even to a reversal, of the judgement. But this can be only if, through my theoretical analysis of it, I am first led to a revision of the experience itself, so that I no longer have the same perception of beauty as I had before. Musical theory is itself drawn from musical experience and from nothing else, and can be verified in no other way than by appeal to such experience. I read also with some eagerness what the critics have to say about that particular piece of music, and I am interested to know what is thought about it by lovers of music in general, and if these find little beauty in it, I may be much shaken in my own judgement, but clearly this does not settle the issue for me, or conclude the process of verification, unless or until what they say leads me myself to

[1] Ibid., p. 71.
[2] *The Self and the Dramas of History* (1956), p. 111.

hear the music differently from before; just as it may be some-body else's scepticism that prompts me to have a closer look at the supposed tulip in the garden and to see it now as what it really is. If I cannot myself hear the music differently, and if yet I remain shaken in my judgement through the suspicion that their faculty of musical perception may be more developed than my own, then my only recourse must be to train myself in such perception by listening to more and more music. And of course what I have here said about musical appreciation applies equally to our judgement in respect of all other arts. Each is verifiable only by an appeal to the region of experience out of which it arose.

§ 17

But the same principles apply also to our ethico-religious judgements. These, as we have seen, are judgements relating to 'our ultimate concern'. They too are verifiable, but in their own kind and on their own level. They are verified by appeal to our ethico-religious experience and to that alone; and cer-tainly not by appeal to our sensible experience of the corporeal world.

The proper name of religious experience is faith. It is by faith that we apprehend the things of God. 'Faith is the evid-ence of things unseen.'[1] There was lately a tendency among certain theologians to say that our faith is *founded* on our religious experience—to say, for example, that we believe God forgives sins because we have experienced the forgiveness of our own sins, or that we believe in prayer because our own prayers have been answered. It would, however, be truer to say that only by believing in a God who forgives sins can we experience the forgiveness of our own; and that only through faith, only by believing in a God who answers prayer, can we have experience of our own prayers being answered. We must 'make our requests known to God',[2] but it is contrary to all true faith to suppose that we may hold him to a particular way of responding. It would be frightening to take upon our-

[1] Heb. 11. 1.   [2] Phil. 4. 6.

selves that measure of responsibility. My own son, when he was small, was forward enough in requesting things of me, but if I had given him everything he asked, just because he asked it and without using maturer judgement to determine what would be best for him to have, I think that even at that tender age he might have been afraid to ask anything at all—and certainly, when he himself came to a maturer understanding, he would have reproached me with having neglected my parental duty towards him. As somebody has put it: 'If God granted me the form of my petition, He would be denying me the substance of my desire.' In my own undergraduate days I had a friend in my college year who had fallen deeply in love with a girl whom we both knew and whom he hoped afterwards to marry. He used to pray fervently that the girl might be led to respond to his love, and I remember how he would confess to me that he would make this a test case for the validity of the faith in which he had been brought up. If this request were refused, if the lady remained as indifferent to his advances as she then appeared to be, he would no longer believe in God. As it turned out, he made no progress with his suit, but I hope (for I believe him to be still alive) that he has now been granted a truer faith to which the thought of that kind of 'verificatory experiment' would be wholly repugnant.

The reason why we must not say that faith is *based* on religious experience is that religious experience, if it is authentic, already *contains* faith. Faith is the cognitive element in it, on which the accompanying emotional and volitional elements are utterly dependent. The other way of speaking and thinking has given rise to so strong a reaction against it in the minds of many contemporary theologians, not least those of the Barthian school, that they will not allow themselves to speak of 'religious experience' at all. But while fully sharing their reasons, I cannot agree with them in this result. Faith *is* experience but, like all veridical experience, it is determined for us and produced in us by something not ourselves. We cannot make ourselves believe and we should not try. If it is veridical at all, faith is the gift of God. On the other hand, instead of speaking of faith as a mode of experience, I am equally willing to speak of it as a mode of primary apprehension.

How then, we are asked, are judgements of faith to be verified, so that we may know whether they are true or false? But here we must make a distinction such as will lead us to answer the question in two different parts. The phrase 'judgements of faith' might mean either of two things. My old teacher, Wilhelm Herrmann of Marburg, always insisted on distinguishing between what he called the *Glaubensgrund* and the *Glaubensgedanken*; and my other theological teacher, Hugh Ross Mackintosh, used to work with the perhaps slightly different distinction between 'the immediate utterances of faith' and 'the further implicates of faith'. The not dissimilar distinction I wish to draw is between our Christian faith itself and those theological judgements which, though having no other justification than that they rest upon faith and are seen to be implied in it, are nevertheless drawn out and made explicit only by later reflection.[1] Formally regarded, this distinction is parallel to that between our commonsense knowledge of the corporeal world and the added and refined knowledge of it which science yields; and we must remember with Professor Macmurray that 'The conclusions of some centuries of scientific research into the characteristics of matter constitute only a minute portion of our knowledge of the physical world.'[2] It is formally parallel also to the distinction between aesthetic appreciation and the theory of aesthetics —between for instance, our delight in music and musical theory. We must not indeed make the mistake of thinking that in any of these cases an entirely sharp dividing line can be drawn between the two kinds of apprehension, or even of thinking that the line, such as it is, is equally well defined in each case. Something of rudimentary scientific reflection is

---

[1] Compare also John Hick, *Faith and Knowledge* (1957), p. 198: 'We do well to distinguish between, on the one hand, the basic convictions which directly transcribe Christian experience, providing matter for subsequent theological reflection, and on the other hand, such theological reflection itself and the formulations in which it has issued.'

[2] *Interpreting the Universe*, p. 16.

contained in all our commonsense apprehension of the physical world; some aesthetical theory is contained in all appreciation of beauty; and even more obviously is it true that some theological reflection is contained in even the simplest kind of 'simple faith'.

This being understood, however, the distinction between faith and theology still stands, and we must therefore first ask, How are *theological* judgements verified? But if we are already agreed that all theoretical judgements are to be verified by a return to the area of primary apprehension (or experience) which first suggested them, then our answer must be that theological judgements can be verified only by a return to the area of primary apprehension which we call faith. We are constantly being reminded by contemporary philosophers that the true significance of any statement is best understood from a consideration of the kind of verification which it demands. With regard to the propositions of physical science this principle may now be taken as generally accepted. 'The meaning of a scientific statement', wrote the late Professor Eddington, 'is to be ascertained by reference to the steps which would be taken to verify it.'[1] But the philosophers desire to extend the same principle to all statements; as for example Professor Ayer:

We say that a sentence is factually significant to any given person if, and only if, he knows how to verify the proposition which it purports to express—that is, if he knows what observations would lead him, under certain conditions, to accept the proposition as being true, or reject it as false.[2]

I think the philosophers are right. Certainly there is no better way of ascertaining the true import of a theological doctrine than by asking what exactly it is in faith's apprehension of the divine which has led to its being put forward and by reference to which it can afterwards be checked. No doctrine has any right of place within a system of Christian theology unless it can make good its claim to yield the best available explication

[1] A. S. Eddington, *The Philosophy of Physical Science* (1939), p. 189.
[2] Op. cit., p. 35.

of some constituent strand of that knowledge of God which has been revealed to the Christian community and received and enjoyed by faith; and it is only by appeal to this existent knowledge, which is precedent to all doctrinal or dogmatic formulation, that the true meaning and relevance of any doctrine or dogma can be understood.

The formal pattern of the verificatory procedure is thus the same in theology as in physical science, the difference being that in the latter case the appeal is to what is 'revealed' to ordinary sense perception, but in the former to what is revealed to the 'eye' of faith. And as to the deepening and refining of faith itself, all that was said above about the deepening and refining of our aesthetic appreciation may now *mutatis mutandis* be applied to this also. Just as there is no way of developing a juster sense of what is excellent in poetry except by living with poetry, by hearing and reading more and more of it, so there is no way of deepening and refining our faith, save by living the life of faith, which is the same as to say by being more humbly open to receive, and more diligently prepared to attend to, what is being divinely revealed to us. Yet here also, just as in the other case, we shall do well to hear what others have to say; not placing too much reliance upon our own individual divinings, but allowing these to be tested in relation to the fuller and maturer faith of our fellow believers, of the religious community to which we belong, and of the long tradition in which we stand; though here again such a process avails for us only in so far as we are thus enabled to see things differently for ourselves, so that our own personal faith is thereby deepened and refined. Even of natural science this is true. The scientist is not content if it is only by his own individual experience of the external world that he can verify his results. He does not much trust his own perceptions if others perceive nothing similar.

§ 18

But the philosophers will further press their challenge, applying their principle not only to the question how we can ascertain the meaning of a statement, but also to the question how we can acquire any right to hold it. We must not, they will say, believe anything unless we are able to define some experience or experiences which we would accept in refutation of it. Under what circumstances, they will ask, would we be willing to abandon the doctrine we now profess? If there are no such circumstances, then the doctrine in question cannot be grounded on veridical experience of any sort, since a statement which is consistent with every conceivable *possibility* obviously tells us nothing about *actuality*. Here are two brief formulations of this challenge from the pens of two different contributors to the same volume of essays:

What would have to occur or to have occurred to constitute for you a disproof of the love of, or of the existence of, God?

If, then, religious 'statements' are compatible with anything and everything, how can they be statements? How can the honest enquirer find out what they mean, if nobody will tell him what they are incompatible with?[1]

In accepting this challenge, it may be necessary to begin by repeating that a body of doctrine which was not in the first place derived from empirical observation of the corporeal world, and which makes no claim to have been so derived, obviously cannot find its verification or falsification in a return to such observation; for to insist that it should is merely to reiterate the former dogmatic assumption, with which we have already fully dealt, that (apart, no doubt, from our apprehension of analytic propositions, such as those of mathematics) we have no knowledge of anything save the corporeal world. This state of the case may be obscured from us by the fact that the Bible, the total contents of which have often been identified with that revelation on which Christian doctrine is founded, does undeniably contain many affirmations which are capable of being tested, and in some part also refuted, by appeal to scientific results resting ultimately on the evidence of the bodily senses. So long as these remained

---

[1] *New Essays in Philosophical Theology*, ed. by Antony Flew and Alasdair MacIntyre (1955), pp. 99, 110.

unchallenged by advancing scientific and historical knowledge, the stimulus was lacking to make the necessary discrimination between them and the authentic message of revelation with which they were intertwined, but this discrimination is now a commonplace of theological procedure. It is now agreed by responsible theologians that for our knowledge of such things as can be perceived by the senses, for our knowledge of 'things seen', we are dependent alone on the evidence of those senses and the scientific reflection that builds on such evidence. Needless to say, this does not mean that faith has nothing to say about the corporeal world. It has very much to say. There is a Christian doctrine of the body and there is a Christian doctrine of the world, but the affirmations which these contain are not such as a truly empirical physical science would ever venture either to affirm or to deny.

Sufficient evidence that circumstances can be defined which would force the theologian to the surrender of any particular theological proposition (as distinct from the primary apprehensions of faith which I would not regard as particular theological propositions, and of which more anon) is furnished by the fact that the truth or falsity of these is all the time being discussed by theologians and that such discussion does in fact very often lead to their surrender. Protestant theology at least is constantly changing its mind, and certainly individual Protestant theologians are constantly changing theirs. One instance of this has just been mentioned: most Protestant theologians have now surrendered the doctrine that Holy Scripture is inerrant. To take another example, I remember listening in my student days to a three-way debate involving those who supported the doctrine of everlasting punishment and those who supported the doctrine of universal salvation, as well as those who supported the doctrine of conditional immortality with the extinction of the obdurately wicked; and I remember that my interest on that occasion was not so much in the particular issue disputed as in taking careful note of the type of consideration to which each of the disputants was making appeal for the settlement of the issue, the type of consideration which he was bringing forward in the hope that it would convince the others, and the type of consideration which, if it could be substantiated, he seemed most likely to be willing to accept as a refutation of his own conviction. Since then I have often listened to other discussions with something of the same (I fear rather academic) interest, as recently when the disputed question was whether infants are regenerated in baptism, and again when the question was whether the statement 'Jesus is God' is a true way of speaking when standing by itself in this simple form. I think in all these cases I would have found it possible to define a body of evidence, or a type of consideration which, if it could be convincingly produced, would have been accepted by each disputant in refutation of the view he was defending; yet in no case would it be evidence drawn from what could be perceived by the bodily senses or from the discoveries of physical science. The ultimate appeal was always from the particular theological proposition to the *Glaubensgrund*, to the primary apprehension by faith of God's revelation of himself in Jesus Christ, about which there was no dispute, because by the grace of God all were alike held by it. Where they differed was only as to whether the particular proposition did or did not inevitably follow from that primary apprehension, was in some sort contained in it, or was at least fully consistent with it.

§ 19

It is clear, then, that when particular theological statements are challenged, they are habitually referred for their verification or falsification to that which they were originally designed to explicate, namely, faith's primary apprehension of the divine. But now our positivist philosophers will press their question further back and will ask what we would accept in refutation of, and as wholly discrediting, that primary apprehension itself. What positive grounds can we have for our faith, if we can conceive and define no grounds which would tell against it? A faith that is consistent with everything possible is not a faith in anything actual.

We speak here of faith itself (as distinguished from the many theological propositions which claim to ground themselves upon it) as being a single apprehension, a single disposition of the believing mind. This appears to be justified. Christian faith does not consist in believing a list, short or long, of disparate and mutually detachable things. It is a single illumination, a single reception of and commitment to the light revealed. 'This faith', as the Westminster Confession says, 'is different in degrees, weak or strong';[1] but it is always faith in the same reality; and its essence is trust in that reality—a trustful commitment leading to obedience to its claims. This is what *pistis* means in the New Testament.

When therefore we are asked under what circumstances we should be forced to surrender our faith, we are really being asked under what circumstances we would find ourselves altogether discrediting a whole mode of primary apprehensions which we have hitherto regarded as veridical. The question is thus formally parallel, not to the question as to what would lead me to the reversal of a particular judgement of sense perception or a particular scientific conclusion, but to the question as to what would lead me to distrust my sense perception as a whole and consequently to surrender my belief in the objectivity of the corporeal world. Or again it is parallel, not to the question how I come to revise my particular aesthetic judgements, but to the question what would lead to so complete a destruction of my sense of beauty that for me there would be no longer any distinction between the beautiful and the ugly at all. Or once more it is parallel (though indeed to my thinking this is not so much a parallel as part of the same thing), not to the question how I might come to think that I was not really under some particular moral obligation which I had hitherto considered binding, but to the question how I might conceivably come to think that I was not obliged to do or to be any one thing rather than another.

These are all questions for which it is very difficult to find an answer; and not least the question how I can be quite sure (as

[1] Chap. XIV. 3.

I am) that what I call my waking life is not after all a dream, so that the supposed corporeal world (including my fellow men by whose independent witness I might otherwise test the objectivity of my own individual hearing and seeing) is not 'there' at all. It would appear that the veridical nature of any primary mode of apprehension cannot be tested by reference to anything outside itself. Each must carry its own witness or must collapse. If the trust we repose in it be not self-authenticating, there is no other apparent way of authenticating it.[1]

Thus when we are asked to conceive and define a set of circumstances which would lead to a total dissipation of the faith that is in us, we can only remind ourselves of how that faith was first gained and how it has continued to be nourished. As we have already indicated, our faith was born within us through our divining a profounder meaning in certain encountered events than is evident to our ordinary senses. Through the impact of these events we found ourselves apprehending a reality which evidenced itself as such by setting a resistant limit to the free expansion of our own desires, constraining us to a recognition of its sovereign claim. It follows that faith would be lost only if this primary apprehension should itself utterly fail, if we were no longer able to discover *any* such meaning in *any* events but came to regard the whole of our experience and everything that has ever happened as a meaningless jumble.

The answer is as simple as that. Nor was there any need to guess at it. For if faith has in fact ever been lost, we know that

[1] Compare John Hick, op. cit., p. 132: 'There is in cognition of every kind an unresolved mystery. The knower-known relationship is in the last analysis *sui generis:* the mystery of cognition persists at the end of every enquiry—though its persistence does not prevent us from cognizing. We cannot explain, for example, how we are conscious of sensory phenomena as constituting an objective physical environment; we just find ourselves interpreting the data of our experience in this way. We are aware that we live in a real world, though we cannot prove by any logical formula that it *is* a real world. Likewise we cannot explain how we know ourselves to be responsible beings subject to moral obligations; we just find ourselves interpreting our social experience in this way. . . . The same is true of the apprehension of God. The theistic believer cannot explain *how* he knows the divine presence to be mediated through his human experience. He just finds himself interpreting his experience in this way. He lives in the presence of God, though he is unable to prove by any dialectical process that God exists.'

that is how it happened. We know also that our own faith is being constantly 'tried'; that, as the Westminster Confession says, it 'may often and many ways be assailed and weakened'.[1] And we know how this comes about. Faith is 'tried' as often as we are confronted with events in which it is difficult to believe that there *is* any divine meaning. 'As for me', cries the writer of the seventy-third psalm, 'my feet were almost gone, my steps had well nigh slipped . . . when I saw the prosperity of the wicked.'[2] Trials of this kind are always with us in some degree; for we cannot hope so to penetrate each single event as to find meaning in it. One of the things it *is* given faith to see is that God's 'judgements are unsearchable, and his ways past finding out',[3] that the divine strategy is so grand in its conception that (as we might say) the private soldier cannot be expected to understand all its moves—and indeed that it would be far from grand if he could.

But the psalmist, it will be remembered, recovered his foot-hold when he 'went into the sanctuary of God' and was given the reminder 'Nevertheless I am continually with thee: thou hast holden me by my right hand.'[4] Here is another instance, also from the Psalms:

Will the Lord cast off for ever? and will he be favourable no more? Is his mercy clean gone for ever? doth his promise fail for evermore? Hath God forgotten to be gracious? hath he in anger shut up his tender mercies?
And I said, This is my infirmity; but I will remember the years of the right hand of the most High.
I will remember the works of the Lord; surely I will remember the wonders of old.
I will meditate also of all thy work, and talk of thy doings.[5]

This means that certain highly significant encounters yield the assurance that even those other encounters which are most opaque to our understanding and appear least patient of an interpretation consonant with trust in God, are nevertheless charged with divine meaning; nor is the harbouring of such

---

[1] Chap. XIV. 3.   [2] Psalm 73. 2–3.   [3] Job 9. 10; Rom. 11. 33.
[4] Verse 23.   [5] Psalm 77. 7–12.

assurance out of accord, on its own level, with familiar 'empirical' procedure. As A. N. Whitehead wrote in a well-known passage,

Religion claims that its concepts, though derived primarily from special experiences, are yet of universal validity, to be applied by faith to the ordering of all experience. Rational religion appeals to the direct intuition of special occasions, and to the elucidatory power of its concepts for all occasions. It arises from what is special, but it extends to what is general.[1]

That distinguished sociologist, the late Karl Mannheim, has taught us to speak of such highly significant encounters as 'paradigmatic experiences'. 'The religious focus', he writes, ' . . . is a way of interpreting life from the centre of some paradigmatic experience.'[2] The faith of Israel in the prophetic period had its focus in the paradigmatic event of the Exodus or the paradigmatic constellation of events represented by the Exodus, the journey through the wilderness and the entry into the Promised Land. Christian faith finds its focus in the paradigmatic event of Christ's Advent or in the paradigmatic constellation of His Advent, Passion, Cross, Resurrection and Exaltation, and the Coming of the Spirit at Pentecost. Thus if Christian faith is ever completely lost, it must be *either* because certain events are now encountered whose contrary witness is so overpowering as altogether to undermine our reliance upon these paradigmatic events, *or else* because the divine significance of the paradigmatic events themselves now evaporates from our mind, whether as a result of further consideration of them or from negligently ceasing to think of them at all. Either way it may be said that a man loses his faith only if he now sees things differently from how he had formerly seen them; and, save that it is a different kind of seeing which is here in question, it is in this way also that the physical scientist comes to reject beliefs which he had formerly entertained.

The *naïveté* of the demand of the positivist philosophers that the deliverances of faith should be verifiable by reference to

[1] *Religion in the Making* (1926), New York ed., p. 32.
[2] *Diagnosis of our Time* (1943), p. 134.

ordinary sense perception has often made me wonder. In reality nothing could be more stultifying to faith, or more repugnant to the New Testament understanding of it, than that it should thus become part of the most matter-of-fact common sense, requiring nothing for its nourishment but sufficient intelligence to take in what the bodily senses reveal and to understand the agreed results to which the natural scientists are led through their closer and more co-ordinated observation. Faith would thus shine with no brighter radiance in the saint than in the sinner, in the most spiritually-minded than in the most negligent of their spiritual condition. But 'the secret of the Lord is with them that fear him';[1] and, as St Paul says, 'spiritual things are spiritually discerned'.[2]

§ 20

But the question suggests itself. Is faith ever *completely* lost? We should find it difficult to believe that any man ever experiences the complete dissipation of that mode of primary apprehension which informs him of the reality of the corporeal world; but do some men experience the complete dissipation of this other mode of primary apprehension which alone can inform them of the meaning of existence? If they do, it should perhaps not surprise us too much, because faith is a tender plant in comparison with sense perception. It may be said that the grosser the reality with which we are concerned, the less likely is it to be corroded by the acids of our scepticism. Our awareness of so-called brute fact needs little to fan its flame. Our more delicate perceptions of truth more easily flicker towards extinction if insufficiently nourished.

Nevertheless it is not so certain as is sometimes made to appear that the apprehension of an ultimate meaning in life ever completely fails in any man whose use of his mental powers is still fully alert, though it may, alas, approach vanishing-point in some who have been left by the inhumanity

---

[1] Psalm 25. 14.
[2] 2 Cor. 2. 14: τὰ τοῦ Πνεύματος τοῦ Θεοῦ . . . πνευματικῶς ἀνακρίνεται.

of their fellows to languish in a degrading penury and debilitating inanition. We have already said that there has apparently never been a culture to which some disposition of faith was not native. Certainly our own culture has such a disposition as part of its foundation. Here is a pleasing parable of this:

Viewing a church tower from a train, we almost accept it as a natural growth. We say the church fits in with the landscape, though it would be correcter to say the landscape fits in with the church, which is likely to be older, built before field-pattern was formed or tree-clump planted.[1]

Not a few of our latter-day intellectuals (including some whose names I have already mentioned) may indeed be found protesting that they have rid themselves of the last vestigial shred of faith, the life they live being unaffected by any clue to its ultimate meaning. But I am by no means always inclined to take their word for this, for it is open to me, without discourtesy, to suspect that they are incorrectly analysing their own spiritual condition. I should look to their deeds as well as to their words, to their behaviour when they are off their intellectual guard as well as to their merely theoretical conclusions about themselves; just as there are others about whom it would have to be said, 'They profess that they know God, but in their deeds they deny him.'[2] According to Karl Mannheim, for example,

It is not wholly impossible that what is happening in Russia, apart from conscious intention, is that a very genuine source of religious and primitive experience is using modern sophisticated terminology to translate itself into the idioms of modern society.[3]

For I cannot but agree with the same writer's view of what would be the result of what he calls the total 'depersonalization' of a culture, the total 'evaporation of primordial images or archetypes which have directed the life-experience of mankind throughout the ages'.

---

[1] Andrew Young, *A Prospect of Britain* (1956), p. 120.
[2] Titus, 1. 16.
[3] Op. cit., p. 131.

Without paradigmatic experiences or consistent conduct, no character-formation and no real human existence and co-operation are possible. Without them our universe of discourse loses its articulation, conduct falls to pieces, and only disconnected bits of successful behaviour patterns and fragments of adjustment to an ever-changing environment remain.[1]

If this melancholy result is not more often realized in actual practice, it is because *complete* agnosticism has been less frequently professed than we are inclined to think, and is still more rarely carried out with vigorous consistency. Most of those of our nineteenth-century intellectuals who come nearest to a total rejection of the paradigmatic experiences which lay at the root of the Christian tradition continued to accept the Christian standards of conduct so closely associated with these; and not a few still tenaciously believed these standards to be somehow grounded in a reality that is independent of our own desires. At an earlier point I quoted from some works of what may be called Lord Russell's middle period some very dogmatic denials of such an independent grounding, but 'As we all know, Mr Russell produces a different system of philosophy every few years'.[2] In his earliest period he followed Professor Moore in defending the independent reality of moral values, though by 1917 he was writing with reference to his views of 1902, 'I feel less convinced than I did then of the objectivity of good and evil'.[3] Yet it would appear that in his latest period he is beginning to revert, for in 1954 he wrote thus:

If I say that oysters are good, and you say they are nasty, we both understand that we are merely expressing our personal tastes, and that there is nothing to argue about. But when Nazis say that it is good to torture Jews, and we say that it is bad, we do not *feel* as if we were merely expressing a difference of taste; we are even willing to fight and die for our opinion, which we should not do to enforce our views about oysters. Whatever arguments may be

---

[1] Op. cit., p. 136.

[2] C. D. Broad in *Contemporary British Philosophy*, ed. Muirhead, Vol. I (1924), p. 79.

[3] *Mysticism and Logic* (1918), p. v. Compare also Russell's *Portraits from Memory and Other Essays* (1956), p. 90: 'When I was young I agreed with G. E. Moore in believing in the objectivity of good and evil. Santayana's criticism, in a book called *Winds of Doctrine*, caused me to abandon this view, though I have never been able to be so bland and comfortable without it as he was.'

advanced to show that the two cases are analogous, most people will remain convinced that there is a difference somewhere, though it may be difficult to say exactly what it is. I think this feeling, though not decisive, deserves respect, and should make us reluctant to accept at all readily the view that ethical judgements are wholly subjective.[1]

I, for one, find it intolerable to suppose that when I say 'Cruelty is bad', I am merely saying 'I dislike cruelty', or something equally subjective.[2]

§ 21

Perhaps the most tenuous of the residual forms of professed attachment to the traditional paradigm is that which, surrendering altogether its claim to be revelatory of reality, still fondly clings to it as a purely *imaginary* frame of reference for the conduct of life. This view found exemplification in Thomas Hardy and in George Santayana. Hardy was in many ways deeply Christian in his sentiments and remained so to the end, but 'with the top of his mind' he came to adopt a philosophy which seemed to leave these sentiments in mid-air. Hence in 1901, when he was sixty years old, he wrote to a friend as follows:

I do not think there will be any permanent revival of the old transcendental ideals; but I think there may gradually be developed an Idealism of Fancy; that is, an idealism in which fancy is no longer tricked out and made to masquerade as belief, but is frankly and honestly accepted as an imaginative solace in the lack of any substantial solace to be found in life.[3]

Santayana too lived out his life within a Christian frame of reference which he was unwilling to surrender, but his *philosophical theory* about it was that it was an artifact of human imagination and nothing more. 'Christian history and art', he wrote in his autobiography, 'contained all my spiritual traditions, my intellectual and moral language.'[4] But in conversation with such a transcendentalist thinker as McTaggart,

---

[1] *Human Society in Ethics and Politics* (1954), p. 4 f.   [2] Ibid., p. 92.
[3] Florence Emily Hardy, *The Later Years of Thomas Hardy* (1930), p. 90.
[4] *My Host the World* (1953), p. 47.

I soon found, when we began to talk about philosophy, that he had discovered that, apart from technicalities, I could be as transcendentalist as he. Only for me transcendentalism was a deliberate pose, expressing a subjective perspective; whereas for him it revealed the metaphysical structure of reality.[1]

In this way 'each religion, by the help of more or less myth which it takes more or less seriously, proposes some method of fortifying the human soul and enabling it to make its peace with destiny'.[2] 'And so a moral world, practical and social, would become, for our imagination, the theatre of our social action, and a roughly valid representation of the forces actually playing upon us and determining the weal and woe of our lives.'[3] Yet he confessed to have been greatly troubled in his mental life with what he called 'the temptation of the primitive poet to believe his fables'.[4]

This delight in an imagined realm of ideals is, however, only one phase of the religion which Santayana wished to retain, the other being a certain 'reverent attachment' to the real nature of things in spite of this being believed to bear no relation at all to our ideal imaginings. 'Rational religion', he wrote in another of his books, 'has these two phases: piety, or loyalty to necessary conditions; and spirituality, or devotion to ideal ends.'[5] More fully:

The aspiring side of religion may be called spirituality. Spirituality is nobler than piety. . . . A man is spiritual when he lives in the presence of the ideal, and whether he eat or drink does so for the sake of a true and ultimate good. He is spiritual when he envisages his goal so frankly that his whole material life becomes a transparent vehicle which scarcely arrests attention but allows the spirit to use it economically and with perfect detachment and freedom.[6]

But piety, 'cosmic piety', is necessary also; a philosophic piety which has the universe for its object; for 'the universe, so far as we can observe it, is a wonderful and immense engine; its extent, its order, its beauty, its cruelty, make it alike impressive'.[7]

---

[1] *My Host the World* (1953), p. 40.   [2] Ibid., p. 5.   [3] Ibid., p. 2.   [4] Ibid., p. 3.
[5] *Reason in Religion* (1905), p. 276.   [6] Ibid., p. 193 f.   [7] Ibid., p. 190 f.

An identical view has been intermittently defended by Santayana's close friend Lord Russell; and first, I think, in an article published seven years after Santayana's book just quoted. He too argues that in order to remain religious we must break up our religion into two quite disparate and unrelated worships—an 'impartial' worship of existent reality frankly recognized as indifferent to all distinctions of value, and a devoted worship of our ideals frankly conceived as human artifacts. 'The two worships subsist side by side without any dogma: the one involving the goodness but not the existence of its object, the other involving the existence but not the goodness of its object.'[1]

I should wish to claim, then, that these depositions of Hardy, Santayana and even Lord Russell betray some residual presence 'in the bottom of their hearts' of that primary mode of apprehension which is faith, though with the philosophic 'top of their minds' they have played such havoc with it. They are 'seeing' something which is, to say the least, analogous to what the man of faith 'sees'; otherwise how could they speak of worship, piety, spirituality, sanctity and reverence? But, as Professor Moore, Lord Russell's early associate, once wrote, 'The strange thing is that philosophers should have been able to hold sincerely, as part of their philosophical creed, propositions inconsistent with what they themselves *know* to be true; and yet, so far as I can make out, this has frequently happened.'[2]

Lord Russell, indeed, appears to have a particularly confused mind in this matter of faith. In his recent *Human Society in Ethics and Politics*, already quoted from, he writes thus:

We may define 'faith' as a firm belief in something for which there is no evidence. Where there is evidence, no one speaks of 'faith'. We do not speak of faith that two and two are four or that the earth is round. We only speak of faith when we wish to substitute emotion for evidence.[3]

And such faith he himself apparently cherishes. He gives us

---

[1] 'The Essence of Religion' in *The Hibbert Journal*, Vol. XI, No. 1 (October 1912).
[2] *Contemporary British Philosophy*, Vol. II, p. 203.   [3] Op. cit., p. 203.

a clear example of it in the closing words of his book, which are these:

> Those who are to lead the world out of its troubles will need courage, hope and love. Whether they will prevail, I do not know; but, beyond all reason, I am unconquerably persuaded that they will.[1]

But how can he be 'unconquerably persuaded' of the truth of a proposition, while at the same time confessing that he does 'not know' whether or not it is true? That certainly is substituting emotion for evidence, and is 'a firm belief in something for which there is no evidence'. Not only is this a kind of faith to which I myself am quite unable to rise, but the particular utterance by which he here exemplifies it is one that I am unable to affirm. But of course this is not what faith means at all. Certainly we do not speak of faith that two and two are four or that the earth is round; but that is not because faith means believing without evidence, but because it means believing in realities that go beyond sense and sight—for which a totally different sort of evidence is required.

Furthermore, there is some ground for believing that failure of faith is frequently associated with some failure or other of the more delicate modes of primary apprehension. A well-known case is that of Charles Darwin, who very honestly confessed that while 'disbelief crept over me at a very slow rate, until it was at last complete', what he called his 'higher tastes' were at the same time gradually 'atrophied', until at last he could derive little pleasure from fine landscape, 'could not endure to read a line of poetry, found Shakespeare intolerably dull', and could no longer recapture 'the state of mind which grand scenes formerly excited in me, *and which was closely connected with belief in God*'.[2] With equally admirable honesty Mr C. D. Broad writes as follows:

> I am somewhat obtuse to the influence of scenery, painting, music, and the higher kinds of literature. . . . Closely connected with this

---

[1] Op. cit., p. 227.

[2] F. Darwin, *Life and Letters of Charles Darwin*, Vol. I, pp. 100 ff., 304 ff. The italics are mine.

is the fact that I am almost wholly devoid of religious or mystical experience.

Yet

This is combined with a great interest in such experiences and a belief that they are probably of extreme importance in any theoretical interpretation of the world.

And again,

There is one thing which Speculative Philosophy must take into most serious consideration, and that is the religious and mystical experiences of mankind. These form a vast mass of facts *which obviously deserve at least as careful attention as the sensations of mankind.* They are of course less uniform than our sensations; many people, of whom I am one, are practically without these experiences. But probably most people have them to some extent, and there is a considerable amount of agreement between those people of all nations and ages, who have them to a marked degree. . . . It seems reasonable to suppose at the outset that the whole mass of mystical and religious experience *brings us into contact with an aspect of reality which is not revealed in ordinary sense-perception,* and that any system of Speculative Philosophy which ignores it will be extremely one-sided.[1]

The phrases I have taken the liberty of italicizing show Mr Broad's readiness to allow that there may be a mode of primary apprehension of reality other than the single one to which the positivists desire us to confine ourselves. Many other cases could be cited in which the atrophy of religious discernment has been accompanied by, or associated with, a failure of other powers of discernment, but I have thought it better to confine myself to cases in which such failure has been self-confessed.

The task of the Christian apologist would have been very different from what it has proved itself to be, if he commonly found himself defending his faith against an agnosticism which not only professed to be complete but did not even, in the course of articulating such profession, betray some unacknowledged or only half-acknowledged residue of the *gnosis* which was professedly denied. Not least do I know this from the many

[1] *Contemporary British Philosophy,* Vol. I, pp. 80, 99 f.

occasions on which my apologetic has had to be directed against the threatened failures of my own faith, and when I have had to fall back for its re-establishment upon the search for those things which in the bottom of my heart I found it impossible to doubt. But if the unbeliever should seem to be genuinely without any 'ultimate concern', any 'sense of the holy' and impulse to worship, any sense of obligation, or any conscience that was more than an attachment to his own individual preferences and an honouring of his own more stable desires, no argument with him would then be possible; any more than it would be possible, or sensible, to argue with one who appeared to have genuinely lost all sense of the reality of the external world and all ability to distinguish it from his dream-world; or with one who was no mere theoretical solipsist but had apparently lost all *sense* of the independent existence of his fellow men. In such a case there would be no *Anknüpfungspunkt* at all, no premise from which argument could begin.[1] If faith is really a primary mode of apprehension, it follows that no theological proposition can be validly deduced from any proposition that is not already theological. The most the apologist, or rather the evangelist, could do in such a case would be to endeavour to introduce his fellow into what might become for him a 'revelatory situation', in which he would be confronted with certain events such as might give rise to 'paradigmatic experiences'. Much the commoner case, however, to say the very least, is that the apologist has to deal with an agnosticism that is significantly less than total; an agnosticism into which some alternative faith, or surrogate for faith, is surreptitiously, however honestly and unsuspectingly, introduced to fill the distressing gap left by that which was surrendered. Perhaps the most familiar of these within the modern period, though it is one to which some like Thomas Hardy were much too clear-sighted to be tempted, has been some form of the belief in progress, which deluded itself into supposing that it was capable of empirical verification and thus consistent

---

[1] 'Belief cannot argue with unbelief: it can only preach to it'—Alasdair MacIntyre in *Metaphysical Beliefs* (1957), p. 211.

with a positivist profession. Such a delusion was very natural and very human in the circumstances and, as I have written elsewhere, its recent evanescence is something 'in which none can be so insensitive or hard-hearted as to rejoice; a situation the possible disastrous consequences of which it is difficult to overestimate. For what, after all, is left for modern man to believe in, if he can no longer believe that the future is likely to be better than the past, or that his children's children are likely to inhabit a world less full of wrong than he himself has had to live in.'[1]

I have spoken of our convictions of the reality of the external world and of other selves than our own; and of the theoretical doubts by which these convictions have on occasion been assailed. The former of the two certainly seems to have been doubted by some philosophers. Nor is it only the idealists, from Plato to Bradley, who have spoken of the external world as mere 'appearance', but also not a few empiricists. 'Doubt of the existence or reality of an external world', writes Mr G. A. Paul, 'has not been peculiar to those philosophers whom we primarily think of as speculative or metaphysical';[2] and he quotes Lord Russell's remark that 'the common-sense belief in fairly permanent bodies—tables, chairs, mountains, is a piece of audacious metaphysical theorizing'.[3] As for myself, I cannot claim that such doubts are entirely foreign to my own mind, but if I am asked how I am able to overcome them, I shall have to confess that for me their ultimate refutation is theological and incarnational. Already at an earlier point I argued that my sense of the reality of the corporeal world is dependent upon my apprehension of it as a shared world and is thus 'in some sort a derivative [from my recognition] of the reality of other selves'.[4] But the most effective way to counter in its turn such tendency as I have to the non-recognition of these other selves is to remind myself that it betokens a failure of duteous obligation, or failure of love. I have no *right* to

[1] *The Belief in Progress* (1950), p. 180.
[2] In *The Revolution in Philosophy* (1956), p. 63.
[3] *Our Knowledge of the External World*, p. 167.
[4] See above, p. 35.

ignore the claims made upon me by the presence of my neighbour. When he calls to me out of his need, I am not permitted to 'pass by on the other side', pretending he is not there, that his reality has still to be established. But to say that I am not permitted is to talk the language, not of any merely prudential or humanist morality, but of religious faith.[1] It is to acknowledge that through the need of my neighbour a claim is being made upon me by unconditioned being, which is to say by God. 'If we love one another, God dwelleth in us.'[2] Where there is no recognition of the neighbour, there can be no recognition of God; and furthermore, where there is no recognition of the reality of the corporeal world, there can be no recognition either of the neighbour or of God, since it is in the world that I encounter my neighbour, and God through my neighbour, and my neighbour through God. The substantiation of each of these three realities is thus dependent upon our awareness of the other two.

Yet for the Christian the refutation of solipsism is not only theological but also incarnational and Christological. Where there is lacking, as in Indian religion and in many forms of Western idealism, any apprehension of God as incarnate, there is likely to be lacking also a full apprehension of the reality of the corporeal world; and we know also how arduous was the struggle of the early Christian Church within its Hellenic environment against the docetic heresy. Ultimately it is because this world of sense and time is the world into which God came, the world in which my salvation has been procured, that I am unable to doubt its reality. Here are some relevant words of Archbishop William Temple:

In the great affirmation that 'the Word was made flesh and we beheld his glory' is implicit a whole theory of the relation between spirit and matter. Christianity is the most materialistic of all great religions. The others hope to achieve spiritual reality by ignoring matter—calling it illusion (*maya*) or saying that it does not exist. . . .

---

[1] 'Dostoievsky wrote, "If God did not exist, all would be permitted"; That is existentialism's point of departure'—Jean-Paul Sartre, *L'Existentialisme est un Humanisme*, p. 36.

[2] 1 John 4. 12.

Christianity, based as it is on the Incarnation, regards matter as destined to be the vehicle and instrument of spirit, and spirit as fully actual so far as it controls and directs matter.[1]

I have been concerned in all this to indicate the way in which the profession of a total atrophy of faith is met by the Christian apologist or evangelist. I have said that if the atrophy were really total, no argument would be possible; but I have also said that in numerous cases we are constrained to doubt its totality, whether because some element of belief is surreptitiously (though unsuspectingly and in all good faith) introduced into the professed outlook itself, or because the professed un-believer's behaviour belies his profession of complete unbelief, betraying the presence somewhere in his make-up of a remnant of faith that is not conscious of itself. But here I must remind myself of the wise words of a nineteenth-century Scottish preacher: 'There is such a thing as "unconscious faith", but those who plead it in their own behalf do not possess it. With them it is conscious unbelief.'[2]

---

[1] *Readings in St. John's Gospel*, First Series (1939), p. xx f.
[2] John Ker (1819–86), *Thoughts for Heart and Life*, p. 112.

CHAPTER V

The Nature and Office of Theological Statements

§ 22

In order to carry our argument further, we may now remind ourselves of some things that were advanced at an earlier point in it. We then drew a distinction between knowledge of truth and knowledge of reality, or between knowledge of propositions and knowledge of being; and for the latter of these two kinds of knowledge we used Lord Russell's term, knowledge by acquaintance. But we found ourselves differing very radically from Lord Russell's catalogue of things with which we are thus acquainted. In his essay of 1911, which was then quoted, he contended that our direct acquaintance is only with sense data such as patches of colour, noises and bodily pains; with concepts or universals such as colour, noise and pain; 'and possibly with ourselves, but not with physical objects or other minds'. 'Our knowledge of physical objects and of other minds', he wrote, 'is only knowledge by description'; and this, I take it, is the same as to say that the object of our knowledge is not these realities themselves but certain propositions concerning them.[1]

As against this, I ventured to affirm that we are directly aware of reality, and of such realities as the external world, ourselves, our fellow men and God. It is this direct awareness (our knowledge of S) that is primary, our propositional affirmations (our knowledge that S is P) being secondary and derivative and always more tentative. But what I have been particularly concerned to argue is that faith is one such primary mode of awareness. Faith does not deduce from other realities

[1] Reprinted in *Mysticism and Logic* (1918), p. 231.

that *are* present the existence of a God who is *not* present but absent; rather is it an awareness of the divine Presence itself, however hidden behind the veils of sense. Apart from such awareness there can be no true religion, and therefore no full humanity. Here I take the liberty of quoting some words of Professor H. A. Hodges:

It has been traditional to say that man is man by virtue of his possession of reason, and no doubt it is possible to read a rich and true meaning into this; though it may also be taken to mean mere cunning, as if man were superior to the dog simply because he can catch his rabbits more efficiently and can bury his bones without forgetting where he put them. That is not what makes him man. He is what he is because he is capable of a kind of double awareness; while seeing around him the same physical world in which his dog moves, and controlling it much better than his dog does, he can also discern a Presence half-hidden and half-revealed by the façade of physical things and processes. This insight gives to his own existence and activity a quite new significance. Man stands before nature as its potential master, but in face of the Presence he is conscious of responsibilities and obligations. It gives him a new dignity, and it brings him a new kind of risk; since if he gets out of harmony with the all-pervading Presence he will get out of harmony also with himself, and will begin to tear himself in pieces.[1]

Finally, however, we must remind ourselves again that, if we allow ourselves to speak of a *sense* of the presence of God, or of a sense of duty or a sense of humour, these are not on all fours with the senses by means of which we apprehend the external world. They are not like the latter prior to all reflective thought, but are developed on a higher level with the aid of such thought. Only a thinking being can see the funny side of things, or distinguish right from wrong, or be aware of God. We may affirm the perceptional element in faith without denying the conceptional element in it.

Having given ourselves these reminders, we may now advance a stage further. Each of those perceptional modes which goes beyond ordinary sense perception calls for a characteristic response on the part of the percipient. Perhaps the most

---

[1] *The Christian in the Modern University* (S.C.M. Press, 1946), p. 12 f.

general term for such responses is 'appreciation', but that term
is too narrow in its associations to cover all the varieties very
comfortably. We speak of our appreciation of virtue, of humour,
of beauty and so forth, but it will not do to speak of our appreciation of our fellow men or of God. When our apprehension is
of other selves than our own, we are above all aware of the
claim they make upon us, and the response they demand is
what we call an attitude of respons-ibility towards them. In
the ethico-religious sphere, where we have to do with personal
relations, we do but evade the realities presented to our apprehension if we face them otherwise than responsibly. Nor can
we bring the least reason into the discussion of these matters
if we approach them disinterestedly, or without full recognition
of the demands they make upon our own will and action.
Our thinking about them is quite unreal unless it be, in
Kierkegaard's phrase, 'existential'.

Our present particular concern is with the apprehension of
the divine, and the response which is here demanded of us
may be spoken of as 'obedient commitment'. Faith is apprehension through commitment. This alone is true faith, *fides
salvifica* as distinguished from mere intellectual acceptance, for
one reason or another, or from one cause or another, of certain
propositions which men of faith are also accustomed to affirm,
such as that a Supreme Being exists, that there is a providence
that shapes our ends, or that there is a life beyond death.
Faith is thus at one and the same time a mode of apprehension
and a mode of active response to that apprehension. This is a
region of experience in which there can be no apprehension
without commitment, but it is equally true to say that there
can be no commitment without apprehension. I have elsewhere[1] pointed out how in one of his books Dr Emil Brunner
remarks that 'Faith is obedience; nothing else; literally nothing
else at all';[2] while in another he repeats this only to add that
it is impossible for us to resolve the two words, 'obedience'
and 'faith', into one, because there is in faith both a cognitive

---

[1] *The Idea of Revelation in Recent Thought* (1956), p. 134 f.
[2] *Der Mittler* (Tübingen, 1927), '*Schluss*'.

and a volitional element, making it necessary to keep moving back and forth in our speaking of it between the indicative and the imperative moods.[1] So also Dr Rudolf Bultmann, in expounding St Paul's view of 'the structure of faith', writes in his *Theology of the New Testament* that 'Faith is the acceptance of the *kerygma* not as mere cognizance of it and agreement with it but as that genuine obedience to it which includes a new understanding of one's self.'[2] Again, in expounding the Johannine view of faith in Christ, he writes: 'It is not as if one first had to believe Him, trust Him, *in order that* one might believe *in* Him, but that one ought to believe Him, and in so trusting Him is in fact believing *in* Him; one can do neither without doing both.'[3] So also Dr Ethelbert Stauffer in his *New Testament Theology*:

In Paul the accent falls upon the revelation of the Word. It is the Word of the gospel that calls out faith from men. Hence faith is said to come from hearing, according to a formula that appears in a number of forms. But the hearing that is of faith expresses itself in the obedience of faith. This obedience of faith has nothing at all to do with subjecting the human intellect to some dogmatic formula. What Paul has in mind is much more the subjection of man's self-glorification to the sole glory of God.[4]

There is no doubt, then, that the faith of which St Paul and St John speak claims to be a veridical apprehension of the divine at the same time as it is an obedient commitment to it, and a commitment at the same time as it is an apprehension. Such faith cannot indeed be sundered from assent to theological doctrines and ecclesiastical dogmas by any clean-drawn line, yet the distinction between the two must be carefully maintained. It is God himself, as he comes to meet us in Christ, of whom the Christian is indefeasibly certain, and not such statements as he can make about God; and the degree of his assurance in holding to such statements will vary directly with the degree of their proximity to, or remoteness from, the

---

[1] *Das Gebot und die Ordnungen* (Tübingen, 1932), p. 68.
[2] *Theology of the New Testament*, Vol. I, Eng. trans. (1952), p. 324.
[3] Ibid, Vol. II, Eng. trans. (1955), p. 71.
[4] *New Testament Theology*, Eng. trans. (1955), p. 170.

elements of reflective insight already present, in however latent a form, in faith's own awareness of the God who thus comes to meet him.

This is to express it in terms of the individual; but if we so express it, we must at once remind ourselves that it is not to the individual Christian in his solitude that God reveals himself, but to the faithful community, and to the individual only in community. 'For where two or three are gathered together in my name, there am I in the midst of them.'[1] Hence the measure of assurance with which the believer will hold to any doctrine will be affected by other factors than his own individual insight into its truth. In cases where his own insight does not yet extend, or extends with only a weak measure of assurance, to affirmations which are confidently made by his fellow Christians, he will think it quite likely that it is they who are right and he who has not understood. So much is true *mutatis mutandis* of the scientist as over against his fellow scientists, or of the literary critic as over against his fellow critics; or ought to be. The critic who can find little to admire in Milton or in Pope should be humble enough to suspect that it is his own sensibility that is defective, rather than that there is nothing admirable to be found in them. But the Christian looks back on a longer and more solid *paradosis* or tradition than the literary critic or the natural scientist is able to do; and certainly any belief that comes anywhere near to satisfying the Vincentian canon, *quod semper, quod ubique, quod ab omnibus*, will be treated by him with the greatest respect.

For the Christian, of course, the Bible possesses an authority which is all its own. Certainly he has no right to the assurance that all its particular affirmations are veridical, yet it is to the prophetic and apostolic witness which it contains that he himself owes his whole ability to apprehend the presence of God in Christ and so to have any Christian faith at all. He will thus be very slow, in any matter touching the intellectual explication of the essential nature of that faith, to attach more value to his own insight than to that of the Biblical

[1] Matt. 18. 20.

writers. To a lesser, but still to a most significant, extent this will be true also of his attitude towards the later development of dogma. This question of the kind of authority to be ascribed to the Bible, to later tradition and to catholic dogma, is a large one, about which much has been written, and about which I myself have ventured to write elsewhere, but my present concern is only to make the point that the measure of assurance with which the Christian makes any doctrinal affirmation ought clearly to be affected by other factors than his own direct insight into its truth. Only the most arrogant individualist could think otherwise.

§ 23

We must now endeavour to define more precisely the nature of those affirmations in which Christians, beginning with the New Testament authors, have sought to draw out the latent intellectual content of the faith that is in them. We have said that while each of these claims to express something of the reality with which faith is confronted, no claim is made that they are fully adequate to that reality. On the contrary, their far-reaching inadequacy is something which our very faith itself constrains us to affirm. The incomprehensibility of God is a Christian dogma. It has never been a cause of distress for the Christian mind, but rather of rejoicing—

> Like aught that for its grace may be
> Dear, and yet dearer for its mystery.[1]

For the old Latin fathers had it that *deus comprehensus non est deus*. There is a prayer of St Athanasius which begins, 'O God, incomprehensible because Thou are blessed, and blessed because Thou art incomprehensible'; and St Augustine prayed, 'Let us delight to find Thee by failing to find Thee, rather than to fail to find Thee by finding Thee.'[2] This balance of emphasis between knowing and unknowing, between the *deus revelatus* and the *deus absconditus*, pervades the New Testament,

---

[1] Shelley, *Hymn to Intellectual Beauty*.   [2] *Confessions* I, 6.

and has its manifest roots in the Old, but there is as yet little attempt to relieve the pressure of the antinomy by a closer determination of the threshold separating them. As A. B. Davidson wrote in his *Theology of the Old Testament*, posthumously published in 1904, 'Scripture does not say in what sense God may be seen and may not be seen, how He may be known and may not be known. It assumes that men themselves understand this, and merely alludes to the two facts as things undoubted in men's thought and experience.'[1]

The thinkers of the medieval and modern world have not, however, been content to leave the matter there, but have busied themselves to fix the standing as knowledge of our theological affirmations by a clearer definition of the respect in which they fall short of an adequate understanding of the realities of which they speak—of the respect in which, as it has sometimes been put, our apprehension of the divine falls short of comprehension. To this end a great variety of terms and concepts have been pressed into service, and we may now remind ourselves of some of these.

It is well known that medieval theology, especially as represented in St Thomas Aquinas, operated chiefly with the concept of *analogy*, and that on this concept Roman orthodoxy still relies. St Thomas is an empiricist in what we have distinguished as the narrower sense of the word, believing that we have no direct knowledge either of other human selves or of God, but only of the things of sense. Such positive statements as we are able to make about God can therefore be made only on the analogy of our experience of the created world. Since, however, I have in mind to devote much of the next chapter to a critical examination of this teaching, it will be convenient to postpone a fuller characterization of it to that place, and meanwhile to give account of certain other concepts which have been called into play by later thinkers, since the break-up of the medieval world.

There is first Spinoza, who in his *Tractatus Theologico-Politicus* goes so far as to hold that the office of theological

[1] Op. cit., p. 82.

doctrines is not to offer us truth but to encourage in us obedience and piety. He does not deny that there is some truth in them, but the truths they contain are of the simplest kind, and even these are put forward rather for our practical guidance than for our intellectual assent. Faith does not so much demand that our doctrines should be true as that they should be pious.

It is not true doctrines that are expressly required by the Bible, so much as doctrines necessary for obedience, and to confirm our hearts in the love of our neighbour, wherein (to adopt the words of John) we are in God and God in us.[1]

I do not wish to affirm absolutely that Scripture contains no doctrines in the sphere of philosophy . . . but I go so far as to say that such doctrines are very few and very simple . . . Scripture does not aim at imparting scientific knowledge, and therefore it demands from men nothing but obedience, and censures obduracy but not ignorance.[2]

Furthermore it appears that the measure of truth contained in such doctrines must be left entirely to speculative philosophy. 'The Holy Spirit only gives its testimony in favour of works . . . and is in itself nothing but the mental acquiescence which follows a good action in our souls. No spirit gives testimony concerning the certitude of matters within the sphere of speculation save only reason, who is mistress of the whole realm of truth.'[3] It is to the imagination, not the reason, that divine revelation is addressed, and it was by means of images that the sacred writers received it;[4] but only rational philosophy can assess the measure of speculative truth which these images embody. Clearly such a view of the nature of theological affirmations bears no resemblance to that of St Thomas, yet many later writers have, as we shall see, occupied positions which are intermediate between them in the limited sense that on one side of them they resemble St Thomas's view and on the other Spinoza's.

[1] Op. cit., chap. XIV; Elwes's trans.
[2] Ibid., chap. XIII.
[3] Ibid., chap. XV.
[4] Ibid., chap. I.

Kant agrees with Spinoza that theological affirmations are practical and not speculative or metaphysical in character and function, but unlike Spinoza he believes them to be apprehended by reason. For there is, he believes, a practical as well as a theoretical exercise of reason, and it is upon this rather than upon our imagination that religious faith rests. Nevertheless, fully rational as it is, he will not (as we saw at an earlier point) allow to such faith the name of knowledge. Not that it is mere opinion; 'to say opinion (*Meinen*) is to say too little, but to say knowledge (*Wissen*) is to say too much'.[1] 'Sufficient ground is still left to you for speaking, in the presence of the strictest reason, of a firm-established *faith*, if at the same time you feel constrained to renounce the language of knowledge.'[2]

What then, according to Kant, is the precise status and function of such faith? It operates always with transcendental ideas, that is, with ideas which carry us beyond the sphere of sense experience. Yet these, though transcendental themselves, must not be put to a transcendent use, as though yielding knowledge of objects outside sense experience. Their only legitimate use is the *immanent* one of helping us to organize our sense experience. Their function is always *regulative*, never *constitutive*. The objects to which they refer must not be taken to be actual objects in the real world, about which we can know what they are in themselves; rather are they ideal beings which reason finds it imperatively necessary to postulate in order to understand and to organize into some sort of unity the things which we do empirically know. Three such are enumerated by Kant, the Ego, the Universe and God. It is the last of these that here particularly concerns us and of this he says:

The third idea of pure reason, which encloses the merely relative supposal of a being who is the one and all-sufficient cause of all cosmological series, is the rational concept of God. We have not the least ground for affirming absolutely the existence of an object corresponding to this idea. . . . All the idea has to tell us is that reason compels us to regard the interconnection of things in the

---

[1] *Kritik der reinen Vernunft, Kanon, Dritter Abschitt.*
[2] Op. cit., *Disciplin d. r. V., Zweiter Abschitt.*

world in accordance with the principles of systematic unity, that is, to regard them *as if* they all took their origin from one single all-embracing Being who is their supreme and all-sufficient cause. This makes it clear that reason has no other interest here at stake but its own formal rule for the extension of its empirical procedure, without ever extending itself beyond the limits of such procedure; and that no constitutive principle such as would extend it to further possibilities of experience lies here concealed.

The highest formal unity, which rests upon the concepts of reason alone, is the *purposive* unity of things, and the speculative interest of reason makes it necessary to regard the whole ordering of the world *as if* it had sprung from the design of a Supreme Reason.[1]

In the same context Kant anticipates the question whether we are to take it that there is any reality at all corresponding to the idea of God, 'whether there is *something* distinct from the world which is the ground of its order'. His answer is 'without doubt; for the world is a sum of appearances, and must have some transcendent ground'. Of what this something is, beyond that it is 'a something', we have no *knowledge*, and therefore we cannot make the smallest constitutive use of it so as to construct the beginnings of a speculative theology. Yet he continues:

It may then be asked whether we *can* in this situation presuppose a single wise and all-powerful Author of the world. *Without any doubt* we can; and not only so, but we *must* presuppose this. But do we thus extend our knowledge beyond the sphere of possible experience? *By no means.* For we have only presupposed a something, of which we have no conception as to what it is in itself—for it is a purely transcendental object; but in relation to the systematic and purposive ordering of the universe, which our study of nature compels us to presuppose, we have conceived this unknown being on the *analogy* of an intelligence, endowing it with those attributes which in the case of our own reasons would be the ground of such a systematic unity.[2]

In one of the closing sections of the first *Critique* (from which all the above quotations have been taken) Kant justifies the use of the word *Glaube* (belief or faith) for the kind of assent

---

[1] Op. cit., *Von der Endabsicht der Natürlichen Dialektik.*
[2] Ibid.

we give to the idea of God as thus regulatively and immanently used for our better understanding of the sensible world. But he here calls it doctrinal faith, because he now wishes to distinguish it from another kind of belief or faith, which is not thus theoretical but rather practical in its use; and indeed he says that it is only because the former bears a sort of analogy to the latter that the use of the word *Glaube* to designate it can properly be justified. The other kind of faith of which he now comes to speak he calls *moral faith*. He introduces his discussion of it by saying that after all 'a purely doctrinal faith has a certain instability in itself, for it often deserts us in consequence of difficulties which meet us in our speculation, though we find ourselves inevitably returning to it again and again'. But, he continues, it is quite different with moral faith. This is a faith in which I cannot waver, for it follows from the nature of the moral law, and to that law I am absolutely committed.

The end is here incontrovertibly established and, according to all the insight I possess, there is no other possible condition under which this end can harmonize with all other ends, and so have practical validity, save that there be a God and a future world; I know quite certainly that no one knows of any other conditions under which the unity of ends under the moral law could be assured. . . . Thus I shall unhesitatingly believe in the existence of God and a future life; and I am certain that nothing can make me waver in this faith, since thereby my moral principles would themselves be overthrown, and these I cannot renounce without becoming abominable in my own eyes.[1]

Yet when all is said, this is faith, not knowledge.

In this way there still remains to us, after all ambitious endeavours of a reason that attempts to range beyond the limits of experience have proved vain, quite enough to satisfy us practically. No one indeed will be able to boast that he *knows* there is a God and a future life; for if he knows this, he is just the man whom I have long wished to meet.[2]

This then is the teaching of the *Critique of Pure Reason*. That of the *Critique of Practical Reason*, published seven years later, follows it on the whole very closely. But the point is now definitely made

[1] Op. cit., *Kanon, Dritter Abschnitt*.   [2] Ibid.

that our moral faith in God and in the objects of the other transcendental ideas not only does not share the 'instability' attaching to the so-called doctrinal faith which employs these within the theoretical sphere for the organization of our sense experience, but is of aid to that doctrinal faith itself by removing the instability. The facts of the moral life ensure for us, in all the uses to which we put them, the reality of the transcendental objects, though without enabling us to say anything more of a theoretical kind about them than we had already done. To that extent the transcendental ideas with which such faith operates are even said by Kant to become constitutive rather than merely regulative in function. He writes as follows:

By this means the theoretical knowledge of pure reason certainly obtains an accession, which however consists only in the fact that those concepts which would otherwise be problematic (merely thinkable) are now definitely declared to have objects corresponding to them, since practical reason has indispensable need of these for the possibility of its own object of the *summum bonum*, which is absolutely necessary to it practically; and thus the theoretical reason is justified in assuming them. . . . Thus through the agency of an apodictic practical law, and as necessary conditions of the possibility of what that law bids us *make into an object*, these concepts acquire objective reality; that is, we are shown in this way *that they have objects*. This still falls short of knowledge of *these objects*, for we cannot thereby make any synthetic judgements about them or determine their application theoretically. Indeed we cannot make of them any such theoretical rational use as that wherein all speculative knowledge consists. Nevertheless the theoretical knowledge, *not indeed of these objects*, but of reason in general, is thereby so far extended that through the practical postulates *objects have been given* to these ideas, and what was a merely problematic thought has for the first time acquired objective reality. There is no extension of the knowledge of *given supersensible things*, but an extension of the theoretic reason and of its knowledge in respect of the supersensible in general; in that it is forced to allow *that there are such things* without being able to determine their nature more closely. . . . For this accession, then, pure theoretical reason, for which all such ideas are transcendent and without object, is wholly indebted to the pure practical exercise of reason. In this region these ideas become *immanent* and *constitutive*, as providing the possibility of *giving reality to the necessary object* of the pure practical reason (i.e. the *summum bonum*), whereas otherwise they would remain *transcendent* and purely *regulative* principles of speculative reason such as do not constrain it to assume a new object beyond experience but only to bring its exercise within experience nearer to completeness.[1]

This is soon followed by an interesting passage in which Kant briefly indicates how far he is prepared to go in endowing the God whose reality is thus assured with the attributes traditionally ascribed to him in the Christian tradition:

I now endeavour to attach this concept to the object of the practical reason, and here I find that the moral principle allows it to be possible only by assuming a Creator of the world possessed of the *highest perfection.* He must be *omniscient,* in order to know my conduct up to its innermost springs in the disposition of my mind, in all possible cases and into all future time. He must be *omnipotent* in order to allot to my conduct its fitting consequences. He must similarly be *omnipresent, eternal,* etc.[2]

Such then is Kant's attempted contribution to the solution of our problem of the epistemological status of faith and of the theological tenets in which the content of faith is accustomed to be explicated. The strong agnostic strain in it is indeed very evident—as it must surely also be in the teaching of Spinoza. It will readily be understood from what I have already advanced that the root of all my own difficulties with it lies in the fact that, having accepted the irreproachable doctrine that all our knowledge derives from experience, he then confines our 'experience' to that gained through the bodily senses. Nothing for him qualifies as veridical experience save our perception of the phenomena of the external world. We thus have no knowledge save that which natural science allows or provides—and for Kant this meant Newtonian natural science. Spinoza had anticipated him in this, holding mathematical science to be the only true type of knowledge, so that even his ethics were *ordine geometrico demonstrata.* And, as we have seen, he has found plenty of our contemporary philosophers to

---

[1] *Kritik der praktischen Vernunft, Erster Teil, Zweites Hauptstück, VII.*
[2] Ibid. All the italics in this and the other passages quoted are Kant's own.

follow him—we remember, for instance, Wittgenstein's pro-
nouncement that 'the totality of true propositions is the total
natural science'.[1] 'But', as Clement Webb has written, 'it is not
necessary to follow Kant in making mathematics and physical
science the sole standard of genuine knowledge, or in consequence to treat experiences in which the whole of our personality is engaged as somehow inferior in validity to the results
of abstraction.'[2] Not all that Kant proceeds to say about the
unconditionality of moral obligation and the thoughts of God
to which by this very unconditionality we are ineluctably
constrained, compensates, or nearly compensates, for the
impoverishment of our total spiritual life involved in this starting-point. We remember Heinrich Heine's caustic suggestion
in his *History of Religion and Philosophy* in Germany that the
'moral theology' which Kant appends to his two *Critiques* was
added for the sake of his pious old man-servant Lampe, whose
distress at the direction in which his master's teaching was
tending would otherwise have been inconsolable. Even if
spoken half in jest, this grievously slanders Kant's stature as
both a profound and an honest thinker. What the facts do
point to is rather an imperfectly resolved tension between two
parts of Kant's own total outlook on life.

Nevertheless our debt to him is immense. He has done more
to illuminate our problem than any other single thinker since
the Middle Ages. It is altogether remarkable—and this must
be my excuse for having set out his views at what may seem a
disproportionate length—how difficult later thinkers have
found it to escape from his influence, to find approaches to the
problem that are radically different from his, or to dispense
with many of the distinctions and much of the terminology
which he first introduced.

§ 24

Let us now very briefly remind ourselves of what some of these
later thinkers have had to say to us regarding our problem of

[1] *Tractus Logico-Philosophicus*, 4. 1.
[2] *Kant's Philosophy of Religion* (1926), p. 211.

the epistemological standing of those theological judgements in which we attempt to explicate the faith that is in us. It is agreed that these cannot claim to be fully adequate to their objects, but what is wanted is a closer definition of the nature of their inadequacy. It is also agreed, and is indeed quite obvious, that the language in which they are expressed is very far from being that of flat common sense or even of that in which the findings of the natural sciences, which are a sort of extension of common sense, are accustomed to be clothed. We are therefore told on all hands that much or all of it is not to be taken 'literally' or understood in the 'straightforward' sense, that it is in the more technical meaning of the word 'improper', or that it is 'logically odd'—this latter term being the one chiefly employed by Professor Ian Ramsey in his book on *Religious Language* published in 1957. But again we desire to know wherein exactly this oddness or impropriety consists.

I begin my list with Hegel, but his view of the matter is in all our minds and the briefest reference will suffice. In one important respect he carries us back behind Kant to Spinoza. He believes that the religious mind operates, not by means of *Begriffe*, exact concepts or notions, but by means of imaginative representations or *Vorstellungen*. Religion is picture-thinking, which means that it is thinking of super-sensible reality in terms of sensible things, and of the invisible in terms of the visible. Philosophy, on the other hand, can offer us adequate knowledge of the super-sensible realm, which to him is the realm of reality as distinct from appearance, because *Begriffe* are its natural currency. Yet this it could not do were it not preceded by the imaginative representations of religion. 'In point of time the mind makes general *images* of its objects long before it makes *notions* of them.'[1] Religious faith has thus a double justification; it is sufficient for the ends of practical piety, and it is a necessary precursor of a true understanding of reality, though not itself yielding such an understanding.

Of the later Hegelians I need mention only Bradley, who

[1] *Logic*, Wallace's trans. p. 1.

here follows his master very closely. Religion, he tells us, 'is a necessity', and yet it is 'a mere appearance'.[1] 'It is clear that religion must have some doctrine, and it is clear again that such doctrine will not be ultimate truth.'[2] Religion necessarily operates with the idea of God, but 'God is but an aspect, and that must mean but an appearance, of the Absolute.'[3] All mere appearances suffer from an internal contradiction which constrains them, when fully thought out, to pass beyond themselves; and thus 'in religion God tends always to pass beyond himself. He is necessarily led to end in the Absolute, which for religion is not God.'[4] 'Hence, short of the Absolute, God cannot rest, and, having reached that goal, he is lost and religion with him.'[5] But if this is true of God, so by the same reasoning is it true of man; and if we say that in that case both are 'illusions and not facts', Bradley replies that 'if facts are to be ultimate and real, there are no facts anywhere or at all. There will be one single fact which is the Absolute.' The only question is therefore what rank within the hierarchy of appearances we can ascribe to the God of religion, what degree of reality short of ultimate reality we are to ascribe to him; and Bradley's answer is that he is more real than anything within the temporal or finite world. 'The man who demands a reality more solid than that of the religious consciousness seeks he does not know what.' And here he begins to speak a little differently from Hegel, refusing to say that something more solid can be found in philosophy. To Bradley 'philosophy itself is but appearance', and though *as knowledge* it must be allowed to stand higher than religion because it is its particular business to discourse of the Absolute which alone is ultimately real; yet religion, whose essence is not knowledge though it involves knowledge, but is rather 'the attempt to express the complete reality through every aspect of our being', is in that regard 'at once something more and therefore something higher than philosophy.'[6]

Reference may next be made to the views of Dean Mansel,

---

[1] *Appearance and Reality*, 2nd ed. (1897), p. 446.   [2] Ibid., p. 451.
[3] Ibid., p. 448.   [4] Ibid., p. 446.   [5] Ibid., p. 447.   [6] Ibid., p. 448 f.

whose Bampton Lectures on *The Limits of Religious Thought*
aroused so much controversy in the Church of England just a
hundred years ago. Mansel is obviously under great debt to
Kant, a debt of which he shows himself well aware in spite of
his somewhat violent repudiation of some of the most characteristic elements in Kant's construction. He goes at least as
far as Kant in denying that any theological proposition we are
capable of making can claim to be absolutely true. He is indeed
something of what would nowadays be called a fundamentalist
in his apparent acceptance of the whole contents of Scripture
as being divinely revealed, but he does not take this to mean
that they provide us with absolute truth, since the Scriptural
revelation carries 'on its face the marks of subordination to
some higher truth, of which it indicates the existence, but does
not make known the substance'.[1] Nor does he believe with
Spinoza and Hegel, any more than did Kant, that philosophy
can lead us any nearer than can religious thought, to the
absolute truth of things. Yet he will not allow that the limits
thus set to our knowledge need cause us any kind of distress,
since 'Action and not knowledge is man's destiny and duty in
this life; and his highest principles, both in philosophy and in
religion, have reference to this end.'[2] This being understood,
'man is content to practise where he is unable to speculate'.[3]
Mansel is as emphatic as possible in holding that we cannot
practise without some degree of knowledge to guide us, but
such knowledge is sufficiently given us in Scripture, though
always in the form of images and imperfect analogy rather
than of exact concepts. Moreover even philosophy, or natural
as distinct from revealed theology, here comes to our aid; since,
as he writes, acknowledging here his agreement with Aquinas,
'The conviction *that* an Infinite Being exists seems forced upon
us by the manifest incompleteness of our finite knowledge; but
we have no natural means whatever of determining *what* is the
nature of that Being.'[4]

　　Mansel therefore adopts the terminology of Kant in saying

---

[1] Op. cit., 4th ed. (1859), p. 95.　　　　[2] Ibid., p. 98.
[3] Ibid., p. 84.　　　　[4] Ibid., p. 117 and note on p. 274.

that such ideas of God and things divine as we are able to possess are *regulative and not speculative* in their character and function. We must, he says, 'be content with those *regulative* ideas of the Deity, which are sufficient to guide our practice, but not to satisfy our intellect; which tell us, not what God is in Himself, but how He wills that we should think of Him'.[1] Finally, I shall allow myself one fuller quotation:

It is thus strictly in analogy with the method of God's Providence in the constitution of man's mental faculties, if we believe that, in Religion also, He has given us truths which are designed to be regulative, rather than speculative; intended, not to satisfy our reason, but to guide our practice; not to tell us what God is in His absolute Nature, but how He wills that we should think of Him in our present finite state. . . .

We must remain content with the belief that we have that knowledge of God which is best adapted to our wants and training. How far that knowledge represents God as He is, we know not, and we have no need to know.

The testimony of Scripture, like that of our natural faculties, is plain and intelligible, when we are content to accept it as a fact intended for our practical guidance: it becomes incomprehensible only when we attempt to explain it as a theory capable of speculative analysis.[2]

Returning from England to the Continent, let us next briefly remind ourselves of the teaching of two other schools of nineteenth-century thought. The first of these is the widely influential movement deriving from Albrecht Ritschl. Ritschl's thought is clearly set within a Kantian frame, though the influences upon it both of Luther and of Schleiermacher are equally apparent in their different ways. Like Kant he desired to extrude all metaphysical speculation from the concerns of faith, and like Kant he conceived these latter to be practical rather than theoretical in character. Religious judgements, he insisted, are always judgements of value (*Werturteile*), their office being, not to satisfy our intellectual curiosity, or to answer our speculative questions, concerning the divine

[1] *The Limits of Religious Thought*, p. 84.
[2] Ibid., pp. 94–97.

realities of which they discourse, but to define the bearing of these upon our own situation and our own behaviour. We know God and Christ and the eternal world 'only in their value for us'. Nor is there any further kind of insight into these to which philosophy can conduct us.

The other continental school is that of the *Symbolofidéists* in France, whose chief representatives were Auguste Sabatier and Eugène Ménégoz. As the chosen name of the school implies, they preferred to define the standing of theological propositions by speaking of them as *symbolical* in nature.

Religious knowledge is symbolical. All the notions it forms and organizes, from the first metaphor created by religious feeling to the most abstract theological speculation, are necessarily inadequate to their object. They are never equivalent, as in the exact sciences. The reason is easy to discover. The object of religion is transcendent; it is not a phenomenon. But in order to express that object our imagination has nothing at its disposal but phenomenal images, and our understanding logical categories, which do not go beyond space and time. Religious knowledge is therefore obliged to express the invisible by the visible, the eternal by the temporal, spiritual realities by sensible images. It can speak only in parables.[1]

§ 25

Passing now from the nineteenth century to the contemporary theological scene, let us consider some of the terms that are preferred by different writers to describe the peculiar character of theological propositions. Those who at present principally discourse on this matter may, I think, be roughly grouped into four schools—the Thomists, the Barthians, the existentialists and the linguistic analysts.

Dr Barth has consistently opposed the Thomists and their doctrine of the *analogia entis*, but his views are not without some affinity to those of the other two schools. Like the analysts, he is very much aware of the radical difference between 'other human language' and 'language about God', and it is to an

---

[1] A. Sabatier, *Esquisse d'une Philosophie de la Religion* (1879); Eng. trans., *Outlines of a Philosophy of Religion*, p. 322 f. I have slightly amended the translation.

explication of this difference that he devotes the opening sections of his monumental *Dogmatics*. As to the existentialists, he has often enough in his maturer writings expressed his opposition to them, yet in his early commentary on the Epistle to the Romans he certainly betrayed some indebtedness to Kierkegaard, from whose thought they drew their original inspiration. What was required for the understanding of such a text was, he said, 'a relentless elastic application of the dialectical method'.[1] In that early period his theology was therefore spoken of, and not without his consent, as the Dialectical Theology. This use of the term 'dialectical' to describe the proper character of religious thought certainly derives from Kierkegaard, whose use of it I mentioned at an earlier point and described roughly as follows. When we turn aside from direct confrontation with God, which is the 'existential' situation, in order to think about him, which is what theology tries to do, our thought falsifies its object unless we allow it, as it were, to be diffracted in two opposite directions at once, so that every affirmation we make about God must be complemented by another from which this non-existential standpoint will appear to be its opposite. But now in its turn this usage of Kierkegaard's derives from Kant. Whenever, according to Kant, we attempt to extend our knowledge to the realm of supersensible realities, we find ourselves landed in what he calls antinomies, that is, we are forced to say two apparently contradictory things about them. Yet these are not really contradictory in the proper logical sense, for of two contradictory propositions one must be false and the other true. They are rather *dialectical* opposites, both of which are false. Hence Kant arrives at his conclusion that we can have no knowledge whatever of supersensible reality.[2]

It is here we have the source of the Hegelian criticism of all religious thinking, as also of the argument used by Mansel for the destruction of the claims of speculative theology. A single quotation from the Hegelian Bradley may suffice in illustration:

[1] Preface to the 2nd ed.
[2] See e.g., *Kritik der reinen Vernunft, Die Antinomie, Siebenter Abschnitt.*

Religion prefers to put forth statements which it feels to be untenable, and to correct them at once by counter-statements which it finds are no better. It is then driven forwards and back between both, like a dog which seeks to follow two masters.[1]

This sounds very like what we have been accustomed to hear from the champions of the Dialectical Theology, but the difference is that according to these latter the two dialectical opposites, when allowed to correct each other by being held together in the mind, do conduct towards a true understanding of the reality to which they refer.

Coming now to contemporary thinkers of the existentialist school, we may note first what is said by Dr Karl Jaspers in his latest work, *Philosophical Logic*. The concept with which he prefers to operate is that of the cipher (*Chiffer*). We cannot, he teaches, directly apprehend the ultimate or divine reality. We apprehend it always through the mediation of the finite or phenomenal world, and thus the only cognition of it which is available for us is in the form of cipher. In principle any event or any thing in the world may thus become for us a pointer to the divine. Potentially as least, the whole world has the character of *Chiffersein*, or is a code of ciphers. But we cannot decode or decipher it into any more ultimate form of knowledge. Rather must we accept the ciphers as such, and devoutly and duteously respond to the claims they make upon us.[2]

On the other hand, Dr Rudolf Bultmann's preference is for the term 'myth'. This term he uses to define the epistemological status of many of the traditional Christian affirmations; though not indeed of all, because there are some which are so grounded in historical fact that they cannot be thus dissolved. By myth he means 'the use of imagery to express the otherworldly in terms of this world, and the divine in terms of human life, the other side in terms of this side. For instance, divine transcendence is expressed as spatial distance.'[3] Such a state-

---

[1] *Appearance and Reality*, 2nd ed., p. 446.

[2] Brief expositions and criticisms of this teaching of Jaspers will be found in F. H. Heinemann, *Existentialism and the Modern Predicament* (New York, 1953) and in David E. Roberts, *Existentialism and Religious Belief* (New York, 1957).

[3] *Kerygma and Myth*, ed. Bartsch (Eng. trans. R. H. Fuller, 1953), p. 10, note 2.

ment closely resembles the language of many of the other writers to whom I have referred, and also that of some others to whom I am about to refer. But the difference is that unlike these Dr Bultmann believes that we can dispense with the imagery, so penetrating behind it that we can restate our affirmations in a form more adequate to the truth they endeavour to express. As is well known, his programme is one of 'demythologizing'. On the other hand, his disagreement with these other writers is much less radical than it would otherwise be, in view of the fact that the restatement which thus ensues is not an ontological one, in terms of what the divine reality is *per se*, but an 'existential' one in terms of man's understanding of himself in relation to that reality. As he writes:

The real purpose of myth is not to present an objective picture of the world as it is, but to express man's understanding of himself in the world in which he lives. Myth should be interpreted, not cosmologically but anthropologically or, better still, existentially. . . .
Thus myth contains elements which demand its own criticism— namely, its imagery with its apparent claim to objective validity. The real purpose of myth is to speak of a transcendent power which controls the world and man, but that purpose is impeded and obscured by the terms in which it is expressed.
Hence the importance of the New Testament mythology lies not in its imagery but in the understanding of existence which it enshrines. The real question is whether this understanding is true. Faith claims that it is, and faith ought not to be tied down to the imagery of New Testament mythology.[1]

The third school of contemporary thought which I have mentioned is that of the linguistic analysts, and I shall here content myself with brief quotation from two Oxonians who, whatever their connexion or lack of connexion with it, may at least be said to move within its atmosphere. The main thesis of Dr Austin Farrer's Bampton Lectures for 1948 was that the divine is characteristically apprehended by us in the form of images. Theological propositions are attempts to express what the images reveal, but they can never do this in a way that leaves the images behind. In Dr Farrer's words:

[1] *Kerygma and Myth,* p. 10 f.

I have heard it wisely said that in Scripture there is not a line of theology, and of philosophy not so much as an echo. Theology is the analysis and criticism of the revealed images; but before you turn critic or analyst, you need a matter of images to practise upon.[1]

The Scholastics of the Middle Ages, he complains, hunted through Scripture for theological propositions out of which a correct system of doctrine could be deduced by logical method. But no such system was present in the minds of the Scriptural authors, whose thought was not on the conceptual level but moved round a number of vital images 'which lived with the life of images, not of concepts'.[2]

My other quotation is from an essay by Mr Ian Crombie, who writes as follows:

Statements about God . . . are in effect parables, which are referred, by means of the proper name 'God', out of our experience in a certain direction. We may, if we like . . . try to tell ourselves what part of the meaning of our statements applies reasonably well, what part outrageously badly; but the fact remains that, in one important sense, when we speak of God, we do not know what we mean (that is, we do not know what that which we are talking about is like). . . . Because our concern with God is religious and not speculative (it is contemplative in part, but that is another matter), because our need is not to know what God is like, but to enter into relation with him, the authorized images serve our purpose. They belong to a type of discourse—parable—with which we are familiar, and therefore they have communication-value, though in a sense they lack descriptive value.[3]

Finally, there is Dr Tillich, whose thought cannot easily be fitted into any school but has been so widely influential. His preference among the various terms that we have seen to be employed to describe the nature of religious affirmations is for the term 'symbol'. 'The language of faith', he writes, 'is

---

[1] *The Glass of Vision* (1948), p. 44.   [2] Ibid., p. 45.
[3] *New Essays in Philosophical Theology*, ed. Antony Flew and Alasdair MacIntyre (1955), p. 142. In another essay in the same volume Mr Thomas McPherson writes: 'Religion belongs to the sphere of the unsayable, so it is not to be wondered at that in theology there is much nonsense (i.e. many absurdities); this is the natural result of trying to put into words—and to discuss—various kinds of inexpressible "experiences", and of trying to say things about God.'

the language of symbols.'[1] 'Man's ultimate concern must be expressed symbolically, because symbolic language alone is able to express the ultimate.'[2] Here lies the difference between philosophy on the one hand and a theology that founds itself on faith on the other.

Philosophical truth consists in true statements concerning the ultimate; the truth of faith consists in true symbols concerning the ultimate. . . . The question will certainly be raised: Why does philosophy use concepts and why does faith use symbols if both try to express the ultimate? The answer, of course, is that the relation to the ultimate is not the same in each case. The philosophical relation is in principle a detached description of the basic structure in which the ultimate manifests itself. The relation of faith is in principle an involved expression of concern about the meaning of the ultimate for the faithful.[3]

But if now we ask what 'true statements' can be made about God, as distinct from using 'true symbols' concerning him, Dr Tillich replies that we can make only one such statement, namely that God is absolute being.

The statement that God is being-itself is a non-symbolic statement. It does not point beyond itself. It means what it says directly and properly. . . . Theologians must make explicit what is implicit in religious thought and expression; and, in order to do this, they must begin with the most abstract and completely unsymbolic statement which is possible, namely, that God is being-itself or the absolute. However, after this has been said, nothing else can be said about God which is not symbolic.[4]

If we now look back over the various views which we have so hastily surveyed, we must realize at once that, in spite of many deep-going diversities, and in spite of the heat which many of them engender in controversy with some of the others, they all have something very real in common. Behind this significant element of agreement stands ultimately the Biblical teaching concerning the limited nature of our knowledge of God, concerning the mystery of the Godhead and the inscrutability of the divine mind. Something of it goes back to the

[1] *Dynamics of Faith* (New York, 1957), p. 45.   [2] Ibid., p. 41.
[3] Ibid., p. 91. By the word 'involved' Tillich means committed and responsible.
[4] *Systematic Theology*, Vol. I (Chicago, 1951), p. 238 f.

'negative theology' deriving ultimately from Neo-Platonism and so strongly represented in the Medieval Scholastics. Not a little of it has its source in the new stirrings of thought which manifested themselves in the seventeenth century as seen, for example, in Spinoza. And we have seen how paramount during the last century and a half has been the influence of Kant. We must also have realized that the wide variety manifest in the terminology of the various writers does not really reflect an equal variety of meanings. One prefers to speak of theological thought as analogical, another as symbolic, another as parabolic, another as regulative, another as practical, another in terms of imagery, another in terms of cipher, and still another in terms of myth. Yet, as even the few quotations I have thought it right to include have been sufficient to show, most of them have on occasion varied their language so as to use several, or perhaps even most, of the other terms. At the same time the terms I have listed seem to fall naturally into two groups, which yield different strands of meaning, though both strands may be present in the same thinker. One of these would be fairly represented by the characterization of theological thought as analogical or symbolic, and the other by its characterization as regulative or practical. In what follows I shall say something about each.

CHAPTER VI

Analogy and Symbol

§ 26

Let us now examine the doctrine that all theological statements are symbolic or analogical in nature. In the widest sense of the term all language may be said to be symbolic; the word 'cow' for instance, being the conventional symbol used by English-speaking peoples to denote a certain four-footed animal. The usage with which we are here concerned is, however, the more familiar one according to which some language is symbolic and some is not. Thus the Concise Oxford Dictionary defines a symbol as a 'thing regarded by general consent as naturally typifying or representing or recalling something by possession of analogous qualities or by association in fact or thought.' For our present purpose we may define it a little more narrowly still as a unit of thought or speech that effectively points to a reality which it nevertheless inadequately expresses, and we may define theological symbolism as a way of thinking and speaking which, while pointing to the infinite, the divine and the unseen, describes it in terms of things seen, human and finite. A non-symbolic statement, says Dr Tillich, 'does not point beyond itself. It means what it says directly and properly'. A symbolic statement, on the other hand, is indirect and 'improper'[1]—improper in the sense that the terms it employs do not really belong (German, *uneigen*) to the sphere of reality they are used to denote.

Now, as we saw, Dr Tillich holds that *everything* we say about God is of this kind save the single statement that he is being-itself. This, however, looks more like a formal definition of what we mean by the word 'God' than an informative statement about him; as Dr Tillich perhaps concedes when he

[1] *Systematic Theology*, Vol. I, p. 238.

writes that 'Any *concrete* assertion about God must be symbolic, for a concrete assertion is one which uses a segment of finite experience in order to say something about him.'[1]

Symbolic language is thus essentially analogical in nature, and it will have been noticed that the Dictionary had recourse to the concept of analogy in framing its definition of it. Dr Tillich may then be taken as agreeing rather closely with the contention of St Thomas Aquinas that, once we have established the proposition *that* God is, all further positive knowledge of *what* he is can be reached only by the *via analogiae* from our finite experience; though it is true that within this agreement there is a certain difference:

Can a segment of finite reality become the basis for an assertion about that which is infinite? The answer is that it can, because that which is infinite is being-itself and because everything participates in being-itself. The *analogia entis* is not the property of a questionable natural theology which attempts to gain knowledge of God by drawing conclusions about the infinite from the finite. The *analogia entis* gives us our only justification of speaking at all about God. It is based on the fact that God must be understood as being-itself.[2]

What is here tilted at is no doubt Dr Barth's repudiation of the *analogia entis* as being necessarily bound up with the Thomist natural theology which he so much dislikes.

It is of course quite obvious that our accustomed Christian discourse is replete with symbol and analogy. Or if it is not already obvious to us, all we need do is to open our hymn books or our prayer books, or indeed our Bibles, at any page. We read, for example, of Christ as the Lamb of God, but also as the Good Shepherd who cares for the lambs. If these descriptions were understood non-symbolically, they would contradict one another and lead only to confusion, whereas in fact they lead to no confusion, being understood to be symbols. In his Gifford Lectures on *Symbolism and Belief*, the late Edwyn Bevan drew a distinction between two classes of religious symbols, the symbols behind which we can see and the symbols behind

[1] *Systematic Theology*, Vol I, p. 239. Italics mine.
[2] Ibid., p. 239 f.

which we cannot see. In the former case we have some non-symbolic conceptual understanding of the reality they symbolize and can therefore, if we so desire, express ourselves in language that is no longer 'improper'; whereas in the latter case we have no such access to the reality behind the symbols as would enable us to think of it in conceptual terms, so that we have nothing to work with but the symbols themselves. Of the former he gives the following example:

Even in the case of many symbols used to express things in the life or activity of God we may be said to see behind the symbol. Take such a figure as the Hand of God. If we say that in a certain event we can see the Hand of God, we mean that the event appears to us to have come about in order to realize some particular value— Justice or the good of mankind or an exhibition of beauty—for which we think of God as caring, and the event appears to us to have been brought about by the Will of God as the efficient cause, either directly or working through the natural order. If we put our belief in that way, we should be convinced that we were stating things much more as they really are than when we talk of God as having a hand, though in such a case as this the figure of the Hand may have a truth for feeling greater than the truth in the other, intellectually more correct, statement. The figure of the Hand makes us feel God's action as the simple direct act of an almighty Person more vividly, and this emotional realization may be an apprehension of the truth more perfect than one gets by the other concatenation of more abstract intellectual notions. However, we must, I think, admit that in the case of such a symbol as the Hand of God, we do see behind the symbol, and so can contrast the symbol with a truer view.[1]

Of the other kind of symbolic language, the kind which we are unable to translate into the language of concepts, we have a typical example in the description of the heavenly city and of the end of all things in the Apocalypse of St John the Divine. We have also the pre-Christian example of the myths in the Platonic dialogues. Indeed all religious eschatological discourse, as all religious cosmogonic discourse, must be couched in a symbolical language which we have no means of translating into conceptual terms. It cannot be 'demythologized'.

[1] *Symbolism and Belief* (1938), p. 259 f.

The point I now wish to make, however, is that not all our theological statements are symbolic either in one kind or in the other. I cannot accept the doctrine that all our knowledge of what God is, is reached by analogy from our experience of the finite or created world. Already twenty years ago I ventured a refutation of this doctrine, and I may now be allowed to summarize very briefly what I then wrote.[1] Prominent among the affirmations which the Christian believer is accustomed to make about God are that he is a personal being, infinite, eternal, unchanging, omniscient, omnipotent, 'most holy, most merciful and gracious, long-suffering and abundant in goodness and truth'.[2] It is, however, quite impossible to believe that such characters as these are suggested to us by anything we find in ourselves or elsewhere in the created world. To say that we gain the conception of perfect being by arranging our feeble human approaches towards perfection in an ascending series, and then imagining the indefinite prolongation of this series, is to forget that such an arrangement could not have been made by us save by the aid of a standard of perfection already present to our minds. How can we say that this is nearer to perfection than that unless we already have some conception of what perfection is? The very definition of the infinite is that which cannot be reached by the extension, however prolonged, of a finite series. Yet on the other hand the construction of such a series would be impossible if the idea of the infinite were not at the same time in the mind.

But indeed, already in the thirteenth century, these very considerations were advanced by St Bonaventure and his fellow Franciscans against St Albert and St Thomas and their fellow Dominicans. M. Gilson thus summarizes Bonaventure's argument:

We think we are starting from strictly sensible data when we state as the first step in our demonstration that there are in existence beings mutable, composite, relative, imperfect, contingent: but in actual fact we are aware of these insufficiencies in things only because we already possess the idea of the perfections by whose

---

[1] *Our Knowledge of God* (1939), pp. 250–258.   [2] Westminster Larger Catechism.

standard we see them to be insufficient. So that it is only in appearance that our demonstration begins with sense data. Our awareness, apparently immediate and primary, of the contingent implies an already existent knowledge of the necessary.[1]

As I wrote in my earlier work, 'What is true in the doctrine of the *analogia entis* is that the knowledge of God does not precede our knowledge of man in time but is given "in, with and under" such knowledge, and that therefore no one of God's attributes is ever given us save in conjunction with— that is, in compasison with and in contrast to—some corresponding attribute of man. What is false is the assumption that the comparison moves from man to God instead of from God to man.'[2] Thus while there is no temporal priority of one knowledge to the other, the logical priority lies with our knowledge of God. As I there quoted from Professor Kemp Smith:

In respect of each and all of the ontological attributes, the Divine is not known by analogy with the self, or with any other creaturely mode of existence. . . . If, without any antecedent or independent apprehension of the Divine, we have to start from the creaturely, as exhibited in Nature and man, and by way of inference and analogy —through enlargement or other processes of ideal completion, to construct for ourselves concepts of the Divine, then the sceptics have been in the right; the attempt is an impossible one, condemned to failure from the start. We cannot reach the Divine merely by way of inference, not even if the inference be analogical in character. By no idealization of the creaturely can we transcend the creaturely.[3]

It cannot indeed be too strongly emphasized that God's revelation of Himself cannot be received by us save in the context of our knowledge of finite realities. Only a being who is (a) self-conscious, (b) aware of other selves, and (c) aware of corporeal things can have any knowledge of God. But the point we are at present concerned to make is that the world of created reality cannot be known to us as what we may call a graded valuational field apart from some revelation of the divine perfection. In that sense our knowledge of all ideals is

---

[1] *The Philosophy of St Bonaventure*, Eng. trans., p. 125 f.
[2] *Our Knowledge of God*, p. 254.
[3] *Is Divine Existence Credible?* (1921), p. 13 f.

a priori; not chronologically prior to our knowledge of the actual, but a necessary condition of our ability to ascribe to the actual such characters as good and bad, just and unjust, wise and foolish.

An important example may be found in the conception of personality. Much modern philosophy had taken for granted that personality is the characteristic mode of being of finite spirits, the very hall-mark of our finitude, and had therefore been very naturally contemptuous of all theological attempts to extend such a characteristic by way of analogy to the divine mode of being. As long ago as the middle of the nineteenth century this assumption was powerfully challenged by such thinkers as Albrecht Ritschl and Hermann Lotze, who insisted that, on the contrary, personality was an ideal conception never more than very imperfectly realized in human existence, but it was not until recent psychology began to talk in much the same way that their contention found wide acceptance. The resultant change of outlook found what is perhaps its most notable expression in the late Dr Clement Webb's Gifford Lectures of 1918 and 1919, where it was very clearly shown that the terminology of personality is originally theological, so that men spoke of the Persons of the Godhead long before they came glibly to speak of themselves as persons; and certainly 'philosophical discussion of the nature of human personality is posterior in time to these theological discussions. Nay, it may even be said that it was the religious and theological interest in the Personality of Christ, concerned as being at once God and man, which actually afforded the motive and occasion of undertaking the investigation of the nature of personality in men generally.'[1] Moreover Dr Webb contended that this order of going did but reflect the true inter-relation of the realities being discussed:

Personality is not merely something which we observe in men; rather is it something which, though suggested to us by what we find in men, we perceive to be only imperfectly realized in them; and this can only be because we are somehow aware of a perfection

---

[1] *God and Personality* (1918), p. 20.

or ideal with which we contrast what we find in men as falling short of it. In such cases we rightly begin with thinking out the ideal and then considering the experienced facts in the light of it.[1]

It is for this reason that I cannot agree that all theological statements are of the nature of analogies or are symbolic in Dr Tillich's sense. The Westminster Shorter Catechism is, I believe, using directly applicable and non-symbolic language when it answers the question 'What is God?' by saying 'God is a Spirit, infinite, eternal and unchangeable, in his being, wisdom, power, holiness, justice, goodness, and truth.'[2]

But how much further down the scale of theological statements does the same thing apply? 'Why callest thou me good? None is good but one, that is, God.'[3] Yes; and by the same sign none is wise but he. When therefore we say that God is wise and good, we are using 'proper', non-symbolic and non-analogical language; and it is when we speak of a *man* as wise and good that our language is improper. But how is it, for example, when we speak of God as Father? Is it only by analogy that we call him Father? This is strenuously denied by Dr Barth, who writes as follows:

It must not be said that the name 'Father' for God is a transference to God, figurative and not to be taken literally, of a human creaturely relationship, whereas God's essential being as God *per se* is not touched or characterized by this name. . . . But what is figurative and not literal is that which we characterize and imagine we know as fatherhood in our human creaturely sphere. . . . He is the *eternal* Father, He is that in Himself. It is as such that He is then Father for *us* and reveals Himself to us and is the incomparable prototype of all human creaturely fatherhood; 'from whom every fatherhood (πᾶσα πατριά) in heaven and earth is named' (Eph. iii, 15).[4]

---

[1] Ibid., p. 21.
[2] It may be said that at least the word 'spirit' is an analogical symbol when applied to God, because both itself and its equivalents in many languages literally mean breath or wind—air in motion. But instead of 'literally mean' we should say 'originally meant'. Spirit certainly does not mean breath today. Compare Edwyn Bevan, *Symbolism and Belief* (1938), p. 151 ff.
[3] Mark 10. 18.
[4] *Credo* (1935), Eng. trans., p. 23 f.
S.P.G.—9

And elsewhere:

We must not say that the use of the name 'Father' here is a transferred, *improper*, inadequate one. That could be said only if the
standard of propriety, here and generally, were our language or the
created reality to which our language applies. If the Creative is
the standard of the propriety of the created, and therefore also of
our language, then the reverse is true . . . *God alone . . . as He who
is by Himself, as the eternal Father of the eternal Son, is properly and
adequately to be called Father*. From the power and dignity of this, the
only, proper name of Father there flows by grace and for faith
the improper—certainly not for this reason untrue, but really
improper—application of the name to God as the Creator; and
likewise its application to inter-creaturely progenitorships such as
are called fatherhood in heaven and on earth (Eph. iii, 15)—which
once again is true but improper—is to be understood as dependent
upon the intra-trinitarian usage.[1]

And here perhaps it is necessary to remind ourselves that
fatherhood has not traditionally been enumerated among the
attributes of God, all of which apply to all three Persons of
the Holy Trinity, but as the property (ἰδίωμα, *proprietas*) of the
first Person; filiation and procession being the properties of the
second and third Persons, as paternity is of the first.

   This is indeed high doctrine on the part of Dr Barth. Is it
too high? It certainly seems an assault on common sense to say
that when I speak of my human progenitor as my father, I am
applying the word to him only in a figurative sense. I believe,
therefore, that a further distinction here falls to be made. I
believe the word 'father' applies in the first place, and quite
non-figuratively, to the fact of natural human procreation; so
that when I say 'The man who has just entered the room is my
father', I am in no sense using transferred or improper language.
But some have unfortunately been heard to say 'Yes, he is my
father, but he has been no real father to me'. Clearly, then, the
word is employed by us both in a factual and in a ideal sense.
Not all who are in the bare factual sense fathers display the
character of fatherliness even in a minimal degree. Only God
possesses it and displays it in perfection; and it is only by the

---

[1] *Die kirchliche Dogmatik*, I, i, p. 413 f.

standard of his perfect fatherliness that we can measure the appropriateness or inappropriateness of the attribution of fatherliness to any man. So far, then, Dr Barth speaks truly when he says that God alone is properly and adequately to be called Father, and that it is in no figurative sense that we so call him. The divine is always prior. The ideal is always *a priori*. Only if something of its nature is revealed to us, can we proceed to the grading or valuation of the actual.

A difficulty with this teaching may perhaps be found in the fact that Jesus, in his parabolic discourses, constantly appeals to the analogy between human and divine fatherhood, and uses indeed a certain argument *a fortiori* from the former to the latter.

Or what man is there of you, whom if his son ask bread, will he give him a stone? Or if he ask a fish, will he give him a serpent? If ye then, being evil, know how to give good gifts unto your children, how much more shall your Father which is in heaven give good things to them that ask him?[1]

Or we may think of the so-called parable of the Prodigal Son, which is really a parable from a father's abiding and out-going love for his erring child. Here, however, two points may be made. Jesus is not using the argument *a fortiori* to establish the fatherhood of God. Rather is he addressing those who claimed already to believe in it, and who were wont to sing 'Like as a father pitieth his children, so the Lord pitieth them that fear him';[2] and was urging them, as he so often had to do, to live up to what they believed. Again, in the parable, he is not arguing from *actual* human behaviour to the divine behaviour. The father of the prodigal son was not a portrait drawn from life but an ideal picture. Our Lord's hearers had never known an earthly father behave like that. As in Faber's hymn:

> No earthly father loves like Thee;
>   No mother, e'er so mild,
> Bears and forbears as Thou hast done
>   With me, thy sinful child.[3]

---

[1] Matt. 7. 9–11.   [2] Psalm 103. 13.   [3] 'My God, how wonderful Thou art!'

§ 27

I have contended that our fundamental knowledge of God is such as cannot have been reached by way of analogy from our knowledge of his creatures, but by a mode of apprehension which is no less direct in its own way than that by which his creatures are known. Let us now devote some further attention to the implications of this contention. In placing its reliance upon the argument from analogy the old natural theology was confessedly proceeding upon the assumption that our only direct knowledge is of the created world, but it was convinced that, starting from that knowledge, it could argue its way to the existence, eternity, omnipotence, omniscience and omnipresence of God, and to his providential care for his creatures. For example Plato, who may be regarded as the father of natural theology, uses the following analogy to prove that God's provision for our human welfare extends to the minutest and most apparently trivial particulars (ἐπὶ τὸ σμικρότατον)[1]:

If a physician, whose office is to cure a body as a whole, were to neglect its small parts while caring only for the greater, will the whole ever prosper in his hands? . . . Nor would it be any better with pilots or generals or housekeepers, or indeed statesmen or any other such people, if they cared only for things many and large and not for things few and small. The stone-masons have a proverb that the great stones do not lie well without the small ones. . . . Let us not then judge God to be ever inferior to mortal workmen who, the better they are, the more accurately and perfectly do they complete their works by one and the same skill; nor let us think that God, who is the wisest of beings and both willing and able to exercise care, takes no care at all of those things which, being small, are easier to take care of, but attends only to the greater things— like some idle good-for-nothing who is tired of his work. . . . With this it seems to me that we have given a very reasonable answer to those who are prone to blame the gods for their lack of care over us.[2]

The difficulty we feel with this manner of approach to the knowledge of God is that any practice of religion which founds

---

[1] *Laws*, 903 b.   [2] *Laws*, 902 d–903 a.

upon it must be a quite one-sided one, lacking any mutuality of communion between God and man. On this view neither is our worship to him a response to a gracious approach on his part nor can it in its turn expect any response from him. This is why Francis Bacon said that a knowledge of God obtained in this way may suffice 'to convince atheism, but not to inform religion'.[1] It is indeed remarkable how far even the deistical writers of the seventeenth and eighteenth centuries believed such knowledge could extend. According to Lord Herbert of Cherbury it extended to the propositions (1) that a Supreme Being exists, (2) that he ought to be worshipped, (3) that virtue is the principal part of his worship, (4) that faults are to be expiated by repentance, and (5) that there will be rewards and punishments in a future life.[2] And Spinoza's list is as follows: (1) that a Supreme Being exists, (2) that he is one, (3) that he is omnipresent, all things being open to him, (4) that he has supreme right and dominion over all things, (5) that his worship consists only in justice and charity in regard to our neighbours, (6) that 'all those, and those only, who obey God by their manner of life are saved', and (7) that God forgives the sins of those who repent.[3] Both Herbert and Spinoza describe their lists as comprising 'the dogmas of universal religion', the former contending that they are innately implanted by God in the minds of all men, and the latter that they are either thus 'written on the hearts of all men' or are reached by the use of figures provided by the prophetic imagination. But in neither case is there postulated any present activity of communication of the Spirit of God with the human spirit. Religion is an altogether one-sided thing. As is well known, Spinoza taught that 'he who loves God cannot expect that God should love him in return.'[4]

However, to this inevitable one-sidedness of a worship that founds only on such a natural theology there has been added, since the time of Hume and Kant, a wide-spread doubt of the validity of that theology even within its own acknowledged

---

[1] *Of the Advancement of Learning*, Book II.   [2] *De Veritate* (1624).
[3] *Tractatus Theologico-Politicus*, Cap. XIV.   [4] *Ethica*, Pars V, Prop. XIX.

limits. Does it suffice to 'convince atheism', let alone to 'inform religion'? The Protestant Reformers, who were early in the field of criticism of natural theology, would have replied that at least it *ought* to do so, though actually it seldom does. 'All men of right judgement', writes Calvin, 'will testify that there is engraved on human minds a sense of the divine which can never be expunged';[1] and further that 'not only has God planted in our minds this seed of religion, but has also manifested Himself in the whole fabric of His creation, so placing Himself before our view that we cannot open our eyes without being constrained to behold Him'.[2] But he goes on at once to say that owing to the corruption of our natures by sin, 'scarcely one in a hundred cherishes the conception of Him in his heart, and in not one does it grow to maturity'.[3] But the post-Kantian critics of natural theology go even farther. They contend that the testimony of the world of nature is ambiguous in itself. Coleridge, who was profoundly influenced by Kant, is reported to have remarked on the difficulty of deciding whether nature was 'a goddess in petticoats or a devil in a strait-waistcoat'. And Helmholtz, the celebrated physicist, is reported as having said, with regard to the argument, so much relied on by the natural theologian Paley, from the structure of the human eye to the existence of a wise and benevolent God who designed it, 'If an optician sent it to me as an instrument, I should send it back with reproaches for his carelessness and demand the return of my money.'[4]

It is quite certain that all the theological affirmations defended by Plato, Lord Herbert and Spinoza were suggested to them in the first place by reflection upon living religious experience and could not have been suggested in any other way. But all living religious experience has been understood by those who enjoyed it as a two-sided affair, that is, as an active intercourse between God and man. It is doubtful whether any race of men has ever believed that man could

[1] *Institutio*, I, III, 1.   [2] Ibid., I, V, 1.   [3] Ibid., IV, 1.
[4] Quoted by R. S. Lull in *Christianity and Modern Thought* (Yale University Press, 1924).

discover anything about God if God were not at the same time actively seeking to make himself known. Not even the most elementary practices of divination could proceed, if it were not believed that the gods themselves took the initiative in the provision of certain signs, omens and oracles such as could be interpreted by those in possession of the necessary skill. Cicero begins his treatise *On Divination* by saying that he knows 'of no nation, however polished and educated, or however brutal and barbarous', which does not share this belief. At all events it is certain that Christians have always believed that such knowledge as they can have of God is the fruit of a divine initiative whereby God seeks to make himself known. The faith of which it has spoken has always been conceived as a response to the divine approach. It is the apprehension of a divine communication.

We speak of this apprehension in frankly symbolic language as a hearing, and of this communication as a speaking. God speaks and we hear his word. But of course we do not suppose that he speaks with lips of flesh or that we hear with our fleshly ears. We believe indeed that the words of Christ were divinely spoken, and these he spoke with lips of flesh, yet we do not say that what is divine in them can be received by our fleshly ears. It is only by 'the ear of faith' that we hear what they have to say to us, just as it is only to 'the eye of faith' that his recorded deeds carry their divine message. There were many in the days of his flesh who heard all he said and saw all he did, but who found in it nothing that was divine. Speaking to his disciples about the crowd which out of curiosity had gathered about him, Jesus said that 'they seeing see not; and hearing they hear not; neither do they understand'.

And in them is fulfilled the prophecy of Esaias, which saith, By hearing ye shall hear and shall not understand; and seeing ye shall see, and shall not perceive . . . But blessed are your eyes, for they see; and your ears, for they hear.[1]

As far as anything perceptible to the bodily senses was concerned, the life of Jesus proceeded from first to last on an

[1] Matt. 13. 13.

entirely human level. His post-resurrection appearances may be adduced as an exception to this, but even here it is never recorded that these are manifest to any but those who had faith.

And here we are reminded of Professor John Wisdom's celebrated parable of the invisible gardener. Two people return to their long-neglected garden, and find among the weeds some of the old plants surprisingly vigorous. They therefore wonder whether somebody has been at work in the garden, but after the most exhaustive inquiries they find that no such person has ever been seen there by the neighbours. One says 'I still believe a gardener comes', while the other says 'I don't', but their different minds on the matter 'reflect no difference as to what they have found in the garden, no difference as to what they would find in the garden if they looked further, and no difference about how fast untended gardens fall into disorder'.[1]

But my contention from the beginning has been that faith is a mode of apprehension which perceives something more in the total reality with which we are confronted than is manifest, or is expected to be manifest, to the senses. As far as these latter are concerned, all that transpires, all that happens to us and around us, can be explained in purely human terms, without leaving any remainder, without the need of any further hypotheses. As Professor Hocking has well said:

The world would be consistent without God; it would also be consistent with God: whichever hypothesis a man adopts will fit experience equally well; neither one, so far as accounting for visible facts is concerned, works better than the other. . . . The religious objects (the predicates given by religion to reality) stand at a pass of intellectual equipoise: it may well seem that some other faculty must enter in to give determination to reason at the point where reason halts, without deciding voice of its own.[2]

But it is evident that among the 'visible facts' that can be thus accounted for without hypothesizing a divine element in

[1] See the article 'Gods' in *Proceedings of the Aristotelian Society*, 1944; reprinted in *Logic and Language*, ed. A. Flew, Vol. I, pp. 192–4, and in John Wisdom, *Philosophy and Psycho-analysis* (1953), pp. 154 ff.
[2] *The Meaning of God in Human Experience* (1912), p. 143.

reality is the whole *religious* life of mankind. Men of faith believe that God is active in their experience at every point, and they conceive their religious life as a bi-polar intercourse between him and themselves. At one of these poles they themselves are standing. But to the mere onlooker, who has himself no part in the intercourse and who therefore, because he does not stand at the human end of it, has no means of access to the divine end, all that transpires at the former will be explicable in purely human terms; that is to say, all that happens in the mind of the believer, his resultant action and his resultant worship, is easily susceptible of explanation in terms of his own psychological states.

Yet it is of the first importance to realize that such an explanation can be adopted only if we are prepared to dismiss all that thus happens in the believer's mind as mere delusion, and his resultant action and worship as meaningless nonsense. What, for example, could be more nonsensical than addressing prayers to a being who does not exist? If our dealings with God are a purely one-sided affair, so that the explanation of them in terms purely of our human psychology is the *true* explanation, then the sooner we give them up the better. This state of the case has always been realized by the most hard-headed and clear-sighted critics of religion, though not a few others, being more muddle-headed, have tried to shut their eyes to it, endeavouring to conceive and to practise a kind of worship which was directed to no object beyond themselves and therefore expected no response. This, moreover, is why Schleirmacher, the Ritschlians, Kierkegaard and his followers in our own day, have all in their own different ways, and in spite of the deep differences dividing them, insisted that the truth of religion is evident only to those who stand within the religious relationship, that 'the secret of the Lord is with them that fear him'[1] and must for ever be concealed from the mere spectator or onlooker.

Up to a point, of course, the same thing applies within the sphere of aesthetic appreciation. The man who entirely lacks

[1] Psalm 25. 14.

the relevant aesthetic sensibility, when he looks at a picture or listens to a piece of music, sees exactly the same lines and colours or hears the same sounds, as the connoisseur. The latter is aware of something more, but this something more does not consist of extra lines and colours, or of extra sounds, and cannot therefore be expressed in terms of mere sensory perception. The former will thus have no difficulty in providing a description of what both alike see or hear, which will be complete in itself, requiring no further hypothesis to explain it; but in so doing he reduces the painting to a mere random assemblage of lines and patches of colour, or the music to what Samuel Johnson is said to have called a noise that gave him no new ideas and prevented him from enjoying those he already had. As we say, 'He sees nothing in it.'[1]

Yet this parallel is only partly apposite, since in the life of faith we have to do, not with anything that passively awaits our contemplation or appreciation, but with an interpersonal intercourse. I shall therefore propose a parable of a telephone conversation, a parable which in spite of its crudity may serve to illustrate the point I am desirous of making. We have often seen a man with a telephone receiver in his hand and have clearly heard all he said, seen the changing shades of expression on his face as he spoke, noticed the different tones in which different remarks were made, and perhaps certain bodily gestures—a nodding or shaking of the head or some movement of his free other hand—with which these remarks were accompanied, while all the time what was being said at the other end was completely inaudible to us. Now it is clear that if something is really being said at the other end, if the man is really hearing something that you are not hearing, then what you are hearing and seeing cannot be correctly accounted for without taking that into account. The sequence of his remarks—of his Yeses and Noes, his expressions of surprise or of protest or of delight—as well as the sequence of his facial and other visible reactions, are in fact determined by the words spoken by

[1] Compare John Wisdom, op. cit., 'One says "Excellent" or "Beautiful" or "Divine"; the other says, "I don't see it." He means he doesn't see the beauty.'

another who is far away, and apart from these they are not intelligible. If the conversation is a real one, any attempt you may make to explain the man's behaviour in terms merely of his own mind will be invalid.

On the other hand it is perfectly open to you, if you see good reason for so doing, to suspect that it is not a real conversation at all. The man may, as we say, be 'putting on an act', he may be the victim of a temporary hallucination, or he may be quite insane. If you adopt one or other of these hypotheses, you can, from your point of view as an observer, offer an entirely self-consistent and also a quite complete explanation of the whole affair without supposing that there is anybody at all at the other end of the wire. But if you do this, you will naturally believe that what you have heard spoken and seen done at the near end is mere sound and fury, signifying nothing.

The application of my parable should be sufficiently obvious. It is quite certain that religious worship and all characteristically religious behaviour *sets up* to be but one side of a two-sided traffic, and that it *looks* and *sounds* like this. Nevertheless it can all be quite easily described by the mere observer in purely psychological terms, and exhaustively accounted for by him on the alternative supposal that it is an entirely one-sided thing, revealing only certain strangely persistent aberrations of our human mentality. The outwardly observed facts are themselves ambivalent, patient of either explanation. But if the purely psychological explanation is the true one, then the whole sum of them reduces to meaningless nonsense such as merits at best our amused or pitying indulgence, and at worst our contempt. And such, as I said before, it has received in plenty from the most intelligent among those who have taken this view of it.

CHAPTER VII

The Frame of Reference

§ 28

We have now to consider the sense in which the affirmations of faith may properly be spoken of as practical and regulative, rather than theoretic or speculative. Not all who have drawn these distinctions have intended quite the same thing by them. When Kant says that religious belief is an affair of the practical reason, he means that it arises out of the rational contemplation, not of external nature, but of the principles given us in the moral law for the practical guidance of our lives. He would not, however, for a moment allow that it provides any further guidance beyond what is already offered by those principles themselves. All it does is to enable us to conceive our ordinary moral duties as divine commands. This way of conceiving them is indeed of invaluable help to us in stimulating us to their more diligent performance; but it does not, or rather it must not be allowed to, suggest to us any further duties such as in one passage he rather quaintly calls 'court duties'. God requires nothing of us save the observance of the moral law, and what that law is every man already clearly knows, whether or not he is religious. Matthew Arnold was later to reduce religion to 'morality touched with emotion'; Kant, less romantically minded, reduced it to morality touched with the reflection that it was required of us by God. He did not therefore speak of religious faith as regulative of our action, but only as regulative of certain ideas by which our action ought to be accompanied. And indeed, as we saw, it is principally to another kind of faith that he applied the term 'regulative'—what he spoke of, rather confusingly, as doctrinal faith, and believed to operate not in the practical but in the theoretical sphere, being of a certain modest service to science in its attempt to give coherence to our observations of external nature.

Those later writers who have borrowed this terminology from Kant have, however, spoken differently. When they have said that such knowledge of God as it is given us to possess is regulative and not speculative in character, they have meant that its office is to provide guidance for the ordering of our lives. We must, said Mansel, 'be content with these *regulative* ideas of the Deity, which are sufficient to guide our practice, but not to satisfy our intellect'. But, unlike Kant, Mansel believed that they really do guide our practice, and not merely stimulate us to the more faithful following of a guidance we already possess. I am sure he was right in this. We cannot act responsibly without thinking, and how we act depends on what we think. Kant would indeed have accepted that statement; but would have protested that all the thinking that is here required is to remind ourselves of something that all men know, whatever else they believe or do not believe. The universal moral law, which is alone sufficient and which should alone be allowed to guide our conduct, is, he contended, self-evidencing, so that our knowledge of it is an invariable quantity subject to no growth or change. Here, however, as in more than one other context, Kant appears as a sadly unhistorical thinker. The evidence surely is that men's judgements of duty vary profoundly from one historical tradition to another, and above all from one religious tradition to another. The conscience of each great culture was formed within the matrix of religious ideas apart from which its deliverances could not be easily justified. Admittedly there is much that is common to all such consciences, but so is there to the religious ideas with which they are in this way associated.

In particular, the Christian conscience was formed within the matrix of Christian ideas, and this is part of what Mansel means by saying that the latter exercise a regulative function. Yet it is not the whole of his meaning, for the word 'conscience', as usually employed, hardly covers all that he believes to be thus regulated. Christian behaviour is much more than the diligent performance of duties. It extends to every aspect of the response we make to the whole of our experience. I remember a fellow student saying to me in my youth that one's Christian faith should make a difference even to the way in which one ties one's bootlaces, and I believe it to have been a wise remark, though I shall leave the exegesis of it to the reader.

§ 29

I am going to speak, then, of the Christian faith as a *frame of reference* which enables the believer to make the appropriate response to every circumstance of life or, translating the Latin word, to all that 'stands around him'. Using a mathematical metaphor, I think of it as a system of co-ordinates within which the believer lives and acts and thinks and feels, and which gives position and significance to each event and each reality as he encounters it. It is in essence a way of regarding, a way of facing, and a way of responding to, every situation in which he finds himself placed. He knows now how to assess the relative authority of the multitudinous claims that are made upon him from every side, and how to meet each. He knows now how best to spend his time, and also how best to spend his money, believing himself to hold both only in stewardship to a higher authority. He knows how to face what we call the buffetings of fortune—disappointment, suspense, unrequited love, frustrated ambition, accident, bereavement and all the rest. He knows how to take pain and sickness, and in particular how to think of 'the last enemy' and how to meet it when it comes. But he knows no less how to enjoy the good things of life, how to comport himself in calm weather as well as in the storm, and how to play as well as to work. 'I know', wrote St Paul, 'both how to be abased, and I know how to abound: everywhere and in all things I am instructed both to be full and to be hungry, both to abound and to suffer need.'[1]

But it is necessary for my further argument that we should

[1] Phil. 4. 12.

remind ourselves how this frame of reference was first provided. When we speak of Christianity we are apt to think of it as a new religion which arose in the first century of our era, but that is a very modern and I believe a very misleading way of regarding it. The first Christians never thought of themselves as the adherents of a new faith. On the contrary they continued to be firmly rooted in the faith of their forefathers; and not only of their Hebrew forefathers, for they traced the beginnings of it back to a time when as yet no Hebrews existed, when as yet the human race was not divided into Semites, Hamites and sons of Japheth. They were eager to assert, as for instance in the New Testament Epistle to the Hebrews, that even Abel and Enoch, who represented in their mythology the second and third generations of mankind, and Noah the 'second founder' of the still undivided race, were men not only of faith but of the true faith. That was the Hebrew, and also the earliest Christian, way of recognizing and explaining the common elements that pervade all the religions and therefore all the moral traditions of mankind.

Nevertheless the Christians believed that something new had come into the world in that first century of our era. This new thing was the *Gospel*. And of course that very word implies that it was something new, for Gospel (like their own Greek word *evangel* which that translates) means good news. It was news in the most literal sense, as the announcement of something that had then only just happened, and the date of which could accordingly be very precisely given. The evangelists (and that means the men who were concerned to spread the good news, as Browning's Joris and Dirck brought other good news from Ghent to Aix) thought of it as beginning when St John Baptist came down from the wilderness to the banks of the Jordan river. St Mark calls that 'the beginning of the Gospel',[1] and St Luke fixes the date for us very exactly as 'in the fifteenth year of the reign of Tiberius Caesar, Pontius Pilate being governor of Judaea, and Herod being tetrarch of Galilee, and his brother Philip tetrarch of Ituraea and of the

[1] Mark 1. 1.

region of Trachonitis, and Lysanias the tetrarch of Abilene, Annas and Caiaphas being the high priests'.[1]

There is a sense, then, in which the Gospel is not the whole of our Christian faith. In this sense, it was the part of it which was new in the first century of our era, but there is that in our faith which was already very old.[2] This was taken for granted without need of comment in the first Christian preaching, because the audiences then consisted only of men and women whose minds were steeped in the Old Testament. But when St Paul and his companions proceeded to carry the Gospel to the Greco-Roman world, they soon discovered that it was unintelligible to their hearers unless these were at the same time taught something else too. They therefore found it necessary to indoctrinate them in the faith of the Old Testament at the same time as they were proclaiming to them the Christian Gospel. Recent scholarship has shown that the creed used by the first generation of Christians contained only one article, 'Jesus is Lord' or 'Jesus is the Messiah', but that when the Gentile mission began, a prior article had to be added, so that it read very much like our own: 'I believe in God, the Father Almighty, Maker of heaven and earth: and in Jesus Christ His only Son our Lord.'

Nevertheless there is a deeper and better sense in which the Gospel *is* the whole of the Christian faith. It is the crown and completion of the Old Testament teaching which, because so much of it is concerned with promises not yet redeemed and expectations not yet fulfilled, cries out for some such completion. But further, the Christians believed that the fulfilment, when it came, cast a radically new light upon the expectation. And Christians still believe this, being convinced that the Old Testament can be truly understood only by the aid of the New. They read the Law in terms of the Gospel and they find that, when this is done, the whole Old Testament story comes to life for them in quite a new way. They even find Jesus Christ in the

[1] Luke 3. 1–2.

[2] Compare Gustaf Wingren. *Theology in Conflict*, Eng. trans. (1958), p. 19: 'The gospel is a part, the most important part, in a history of salvation in which creation, the election of Israel, the covenants etc., also belong.'

Old Testament. That last statement can indeed be made in a way that darkens counsel and that has often led, as I believe, to a perverse ingenuity in Old Testament interpretation; but it is true in the sense that the Christian understands all he reads in the law and the prophets through the illumination which has come to him from the things that long afterwards transpired in Galilee and Jerusalem. Indeed the same is true of everything that the Christian reads anywhere. He reads it with Christian eyes, for he has no other. He may read the sacred books of the great pagan religions and find something in each that he can absorb, but the Gospel is the standard by which he judges them and which enables him to separate whatever light and truth may be in them from the error and the darkness which is most certainly in them too.

What then is the Gospel? What is the good news? A full statement of it, as it has always been understood by Christians, had to await the events of our Lord's death and resurrection and of Pentecost; but it was already proclaimed by our Lord himself, and at the very beginning of his ministry. In the first chapter of our earliest Gospel we have the following summary of his first public utterance:

After John was arrested, Jesus came into Galilee, announcing (*keryssōn*) the good news of God, and saying, The *kairos* is fully come, and the reign of God is at hand; change your minds, and trust to the good news.[1]

The noun corresponding to the word for 'announcing' is *kerygma*, and this has now become something of a technical term among theologians for the basic Christian announcement or proclamation, as distinguished from the further instruction which may be based upon it. *Kairos*, which above I left untranslated, is likewise a prominent word throughout the New Testament, and a word which has also been given a leading place in recent theological discussion. But in his profoundly learned and most illuminating treatise on *The Origins of European Thought*[2] Professor R. B. Onians, writing as a classical scholar,

[1] Mark 1. 14–15.
[2] pp. 343–348.

has shown that the word originally meant an opening, such as the hole in the middle of the target through which the arrow was intended to pass. It thus corresponds very exactly to the Latin word *opportunitas*, deriving from *porta* which also means an opening; and in English we have the same usage when we speak of the *nick* of time. Then in my translation I said 'The *kairos* is fully come', but the Greek verb is *peplerōtai*, and this, with the corresponding noun *plerōma*, represents another prominent New Testament concept. *Plerōma* means fulfilment, and the evangelist's Greek rendering of the Lord's phrase has usually been Englished as 'The time is fulfilled'. Thus the Gospel announced by our Lord was that with his advent the day of opportunity had dawned, or that, as we might almost say, he came in the nick of time. St Paul closely echoes this announcement when he writes to the Ephesians that God

has made known to us in all wisdom and understanding the mystery of his will, according to his purpose which he set forth in Christ as a plan for the *plerōma* of the *kairoi*, to bring all things to a head in him . . .[1]

And to the Galatians that

when the *plerōma* of the time (*chronos*) had come, God sent forth his Son . . . to redeem those who were under the law, that they might receive adoption as sons.[2]

Finally, Jesus' announcement of the Gospel is followed by a challenge. This is translated in the Authorized Version as 'Repent ye, and believe the Gospel', but I have ventured to render it as 'Change your minds, and trust to the good news' —though perhaps 'Change your hearts and minds' would come nearer to expressing the full meaning of the Greek verb. My reason for preferring to speak here of trust rather than of belief is that the latter word is too apt to give us the impression that what is demanded is mere intellectual acknowledgement of the truth of the announcement, whereas what is really demanded is a complete re-orientation of the whole of life. But of course this includes a re-orientation of the intellect. Commitment

[1] Eph. 1. 9–10.   [2] Gal. 4. 4–5.

to the good news must be whole-minded as well as whole-hearted. St Paul said, 'I set aside theories and every rampart thrown up to obstruct the knowledge of God, and I make every thought captive to the obedience of Christ.'[1] To orient (or orientate) is to face in the proper direction, and that is exactly what Christians are called upon to do. A Christian is a man whose face, like the faces of the Magi in the story, is properly oriented to Bethlehem in Judaea. It is there that he too finds the long-sought-for clue to the mystery of being, to the meaning of human existence, and therefore to the proper ordering of his own life. Holding fast to this clue, as one who has nothing else to cling to, he commits himself unreservedly to its guidance, knowing that, as the Epistle to the Hebrews says, he has here 'an anchor of the soul, sure and steadfast, which penetrates to what is behind the obscuring curtain'.[2]

Christianity is not itself a New Testament word. The earliest equivalent of it is simply 'the Way' or 'the Road' (*hodos*), and the first Christians spoke of themselves as following this road. Long before anybody called them Christians they spoke of themselves as the *followers* of Jesus; and he himself had so spoken of them, his constant command being 'Follow thou me'. I rather think that we have here a specifically Christian usage. Were the disciples of any earlier teacher spoken of as his followers—except in the colourless sense of those who came after him in time? At all events, when our Lord asked his first converts to follow him, he meant that they should take the road with him—in a quite literal sense. And I believe that when the Christians of the next generation spoke of the Way and of themselves as followers of Christ in the Way, they meant that they were recapitulating the way he himself had travelled, his journey up to Jerusalem and to the crucifixion. The Way was the way of the Cross, in accordance with their Lord's own word, 'He who does not take up his cross and follow me, is not worthy of me.'[3]

Christianity, then, is a way of living, which includes a way of thinking, a way of feeling and a way of behaving. It is the

[1] 2 Cor. 10. 5.   [2] Heb. 6. 19.   [3] Matt. 10. 38.

way which was first lived out in its fulness within the Pentecostal community, that is, the fellowship of the Upper Room
in Jerusalem after Christ's death, resurrection and exaltation.
The words fellowship, community, communion all translate
the same Greek work *koinōnia*, which thus becomes another of
the key-words of the New Testament. To be a Christian meant
to be a sharer in this fellowship. Moreover, to describe what
I might call the peculiar atmosphere or ethos of this fellowship
another Greek word, which had hitherto been rarely used,
was called into constant play. This is the word *agapē*, which
the Authorized Version often renders as charity, but many
modern versions always as love. Neither rendering, however, is
very satisfactory. Whatever charity may have meant in the
reign of King James, it does not carry the right overtones now
—as we may see from the wit's definition of it as wasting one's
substance with riotous giving. Similarly, love is as likely as not
to bear the wrong meaning. It is how we translate the Greek
erōs, a word which meant only sexual intercourse until it under-
went a certain sublimation at the hands of the philosophers
and the adherents of the mystery religions, and which is
wholly absent from the New Testament vocabulary. How often
also in contemporary literature the word means simply and
solely sexual intercourse! I have sometimes made bold to think
that in the many contexts *friendship* would translate *agapē*—
better than either love or charity, in spite of the fact that there
is another New Testament term (*philia*) which must also be so
translated.

The Christian Way, then is the way followed within the
koinōnia of *agapē*, and is a form of togetherness specific to
Christianity in spite of all foreshadowings of it that may elsewhere be found. In all probability it was St Paul who introduced the term *agapē* into Christian discourse,[1] and he used it
to differentiate the characteristic life of the Christian *koinōnia*
from that which he had formerly known within the synagogue.
The togetherness is essentially that of a triangular relationship,

[1] Compare Anders Nygren, *Agape and Eros*, Part I (1930): Eng. trans. (1932),
p. 83 ff.

the three angles of which were oneself, one's fellow Christians, and God as known in Christ; and the relationship is such that from any one angle a second angle can be effectively reached only by way of the third. We can reach God only through our neighbour. We cannot love him except in loving our neighbour. Nor does God reach us or manifest his love to us save through our neighbour—that is, save in our togetherness with him. Christianity is in its very essence a matter of fellowship. No man who keeps to himself can be a Christian. It is, as Christ himself said, when at least two or three are together in his name, that he is there in the midst;[1] and of the occasion on which this experience was first enjoyed in its fullness it is written that 'When the Day of Pentecost had come, they were all with one accord in one place . . . and they were all filled with the Holy Spirit.'[2] This is the only true meaning of the Cyprianic formula *extra ecclesiam nulla salus*, which I should like to translate as 'the man who keeps to himself cannot be made whole'.

But if it is only in our togetherness with our neighbour that the love of God and his Christ effectively reaches us, so conversely is it true that our own love for God and his Christ can find effective expression only in our love of our neighbour. The love of God may seem to be a very rarified and abstruse kind of emotion such as is not easy to produce in oneself, and indeed devout souls have often been troubled about their apparent inability to discover it in themselves.

Lord, when saw we thee an hungred, and fed thee? or thirsty, and gave thee drink? When saw we thee a stranger and took thee in? or naked and clothed thee? Or when saw we thee sick or in prison, and came unto thee?

And the King shall answer and say unto them, Verily I say unto you, Insomuch as ye have done it unto one of the least of these my brethren, ye have done it unto me.[3]

St Paul indeed, though he speaks constantly of God's *agapē* towards us, and of ours towards one another, does not readily

---

[1] Matt. 18. 20; and see verse 19, 'If two of you shall agree'.
[2] Acts 2. 1–4. [3] Matt. 25. 37–40.

speak of our *agapē* towards God. The writer of the article on *agapē* in Kittel's great *Wörterbuch* goes indeed so far as to say that according to St Paul 'the purpose of divine love is not that we should return love to God; . . . it is that he who is called should serve his neighbour in love'. St John speaks more easily of *agapē* towards God, but for him also it is given reality in our service of our brothers:

If a man say, I love God, and hateth his brother, he is a liar; for he that loveth not his brother whom he hath seen, how can he love God whom he hath not seen?[1]

Thus the same article in Kittel has it that 'in John, love to God or Christ takes second place after love to the brethren'; which is, however, not an altogether happy way of expressing something that is undoubtedly true.

Finally, however, we must note that the current of *agapē* within the Christian *koinōnia* flows also round the triangle in the contrary direction. The horizontal path along the base is not viable unless we are at the same time following the longer route via the apex. If we can find God, and God can find us, only in our finding of our brother, so also is it true that we can find our brother only through God's finding of us and our finding of him. That is to say, our brother remains a stranger save as we know him in God and as the object, like ourselves, of God's love. 'It is not', writes Professor Nygren, 'that God's love for man and man's love for his neighbour are two different things; they are one thing. *Agapē* is used to denote God's love, not for human love; God's love present in the human heart.'[2]

§ 30

Those who speak of Christianity as a way of life have often been suspected of reducing it to what is called mere morality, and in not a few cases the suspicion has been justified. A distinction of this kind between religion and morality is, however, wholly absent from all ancient thought, being a most

[1] 1. John 4. 20.   [2] Op. cit., Eng. trans., p. 96.

doubtful product of later philosophical relationalism. Certainly the New Testament knows nothing of it. For in the first place the Christian Way is a way of thinking as well as a way of acting, neither of which makes sense unless it be accompanied by the other; and in the second place its way of acting includes acting towards God as well as acting towards our fellow men. Indeed even that way of putting it is already too disjunctive to do justice to the Christian outlook. For in the first place all authentically Christian thinking not only issues in action but is for the sake of action. Professor Macmurray sums up the central contention of his Gifford Lectures by saying that 'All meaningful knowledge is for the sake of action, and all meaningful action is for the sake of friendship';[1] and here for 'friendship' I should like to be allowed to say *agapē*, just as I have already asked to be allowed for *agapē* to say 'friendship'. And in the second place Christian action towards our fellow men is not a separate thing alongside of Christian action towards God. To serve our fellows in love is the only way open to us of serving God in love. Again I must quote, 'When saw we thee an hungred? . . . And the King shall answer, . . . Inasmuch as ye have done it unto one of the least of these my brethren, ye have done it unto me.' As I have perhaps sufficiently emphasized, the *koinōnia* of the Upper Room in Jerusalem was no mere fellowship of man with man but at one and the same moment a fellowship also with God the Father, God the Son and God the Spirit.

In his Eddington Memorial Lecture, to which reference has already more than once been made, Professor Braithwaite contended that 'the primary use of religious assertions is to announce allegiance to a set of moral principles'; and that the assertions of the Christian religion, which he holds to be epitomized in the assertion that God is *agapē*, find their use, and therefore their meaning, in the Christian's commitment to follow what he calls an agapeistic way of life. Yet though thus assimilating religion to morality, he is at the same time anxious to acknowledge that the two are not identical. There is something more in a religious assertion than in a moral assertion,

[1] *The Self as Agent*, p. 15.

for the former always includes a reference to a certain story or set of stories, these consisting of empirical propositions; such as, for the Christian, statements about the life and death of Jesus and also about the beginning and end of the world. But he holds that it is not necessary for the Christian 'to believe in the truth of the story involved in these assertions: what is necessary is that the story should be entertained in thought, i.e. that the statement of the story should be understood as having a meaning'.

A man is not, I think, a professing Christian unless he both proposes to live according to Christian moral principles and associates his intention with thinking of Christian stories; but he need not believe that the empirical propositions presented by the stories correspond to empirical fact.

Thus the function of the story is a purely psychological one.

It is an empirical psychological fact that many people find it easier to resolve upon and to carry through a course of action which is contrary to their natural inclination if this policy is associated in their mind with certain stories. And in many people the psychological link is not appreciably weakened by the fact that the story associated with the behaviour policy is not believed.

In religious conviction the resolution to follow a way of life is primary; it is not derived from believing, still less from thinking of, any empirical story. The story may psychologically support the resolution, but it does not logically justify it.

Professor Braithwaite is, I understand, himself a professing Christian, and the deep sincerity of his statement cannot be questioned by anybody who reads it attentively. The difficulty we have with it is in believing that the stories will continue to be entertained if none of them is believed to be true; or that even if so entertained, they will continue to exercise the required psychological function. We are reminded here of Thomas Hardy's 'idealism of fancy' and of the views of Mr Santayana, to which reference was made at an earlier point, and of the criticism we then passed upon them. But it is more important that we should understand the difference between what is here advanced and the 'demythologizing' programme of Professor Bultmann as well as the views of Professor Tillich. Professor Bultmann does indeed go very far in reducing the extent of our reliable knowledge of the historical life of Jesus and in regarding many elements in the evangelists' narrative as 'mythical', but there is a point at which he calls a halt to this reductive process; and Professor Braithwaite, who characterizes the Christ-myth theory as 'unplausible', shows, to say the least, no disposition to go further than he. Professor Tillich is more explicit in declaring that by the methods of historical criticism we cannot even reach the certainty that such a man as Jesus of Nazareth ever existed.[1] But neither of these theologians would allow that we are here at the mercy of such methods. Both would hold that the essential Christian affirmations about Jesus—that in him God was incarnate and that through him we have redemption from our sin and misery—are not such as could conceivably be either verified or falsified by such methods. Thus, whatever we may think of their depositions, the all-important difference between them and Professor Braithwaite is that they believe these affirmations to be true and required by Christian faith, whereas he thinks a man may be a Christian without believing any of them. Even the Christian doctrine that there is a God who desires us to do his will is not, he considers, one that we are justified in believing, though it is morally stimulating to entertain it in our minds. 'There is', he tells us, 'one story common to all the moral theistic religions which has proved of great psychological value in enabling religious men to persevere in carrying out their religious behaviour policies—the story that in so doing they are doing the will of God';[2] but it would be a mistake to regard this story as true. This is to go further in the direction of unbelief than Kant did in his *Als ob*, since according to the latter it is an imperative requirement of pure practical reason that we should not only act but also think as if God existed, and so *believe* him to exist, though from this belief we must not allow ourselves to draw

---

[1] See for instance *Systematic Theology*, Vol. II, p. 113 ff.

[2] This and all the previous quotations are from R. B. Braithwaite, *An Empiricist's View of the Nature of Religious Belief* (1955), pp. 22–31.

any speculative inferences. At all events, what I am anxious to affirm is that the life of the Christian *koinōnia* is carried on, from beginning to end, within what I have called a triangular system of relationships in each of which God plays not only an active but the initiating part.

§ 31

There still remains for our consideration what is after all the central phrase in St Mark's summary of the announcement with which our Lord began his public ministry: 'The reign of God is at hand.' The more usual English rendering is 'Kingdom of God', but the other is better because it suggests as it should an administration rather than a realm, and a time rather than a place. In the early decades of the present century there was keen debate among New Testament scholars whether Jesus thought of this reign as being already inaugurated with his advent or as about to be inaugurated in the very near future. The latter or futurist hypothesis, as developed in its radical form by Albert Schweitzer, Johannes Weiss and others, meant that Jesus was calling men only to prepare themselves for a crisis which had not yet come but would come very soon. It is, however, now fairly generally agreed that, whereas there is indeed much in his teaching that speaks of a coming reign of God, there is much also that speaks of a present enjoyment of the powers and blessings of that reign. It was in this way also that the situation was understood within the early Church after Pentecost, though with varying degrees of emphasis upon the two contrasted aspects of it. There is, for instance, a quite unmistakable difference of emphasis in this matter between the Pauline and the Johannine writings. But if we take the New Testament teaching as a whole, it may be said that there is something like an even balance between the note of fulfilment, as of a new age that has already dawned, and the note of expectation, as of a consummation that is still to be awaited. Christians knew themselves to be living in the new age, but they knew also that the old age had not yet passed away, so that they were living in both ages at once. God, writes St Paul, has indeed 'delivered us from the dominion of darkness and transferred us to the kingdom of the Son of his love';[1] yet he has much to say also of the havoc that the powers of darkness are still working in the world and even within the Christian community. Christ has decisively defeated these powers, so that they are now 'under his feet', but they still carry on their guerilla warfare among men; so that, as it has been so felicitously expressed by Dr Oscar Cullmann in his much-quoted simile, men are now living in the interval between the decisive battle and Victory Day.[2]

Thus when the followers of Jesus met in that little room in Jerusalem on the Day of Pentecost, they met under the power of a sequence of events which had only just transpired, but which they believed to have set the course of human history and of human life on an entirely new course for all time to come. They thought of this sequence as extending from the advent of Jesus, through his ministry, passion, crucifixion, death, resurrection and ascension to the Pentecostal coming of the Spirit which they were even now enjoying. They knew that the final event in this same sequence, the 'coming again' of their Lord, still lay in the future; but they were convinced that for those who lived in the light of what had already transpired and in the confident hope of the consummation yet to come, all things had already been made new—a fact of which even the least Christianly-disposed among us has daily reminder as often as he puts a date to a letter he writes or examines the postmark on a letter he receives. Every one of us every day pays at least lip-service to the centrality of the Christ-event, and to the new age in the world's history which it introduced—lip-service to the persuasion of those who divided our calendar into the years B.C. and the years A.D., 'the years of our Lord'.

The encounter with the totality of this sequence of events, which we may speak of in the singular as the Christ-event, is the paradigmatic experience which issued at Pentecost in the *koinōnia* of *agapē*, the fellowship of Christian love, and has ever

[1] Col., 1. 13.   [2] *Christus und die Zeit* (1946), chap. V.

since kept the Christian faith alive in men's hearts and lives. It provides the paradigm in the light of which all other events are to be interpreted, the frame of reference within which they are to be set. This includes not only the daily contingencies with which the individual has to deal in his own personal life, but also all that happens in the wider world around him; and moreover it includes not only contemporary events, but also all that has happened in the past and all that is still to happen in the otherwise unknown future, giving rise alike to a specifically Christian interpretation of history and to a specifically Christian eschatology. In this way a single critically significant encounter is used to give significance to all other encounters, past, present and future. Let me now set out more fully a statement by A. N. Whitehead to which I made reference at an earlier point:

Religion claims that its concepts, though derived primarily from special experiences, are yet of universal validity, to be applied by faith to the ordering of all experience. Rational religion appeals to the direct intuition of special occasions, and to the elucidatory power of its concepts for all occasions. It arises from that which is special, but it extends to what is general. The doctrines of rational religion aim at being that metaphysics which can be derived from the supernormal experience of mankind in its moments of finest insight.[1]

Not all the phraseology Whitehead here employs is such as I myself would have chosen, but the passage as a whole excellently expresses what I have been trying to say. I should like also to place beside it the following remarkable passage from Professor Ethelbert Stauffer's *New Testament Theology*, though again there are phrases in it which seem to me misleading and which indeed I do not fully understand:

The New Testament writers never think of Christianity as absolute. They do not make the doubtful attempt to give absoluteness to some particular interpretation of life, or some special understanding of God. Indeed, men like Paul engage in bitter war against the temptation to give absolute status to some form of Christianity or some ecclesiastical system, and thereby to invalidate the sole

---

[1] *Religion in the Making* (1926), chap. I, § 5.

efficacy and sufficiency of the *sola cruce*. Rather did the primitive Church preach the gospel of salvation wrought out in the Christ-event, which had introduced a new situation between God, the world and the adversary, and had placed the destiny of mankind on a new footing. Every reality in the world and in history is in some way related to this central fact, relative to this absolute point of reference. In this sense we can speak of the absoluteness of Jesus Christ. But the New Testament connects this absoluteness with an historical fact that hides itself in the 'servant's form' of historical relativity. It is this Christ-event that the primitive Church proclaimed: an absolute in the form of the relative.[1]

The New Testament writers employ a considerable variety of concepts to describe the 'new situation' or 'new footing' which is here spoken of. In our Lord's own discourse, as reported in the Synoptic Gospels, it is always described as the inauguration of the reign of God. For apostolic thought it is a new divine 'economy' or, in the Latin translation that was found for that Greek word, a new 'dispensation'. Or again it is a 'rebirth' (*palingenesia*)—a rebirth both of the historical situation to which men were called upon to adjust themselves and of the individuals who were willing so to adjust themselves. The Pentecostal experience made it no less inevitable that life in the new order should be spoken of as 'living in the Spirit'. St Paul constantly so expresses himself, but even more often he speaks of the Christian believer as being 'in Christ'; and sometimes he combines the idioms in one, as when he speaks of those 'who are in Christ Jesus, who walk not after the flesh, but after the Spirit'.[2] When he has particularly in mind the contrast between his life as a Jew and his life within the Christian *koinōnia*, this opposition of flesh and Spirit becomes an opposition of law and grace. 'Ye are not under the law, but under grace',[3] he says to his fellow Christians; and in the same context, as in many others, he speaks of the Christian as a man who has died with Christ, so that his former being was buried with him, but who has now risen with him to 'newness of life'.[4] 'Therefore', he writes again, 'if any

---

[1] *Die Theologie des Neuen Testaments* (1941); Eng. trans. from the 5th ed., p. 159.
[2] Rom. 8. 1.   [3] Rom. 6. 14.   [4] Rom. 6. 4.

man be in Christ, he is a new creation; the old things have passed away, and lo! new things have come into being.'[1] Or once more: 'As in Adam all die, so in Christ shall all be made alive.'[2] In so many varying ways does the New Testament describe the new era which has been inaugurated by the Christ-event, the new society appropriate to this era, the new humanity in which it issues, and the new manner of life for which it provides the paradigm.

[1] 2 Cor. 5. 17.   [2] 1 Cor. 15, 22.

CHAPTER VIII

Meaning and Relevance

§ 32

In his admirably useful summary of the development of English philosophy between the two World Wars Professor J. O. Urmson writes as follows about the latest period of that development:

In place of the dogmatic 'The meaning of a statement is the method of its verification', we were now advised 'Don't ask for the meaning, ask for the use' and told that 'Every statement has its own logic'. . . . The slogan 'Don't ask for the meaning, ask for the use' warns us to stop asking 'What is the analysis (the meaning) of this statement?' expecting to find some equivalent statement; . . . instead we are to ask what is done by the use of the statement. If, for example, it is unverifiable, then its job is clearly not to describe the world about us, but perhaps it is used for some quite different purpose. We shall find out by finding out what the utterance of that sentence enables us to do.[1]

This change of front appears to have been dictated by the following train of thought among the reductive empiricists. The logical positivists had held that moral and theological statements were incapable of verification, since the only verification they would acknowledge was by reference to sensory experience. They therefore concluded that these statements have no meaning, since to have a meaning was taken as equivalent to conveying some information about the real world which was assumed to be the world of sensory experience. It now came to be felt, however, that in spite of their telling us nothing about reality, moral (and perhaps also theological) statements did have their uses, and we were encouraged to investigate their nature by asking ourselves what these uses

[1] *Philosophical Analysis* (1956), p. 179.

are. The general answer given was that they conveyed something, whether to ourselves or to others, either about our emotions or about our intentions or about both together. But to convey something is to have a meaning; and thus the above-mentioned slogan has come to be understood, not as saying that such statements have no meaning, but rather as saying that we can best understand such meaning as they have, not by seeking it directly, but by approaching it through an examination of the uses we make of them. Thus Professor Braithwaite:

> Though a high-minded logical positivist might be prepared to say that all religious statements are sound and fury, signifying nothing, he can hardly say that of all moral statements. For moral statements have a use in guiding conduct; and if they have a use they surely have a meaning in some sense of meaning.[1]

The difference between the old and the new way of it would then be expressed, not by contrasting meaning and use, but by contrasting the verification-principle with the use-principle.

We have already had occasion to note that Professor Braithwaite prefers to follow the conative rather than the emotive theory of the nature of moral assertions, holding that these are essentially announcements how those who use them intend to act, and further that the only use, and therefore the only meaning, of whatever in religious assertion goes beyond merely moral assertion is that we should be fortified in our intention thus to act by the entertainment in our minds of the stories to which these assertions belong.

My present interest in the use-principle is of a limited and rather special kind. When I say 'Ask for the use', I shall have in mind not all possible uses but only usefulness for the practical conduct of our lives; and when I speak of the use of Christian affirmations I shall be thinking of their usefulness as contributing to the frame of reference which serves for the guidance of Christian living. The two things I want to say, then, are that no affirmation has right of place within a system of Christian

[1] Op. cit., p. 10.

theology if it has no such usefulness, and that the meaning of any such affirmation is best understood from an examination of the precise difference it would make to the conduct of Christian life if it were not believed or at least if it were deliberately denied.

It will be remembered that in his little book *After Strange Gods: A Primer of Modern Heresy* Mr T. S. Eliot includes an appendix in which he explains that his first intention had been to append a graduated Exercise Book, beginning with very simple examples of heresy and leading up to those which are very difficult to solve, and leaving the student to find the answers for himself. On second thoughts, however, he decided to content himself with offering only four examples, the first very elementary, the second only slightly more advanced, but the remaining two among the most advanced that he could find. The fourth is from Professor Macmurray's *The Philosophy of Communism* (pp. 62–63) and reads as follows:

Any serious criticism of communist philosophy must start by declaring openly how much of its theory is accepted by the critic. I must therefore preface my criticism by saying that I accept the rejection of idealism and the principle of the unity of theory and practice in the sense in which I have expounded it. And since this is the truly revolutionary principle, such an acceptance involves taking one's stand with the tradition of thought deriving from Marx. The negative implications of accepting this fundamental principle go very deep. They include the rejection of all philosophy and all social theory which does not accept this principle, not because of particular objections to their conclusions, but because of a complete break with the assumptions upon which they are based and the purpose which governs their development. They involve the belief that all theory must seek verification in action and adapt itself to the possibility of experiment. They make a clean sweep of speculative thought on the ground that the validity of no belief whatever is capable of demonstration by argument. They involve a refusal at any point to make knowledge an end in itself, and equally, the rejection of the desire for certainty which is the motive governing speculative thought.

I do not now propose to submit myself to this test in the practice of detection, except in one particular which is of interest for our present argument. 'All theory', Professor Macmurray here says, 'must find verification in action.' I have already quoted from his Gifford Lectures the dictum that 'All meaningful knowledge is for the sake of action, and all meaningful action is for the sake of friendship', and I may now add this further sentence from the same volume, 'If we can understand, to whatever extent, what difference would be made in our intention if we acted in the belief that a certain proposition were true, then that proposition has a meaning.'[1] All this is very like what I have myself been saying; and I agree with it all, if by action is meant not merely active intervention in the created physical and human order, but the total response of our spirits—whether in worship, meditation and prayer, or in sentiments and deeds of love—to the universal reality with which we are confronted, human and divine. Perhaps this is what Professor Macmurray has in mind, though I do not think it is what Marx had in mind. Yet in still another of his books, *The Structure of Religious Experience*, while he speaks of God as 'that infinite person in which our finite human relationships have their ground and their being',[2] he tends to write as if the primary reference of religious experience were to our inter-human relationships, the idea of God being no more than an implicate of these. 'The focus of all human experience is', he says, 'to be found in our relations to one another'; and religion

arises from our ordinary experience of living in the world in relation with other people, and to that experience it refers. . . . So soon as this fact of our relationship to others is brought to focus in reflective consciousness, religion is born. The only way to avoid religion is to avoid the consciousness that we are members of the community.[3]

But I can accept this, and can differentiate the Christian view from the too humanist Marxist one, only if this community is understood as being a community or communion with God. Certainly I cannot enjoy communion with him unless I am at the same time in communion with my fellow men, but the primary truth is the converse one that, as was declared in

[1] *The Self as Agent*, p. 217.   [2] Op. cit., p. 81.   [3] Ibid., pp. 107–109.

the 'Message' issued by the first Assembly of the World Council of Churches in Amsterdam in 1948, 'In seeking Him, we find one another'. My own contention then is that no doctrine has right of place within our Christian theology unless we can show that the denial of it would disturb or distort the pattern of our Christian sharing in that *koinōnia* of *agapē* which goes back to Pentecost and which I have described as a triangular system of relationships between the triune God, ourselves and our fellows. The word *koinōnia* in this specific sense, wrote Dr Anderson Scott in a memorable essay on 'What Happened at Pentecost', to which I wish to acknowledge my great indebtedness for the understanding of this whole matter, 'would appear to denote a fellowship which was not merely a fellowship of believers *inter se*, nor yet a fellowship of the believers individually with the Spirit, but a complex experience which included both'.[1] But the primacy belongs to the relationship with the Spirit. To St Paul the *koinōnia* is 'the fellowship of the Spirit',[2] or alternatively 'the fellowship of His Son Jesus Christ our Lord'[3] into which God has graciously called us; and the unity which is enjoyed in it is 'the unity of the Spirit'.[4]

§ 33

I cannot but here remember how my late brother Donald was always saying to me that the challenge addressed to us by so many of our contemporaries in regard to a particular Christian doctrine, if not indeed to the system of doctrine as a whole, was not so much 'Is it true?' as 'What is its relevance?' He himself gave much time to the counselling of young students in his own University, and again and again would find himself confronted with the question: 'What practical difference does it make to me whether or not I believe this traditional dogma, or whether or not it is true?' The average student was not a metaphysician or even a theologian, and much of what the theologians were saying appeared strangely remote from his vital concerns, having about it an air of unreality.

[1] In the composite volume, *The Spirit*, ed. B. H. Streeter (1919), p. 137 f.
[2] Phil. 21. 1; 2 Cor. 13. 3.   [3] 1 Cor. 1. 9.   [4] Eph. 4. 3.

Those who have been nurtured from early youth in a doctrinal piety are less likely to feel this difficulty, and certainly have less excuse for doing so, since they have had long opportunity of observing how doctrine and piety are inter-related in the life of the pious community. Yet not a few who have enjoyed this privilege today find themselves in much the same case as their less fortunate neighbours. This is due to a complexity of reasons. For one thing, it is probable that some things taught by the theologians are *not* properly relevant to the Christian concern. Many of the early Fathers of the Church inherited, together with the New Testament teaching, a strong interest in the problems raised and the methods employed by Greek metaphysics, and though this was undeniably of invaluable service to them both in providing categories for a further understanding of the intellectual implications of their Christian faith and in enabling them to relate it to the other activities of the human mind, yet they were misled into making that faith itself appear far too much as an affair of the intellect, as if it were in its own essence a metaphysical system. The later history of natural theology clearly testifies to the continuing presence of this danger. But further, this too intellectualist approach persisted even among those theologians who, as has been the case of so many Protestant thinkers, turned aside from natural theology, virtually confining themselves to what was called revealed theology. How many expositions of a Christian dogma have we read, or even listened to from the pulpit, which altogether failed to make clear to us why it was important that we should accept it, beyond perhaps the general statement, to which less and less credit is apt to be given in our own time, that if we did not we should be damned eternally! I call this latter a general statement, and an unconvincing one at that, because it offers no insight into just *how* the presence in our assenting minds of the particular dogma in question is suited to exercise a beneficent effect upon our spiritual well-being either in this life or any other.

Take for example the doctrines that there are three Persons in the one Godhead and that the second of these has two

natures in his one Person. These shadow forth fundamental
Christian convictions such as I believe to be most intimately
relevant to the daily conduct of the Christian life, but they
require much interpretation and even restatement before the
typical modern mind can grasp that relevance. They were
built up in a post-apostolic period of Christian thought,
though, as we are accustomed to say, the 'materials' for the
building of them are already present in the apostolic teaching.
Yet that teaching itself stands only less in need of translation—
translation not merely of word but of idea—if the men of our
time are to grasp what it portends. The thought-forms by
means of which the apostolic authors were enabled to receive
the revelation vouchsafed to them were those which stood
ready to their hand. Belonging as they did to that time and
place, they were also those that would be most readily understood by the men and women to whom the apostles addressed
themselves, but except in the one context of traditional
Christian preaching they have long ceased to form any part
of the furniture of the Western mind. Grave damage has
therefore been done to the Christian cause, not only by those
of our evangelists who still recoil from any attempt at retrans-
lation, but also by the belatedness of such valiant attempts as
have now in fact been made. How many great and good men
of nineteenth-century England, to go no further afield, found
themselves forced to repudiate virtually the whole of Christian
dogma!

I think, among many others, of Thomas Carlyle, of Matthew
Arnold, of Arthur Hugh Clough, of John Stuart Mill, of James
Anthony Froude, of Frederic Harrison, of William Hale White
(better known as 'Mark Rutherford'), of Thomas Hardy, of
Leslie Stephen, of Henry Sidgwick, of John Morley. Most of
these men were fundamentally Christian in temper and were
of a quality of mind and spirit that would have made them
distinguished servants of the Church in another age: Edmund
Chambers wrote of Clough 'He is a sceptic who by nature
should have been with the believers';[1] Lord David Cecil has

[1] Article on Clough in *The Encyclopaedia Britannica*, 11th ed.

written of Hardy as 'one of the most Christian spirits that ever lived';[1] it was said of Morley by one of his most intimate friends 'They call him agnostic, but he lived Christianity';[2] and of Sidgwick it used to be said in Cambridge that 'he exhibited every Christian virtue except faith'. Most of them, like the Arthur Henry Hallam whose struggles led Tennyson to believe that 'there lives more faith in honest doubt . . . than in half the creeds', struggled no less painfully than he; though alas, of none of them could it be said that 'At last he beat his music out' or that

> He faced the spectres of the mind
> And laid them: thus he came at length
> To find a stronger faith his own.[3]

We may indeed wonder that men who, besides being endowed with so much of Christian sentiment as these, possessed also such penetrating intellects, showed so little understanding for the profound truths that underlay the inherited and time-conditioned formulae. Yet we can hardly find it in our hearts to reproach them, since they received so little help to this end from the Christian believers of their time. There were indeed 'liberal' Christian thinkers like Benjamin Jowett and Thomas Arnold, but theirs was a liberalism of so wide (and withal of so faultily designed) a mesh that many of the profoundest elements of the Christian revelation largely escaped it; and of this not a few of the doubters I have mentioned were aware, protesting that this diluted version of Christianity was no easier of acceptance by the intellect than the old one, while at the same time failing to provide that easement of the spirit, that satisfaction of heart and soul, which the old one, if only it could be believed, was well fitted to bestow.

Of course at the bottom of all this distress of mind and 'honest doubt' lay the difficulty of synthesizing the insight into reality contained in the Christian revelation with the very different type and body of insight which has been ours since

---

[1] *Hardy, the Novelist* (1943).

[2] Quoted by Basil Willey, *More Nineteenth-Century Studies* (1956), p. 267.

[3] *In Memoriam*, Canto xcvi.

the *Aufklärung* or, let us say, since the days of Galileo, Kepler, Francis Bacon, Descartes, Newton and Locke. It is a difficulty well understood by many of ourselves who, having in early youth been nurtured in a traditional orthodoxy, were soon afterwards subjected to a modern education at school and college—an education almost the whole of whose direction derived from the *Aufklärung*. The thinkers of the patristic period were able to synthesize the faith of the New Testament with the wisdom of the Greeks in a way that satisfied most of the intellectuals of that age; and the so-called 'medieval synthesis', as fashioned by the doctors of the twelfth and thirteenth centuries, performed a like office for the men of the earlier Renaissance, but there has been long delay in reaching a workable synthesis between what as Christians we believe and the scientific outlook of the modern world which most of us also share. Brave attempts in this direction are now being made, not a few of them by recent Gifford lectures, but though the nineteenth century had already witnessed some such attempts, these proved largely abortive, so that we cannot wonder that so many of its most intelligent sons never reached the fulfilment of their prayer 'That mind and soul, according well, May make one music as before, But vaster'.[1]

§ 34

It will be understood that my immediate concern in offering such an analysis of our present distress has been to expose some of the reasons why so many of our contemporaries profess difficulty in understanding the relevance of much that is given them in the name of Christian doctrine. I have already sufficiently declared my conviction that their demand to be shown the practical bearing of every detail of such doctrine is not only an entirely legitimate one but also a most encouraging sign of their awareness of the real issue at stake. I hope and believe that we are now doing more to satisfy this demand than our forefathers ever did, being less speculatively theological in our

[1] *In Memoriam*, ad init.

exposition of the Christian faith and more concerned to bring
out what Kierkegaard taught us to call its 'existential' significance for the active conduct of our lives and the solution of the
problems we have every day to face. The earliest Protestant
Reformers, with their impatience of medieval scholasticism,
did indeed move most significantly in this direction. I think
especially of Luther and the Melanchthon of the first edition of
the *Loci Communes*, with their declaration that *Christum cognoscere
est beneficia eius cognoscere* and with Luther's saying that 'The
heart of religion lies in its personal pronouns'. While this
initial impulse was largely lost in the Protestant scholasticism
of the succeeding age, it burgeoned again in the best of the
English Puritans—the so-called 'experimental' Puritans who
were concerned always with the bearing of the doctrine they
enounced on the inward personal life of the believer; and at a
later date in Pietism and Wesleyanism and the other movements of evangelical revival. But in the first place, these were
all addressing generations of men to whom the doctrines were
quite familiar and who had in general no difficulty in giving a
purely intellectual assent to them, so that the task of the
preacher was less to show why the doctrines should be accepted
than to summon those who already accepted them with their
intellects to apply them each to his own case. But in the second
place, the application they had in mind was far too narrowly
conceived. It was a very other-worldly application, and in
consequence a very individualistic one, while above all it
remained all but wholly oblivious to the new movements of
thought and insight that were already rapidly developing in
the modern mind, and consequently offered no guidance as to
the relation of these to the Christian faith.

With this we may now contrast the approach to Christian
doctrine represented by such a contemporary theologian as
Reinhold Niebuhr. He consistently defends what he likes to call
the 'classical' Christian teaching against all reductive 'liberal'
versions of it, but he defends it precisely by exhibiting its
detailed relevance to the situation in which modern man now
finds himself—a relevance which extends not only to what (in

Whitehead's phrase[1]) 'the individual does with his own soli-
tariness' but to every phase of our corporate and public life.
In his Gifford Lectures Dr Niebuhr has something to say under
most of the familiar heads of Christian doctrine—the creation
of man in the image of God, original righteousness, the Fall
and original sin, the Atonement, the Parousia, the resurrection,
the Last Judgement and many another, but in each case his
endeavour is to show how only within the frame of these conceptions can we reach a satisfying adjustment to our human
situation and a right-minded attitude to the various exigencies
with which in our time we are faced. He seems to be saying
that if any least detail of that frame is ignored or rejected, the
result is likely to be a dangerously false and over-simplified
solution of this or that social or even international problem.

I remember hearing it said when the lectures were being
delivered that Dr Niebuhr's defence of a particular dogma was
always an 'indirect' one, that he neither offered arguments for
its truth of the kind to which the old natural theologians had
accustomed us nor yet, in the manner of the old revelational
theologians, appealed for its establishment to the authority of
Biblical and patristic texts and ecclesiastical pronouncements,
but was content to demonstrate that without its controlling
presence in our minds some distortion of our Christian life-
in-community was bound to ensue. Moreover, at the same time
I heard the question asked whether the lecturer was really
as much concerned for the ultimate *truth* of the dogma as
he ought to be. If this question had been put with regard to
those who, like Hardy, Santayana and Professor Braithwaite,
are satisfied to regard Christian dogmas as imaginative
constructions whose entertainment in the mind stimulates us
to a more faithful adherence to such resolves as even without
their aid we were able to make, the answer would have to be
in the negative. But with Dr Niebuhr it is not so. If I understand
him aright, his concern is both to clarify the meaning of the
doctrine and at the same time to justify its truth by the demonstration that only by its means can we attain to a realistic

---

[1] *Religion in the Making* (1926), p. 16.

understanding of our human situation as it actually exists, all alternative doctrines being the victims of illusion, of self-deception or, if you like, of wishful thinking.

Many examples of this procedure might be quoted from his pages, but I must content myself with one, which he prints under the heading 'A Synthesis of Reformation and Renaissance', and which I select because it illustrates his keen awareness of the need of such a synthesis.

The defeatism of the Lutheran, and the tendency towards obscurantism in the Calvinist, Reformation must be regarded as a contributory cause of defeat of the Reformation by the Renaissance. It failed to relate the ultimate answers of grace to the problem of guilt to all the immediate and intermediate problems and answers of life. Therefore it did not illumine the possibilities and limits of realizing increasing truth and goodness in every conceivable historic and social situation.

This defeatism is only a contributory cause of its defeat because the general atmosphere of historical optimism in the past centuries seemed to refute even what was true in the Reformation; just as it seemed to validate both what was true and what was false in the Renaissance. There was, therefore, little inclination to discriminate between the true and the false emphases in the Reformation; between the truth of its ultimate view of life and history and its failure to relate this truth helpfully to intermediate issues of culture and social organization.

But when we are confronted with the task of re-orienting the culture of our day, it becomes important to discriminate carefully between what was true and what was false in each movement. There is of course a strong element of presumption in the effort to make such judgements which will seem intolerable to those who disagree with them; and which can be tolerable even to those who find them validated, at least partially, by contemporary history, only if it is recognized that they are made in 'fear and trembling'.

The course of modern history has, if our reading of it be at all correct, justified the dynamic, and refuted the optimistic, interpretation contained in the various modern religious and cultural movements, all of which are internally related to each other in what we have defined broadly as 'Renaissance'. It has by the same token validated the basic truth of the Reformation but challenged its obscurantism and defeatism on all immediate and intermediate issues of life. . . .

No apology is necessary for assigning so great a pedagogical significance to the lessons of history. The truth contained in the Gospel is not found in human wisdom. Yet it may be found at the point where human wisdom and human goodness acknowledge their limits; and creative despair induces faith. Once faith is induced, it becomes truly the wisdom which makes 'sense' out of a life and a history which would otherwise remain senseless.[1]

§ 35

To complete the argument of this chapter, let us now briefly examine the measure of justice in Kant's constantly reiterated injunction against employing for the extension of our theoretic or speculative knowledge the conceptions of super-sensible reality which we are led by faith to entertain. It will be understood from what has already been said that we cannot accept his denial of the name of knowledge to these conceptions nor his doubts concerning the ontological status of their objects, but I believe there lies valuable insight behind his contention—a contention which he was the first clearly to formulate—that they are not of such a kind as to allow us to rest speculative conclusions upon them, making them the foundations of a metaphysical scheme.

The objects of faith are all apprehended by us in a mode of knowing which, though it may be accompanied by full conviction, nevertheless falls far short of full comprehension. Our thought can reach *up to* them, but we cannot, as it were, get our thought *round* them. We see them only 'as in a mirror dimly', and therefore our notions of them are never adequate to their essential nature. The pulse of certainty beats throughout the whole of our Christian knowledge, but we can never quite capture it for our particular formulations. It was with this acknowledgement that our whole argument began, and we subsequently found much confirmation of it in the utterances of theologians of different schools, as for instance that all theological statements are dialectical in nature, that the *deus revelatus* remains to the end a *deus absconditus*, that we do not know God *per se* but only *quoad nos*, and that in our theologizing we

[1] *The Nature and Destiny of Man*, Vol. II (1943), p. 212 f.

are all the time dealing with mysteries that we do not fully understand. In plain words, the light of revelation that has been vouchsafed to us is never enough to satisfy our intellectual curiosity, though it is a light sufficient to illuminate our way, so that we can see to do the work we were meant to do and to adjust ourselves to the situation in which by the will of God we have been placed within the human society but also within the cosmic immensity. Had the true end of our being been 'knowledge for knowledge's sake', we should no doubt have a right to grumble at such a divine disposition of things; but if our end is the love and service of God, we cannot justly demand more light until we have better used the light we already have. If indeed, in Keats's phrase, this world is something like 'a vale of soul-making',[1] then the very limitation of our possible knowledge may be seen as an indispensable part of the probation to which God is subjecting us. Many Christian thinkers have seen it so, and it is interesting to note that Kant saw it so also. He concludes his discussion of the limits of our knowledge in the second *Critique* with the section entitled 'Of the Wise Adaptation of Man's Cognitive Faculties to his Practical Destination', and his last words of all are that 'the unsearchable wisdom by which we exist is not less worthy of admiration for what it has denied us than for what it has granted us'.[2]

It was Kant's keen awareness of this that made him so content, perhaps in his case too readily content, to be forced to 'abolish *Wissen* to make room for *Glaube*'. But indeed it had already been put forward as a cardinal truth by Bishop Butler in the last of his *Fifteen Sermons*, which bears the title 'Upon the Ignorance of Man'. Our condition in this world, he says, is a school of self-discipline, and there would have been insufficient opportunity for the exercise of such discipline if we had what he calls complete sensible evidence of the truth of what we believe by faith.

The strict discharge of our duty with less sensible evidence does imply in it a better character than the same diligence in discharge

---

[1] *Letters*, Forman's ed. (1935), p. 123.

[2] *Kritik der praktischen Vernunft*, Erster Teil, Erstes Buch, Zweites Hauptstück. § IX.

of it upon more sensible evidence. This fully accounts for and
explains that assertion of our Saviour, 'Blessed are they that have
not seen, and yet have believed'. . . . If to acquire knowledge were
our proper end, we should indeed be but poorly provided: but if
somewhat else be our business and duty, we may, notwithstanding
our ignorance, be well enough furnished for it; and the observation
of our ignorance may be of assistance to us in our discharge of it.

The classical dogmas of the Church, as set forth in the
decisions of the ecumenical councils, the confessions and
dogmatic theologies, are all attempts to gather up, to relate to
each other, and to present in precise formulae, the various
elements of insight into reality which are native to the Christian
faith as such. Their purpose was one of conservation and
defence, that faith might be saved from corruption, and not
least from the intrusion of such alien elements as would give a
wrong direction to the practice of Christian piety. If the
accepted formulae now appear to us to be too speculative in
nature, it is because they were preceded by other constructions
which would have disturbed and distorted that practice. In
Whitehead's words which I have elsewhere quoted: 'Wherever
there is a creed, there is a heretic round the corner or in his
grave.'[1] The formulae were certainly speculative to the extent
that they were in the nature of logical deductions from faith's
more immediate utterances. These deductions had to be drawn
by the aid of such categories of intellectual understanding as
were available in that time and place, categories that had for
the most part been provided by Greek philosophy and were
shared by the heretics whom it was hoped to confound by the
use of the very same tools they themselves had used. Such have
been the changes in philosophic thought between that day and
our own that contemporary theologians do not easily work
within these categories, yet they will often be heard to say
something like the following: 'We should not put things that
way today, but that way of putting it served the purpose of
its own time. Of the alternative formulations that were
possible within the thought-forms then available the Church

[1] *Adventures of Ideas* (1933), p. 66.

did actually in each case choose the better ones.' Not a few such contemporary theologians have, however, tried their hands at reshaping the accepted solutions in terms of the very different thought-forms now more generally current among us, or even in terms of one particular modern metaphysical system, like those of Hegel or Bergson or Whitehead. It cannot be denied that for the time being the 'problem of communication' has in this way been frequently eased. How many intellectuals in the England of the second half of the nineteenth century, for instance, were saved from complete unbelief by reshaping the Christian dogma in terms of Hegelian idealism! If they *were* Hegelians in their philosophy, they were partly justified in doing this, though we could have wished that they had rather used such Christian insight as they possessed to save them from the errors of their Hegelianism. As I have already contended and as I think we should all agree, we moderns must do everything we can to understand how our modern outlook hangs together with our Christian faith. Yet we must also allow for a certain looseness of connexion between the two, especially if in 'our modern outlook' we include not only the general spirit animating science but its currently prevailing findings; and more especially still if we include in it a particular *metaphysical* system to which we have attached ourselves. These findings and that system must, if we are wise, be regarded as strictly provisional, destined to be superseded by others in their turn, perhaps very quickly. A too close linkage between them and our faith, while it may yield us present easement and a readier address to the men of our own generation, will be all the more likely to hinder our Christian communication with the men of a later time. Let us then, taking a lesson from past experience, beware of creating for our successors another such distressful situation as our fathers created for us when they not only assumed the finality of the old dogmatic definitions (determined as they were by the prevailing categories) but even made the Christian's unqualified intellectual acceptance of them a test of his loyalty to his Lord and Master.

But the point on which I am most anxious to insist is that, because the dogmas so defined cannot, in spite of the wisdom and skill which went to the making of them and which made them so excellently suited to their practical purpose, be regarded as possessing the type of theoretical adequacy to which we are accustomed in philosophic discourse, we cannot safely proceed from them to further inferences of a theoretical kind. They are themselves deductions from the primary perceptions of faith, but they have not the character of metaphysical propositions and must not be treated as such. St Athanasius himself, well aware of the purpose it was intended to serve, described the Nicene Creed as a notice-board set up to preserve Christian thinking against all the heresies that were then threatening it (στηλογραφία κατὰ πασῶν αἱρέσεων). *If we are minded to reach a fuller theoretical understanding, it is therefore safer to go back to the original foundations, resting it once more upon faith's primary insight rather than upon the dogmas that were so long ago formulated for the preservation of that insight.*

I have italicized that sentence, because it expresses exactly the conclusion I desire to draw. Let us give point to it by means of a particular example. The controversies which so violently agitated the Church of the patristic period, and which issued in the ecumenical definitions, mainly concerned the closely related dogmas of the Trinity and the Person of Christ. The dogma of the Trinity was in essence an attempt to think together three elements that had from the beginning been present in the faith and worship of Christians. That faith took its rise on Hebrew soil and among men who had been nurtured in the uncompromising monolatry, if not monotheism, of the Hebrew prophets. Nothing, therefore, could make these waver in their conviction that there is but one true God who alone must be worshipped. Yet now they found themselves irresistibly constrained to worship Jesus. This, however, could only be if his relation to God was such that in worshipping him they were at the same time worshipping God. Clearly they could not simply identify this Man whom they had known in the flesh and who had died on the Cross with the God of their fathers to whom also he himself prayed; yet just as clearly they could not, without lapsing into ditheism, regard him as other than that one God. Moreover, Jesus had now 'gone away'.[1] When the disciples met on the Day of Pentecost, their Lord was no longer with them as he had been with them in the days of his flesh. But now they found another Presence in their midst, 'another Helper, the Spirit of truth',[2] whom they were likewise impelled to worship, yet whom they could not, without lapsing now into tritheism, regard as simply other than the God of their fathers, nor yet as simply other than the Jesus with whom they had lately companied. Thus from Pentecost onwards the Christians found themselves worshipping a God who was One but at the same time Three in One, and the later dogmas of the Trinity and the Person of Christ are attempts to express this in terms which would preserve it against every wayward direction of thought which tended to simplification at the expense of truth. My revered teacher, H. R. Mackintosh, has written:

History alone, then, is our true point of departure; but when men call a halt at the outer boundary of historical experience on the ground that to transcend fact is to speculate, and that speculation is injurious to faith, it must be answered that all such proscription is unavailing. In the first place, men will *persist* in thinking . . . It is, moreover, illegitimate to insist on restricting the Christian mind to the supremely practical language of the first disciples, whether on the Trinity or on any other aspect of the creed. . . . We search the New Testament in vain for theories; but assuredly we encounter great vital data which it is our duty to cross-examine and explicate and synthesize without being too much concerned with the recurrent charge of having strayed into the domain of metaphysic.[3]

Yet such cross-examination and explication and synthesizing is carried on, as it were, at our own risk and peril. We cannot think that even the first formulations in which it issues are entirely free from error. But if we then attempt to build further inferences upon these earlier ones, this error will be multiplied, and the further we proceed with this process, the greater and

---

[1] John 16. 5–7.   [2] ἄλλον παράκλητον κ.τ.λ., John 16. 16.
[3] *The Doctrine of the Person of Jesus Christ* (1912), p. 513 f.

more numerous our errors are likely to be; for the farther a chain of reasoning travels from the experienced facts on which it founds, the greater is the chance that it is leading us astray.

Let me conclude by quoting the following paragraph from a scholarly Anglican work of some sixty years ago:

For example, it was not until Sabellianism attacked the Tripersonality of the Godhead, extending the unity of nature into a unity of person, that the Church found it necessary to co-ordinate her belief in the Deity of the Son and of the Spirit with her intellectual hold upon Monotheism. Nor was it until Arius rationalistically denied the Eternal Divinity of the Word that she had to discover terms in which to express her faith in the essential unity of the Father and the Son which embraced without destroying the Personal distinctness. Similarly, it was due to the attacks of Apollinarius, Nestorius and Eutyches upon the completeness of either the Humanity or the Divinity of her Lord that the Church was led to work out the right expression of her belief in the Two Perfect Natures united in His own Divine Personality.[1]

'Notice-boards against all heresies' were thus exactly what these dogmas were. It is for this purpose that they were framed, and in arguing for the limitation that it imposes upon their use, I have perhaps sufficiently explained the sense in which I would here apply the Kantian injunction against employing for the further extension of our metaphysical knowledge those ideas of supersensible reality which our faith nevertheless obliges us to entertain.[2]

[1] T. H. Bindley, *The Oecumenical Documents of the Faith* (1899), 2nd ed., p. 2.

[2] In the first volume of his Gifford Lectures, *For Faith and Freedom* (1956), Leonard Hodgson writes as follows: 'But the revelation itself, the *depositum fidei*, is not to be identified with any verbal expression of it. All subsequent theologies are not to be judged by their faithfulness to the original *kerygma*, but by their faithfulness to the revelation of God in Christ to which the primitive *kerygma* bore witness' (p. 86). 'It makes all the difference in the world when we locate the *depositum fidei* not in the apostolic *kerygma* or the prophetic utterance, but in that to which they point, that which they open our eyes to see' (p. 101).

CHAPTER IX

Faith and the Faiths

§ 36

In all that I have so far said I have been speaking from within the Christian faith, while at the same time acknowledging that faith of some kind is present in the hearts of all mankind. There are other faiths than the Christian faith, other religions than the Christian religion, but I have not hitherto so much as touched upon the question how the former are related to the latter. Furthermore, I have made little or no reference to the familiar distinction between natural and revealed religion or theology. These omissions must now be made good.

When in 1885 Lord Gifford founded the lectureships that bear his name, he defined their purpose as the 'promoting, advancing, teaching and diffusing of natural theology in the widest sense of that term', and then went on to say:

I wish the lecturers to treat their subject as a strictly natural science, the greatest of all possible sciences, indeed in one sense the only science, that of Infinite Being, without reference to or reliance upon any supposed special, exceptional, or so-called miraculous revelation. I wish it considered just as astronomy or chemistry is. I have intentionally indicated, in describing the subject of the lectures, the general aspect which I would wish the lectures to bear, but the lecturers shall be under no restraint whatever in their treatment of their theme. . . .

It is plain that Gifford was here relying upon the traditional distinction between natural and revealed knowledge, a distinction which indeed presented no difficulty to the majority of his contemporaries. Among these would be some who, like many eighteenth-century Deists, denied the existence of any revealed, and others who, like Hume and Kant, doubted the availability of any natural knowledge of God; but both parties would have agreed that the terms of the distinction between the two kinds of knowledge were in themselves clear enough. It was the distinction between what men could discover for themselves by 'the unaided light of reason and nature' and what they knew only through authoritative divine communication. Yet there were already some who refused to accept any such dichotomy, placing their reliance upon a kind of knowledge which conformed to neither of these definitions, a knowledge which was neither 'unaided' nor yet given in the form of communicated doctrine. Since not a few of those who were afterwards appointed to the lectureship belonged to this third category, these found themselves in considerable embarrassment as to the line they were to follow. As early as 1890, only five years after Gifford had written his will, John Caird began his Gifford Lectures in Glasgow by protesting that the distinction between a natural and a revealed knowledge of God was 'arbitrary and misleading'.[1] And if I were now to ask myself whether what I have so far said is natural or revealed theology, I should find it difficult to answer unequivocally. I fear Dr Karl Barth and those who follow him would say it was all natural theology, while some others would say that I had infringed the conditions of the Gifford Bequest by my constant mention of revelation.

§ 37

One of the difficulties has been that such a phrase as 'the natural knowledge of God' seems to cover and confuse two very different things. The natural theology which was developed with so much skill and in such great detail by the doctors of the Middle Ages consisted in the construction of philosophic arguments such as would provide, for those who had sufficient philosophic training to understand them, some independent support—a sort of flying buttresses—for the more elementary of those beliefs which, having been given by divine revelation, were already in the possession of the faithful. Prominent among

[1] *The Fundamental Ideas of Christianity* (1899), p. 13.

these were St Thomas Aquinas' five ways of demonstrating the existence of God—the argument from communicated motion to an unmoved First Mover, the argument from the chain of causation to a First Cause, the argument from the contingency of the world to a Necessary Being, the argument from the observed fact of lesser and greater degrees of goodness to a Perfect Goodness, and the argument from the observed design in nature to a Divine Designer.

Such arguments were first put forward by Plato and Aristotle and their disciples, pagan philosophers who had no knowledge at all of the Hebrew-Christian revelation. Yet the beliefs they were designed to establish, or something which in varying degrees approximated to them, were already operative in the minds not only of their own people but of many other pagan peoples. A pagan is not a man who does not believe in and worship deity, but a man who believes in and worships too many deities. He is not a man who has no religion but a man who, as we shall presently find Dr Barth contending, has too much. How then have those pagans who have not had the benefit either of the Greek or of the medieval theistic argument-ation come by such knowledge of the divine as they possess? This question was too seldom put to themselves either by Plato and Aristotle on the one hand or by St Thomas and his fellow scholastics on the other, but when it was put, the tendency was to assume that such knowledge had been reached by processes of thought quite germane to those which the philosophers, in framing their arguments, were afterwards to set out in strictly logical form. It was widely supposed that it was in the course of their attempt to explain the natural world that the notion of divine beings first suggested itself to men's minds.

Such a view, however, finds little support in what we now know, which is altogether more and more accurate than any-thing the Greeks and medievals knew, of early religion. There could not then have been in men's minds any process of infer-ence, in however latent and non-explicit a form, from the contingency of the world to a First Cause or from the design evident in nature to an Arch-Designer; and this for the very simple reason that they did not think of the divinities they worshipped as having caused or designed the world. Even of the ancient Israelites it is true that only at a comparatively late stage in their history did such a thought become dominant in their minds—a fact which is obscured for us by the placing of the story of creation at the very beginning of the Old Testament canon, though in fact it dates only from the period of the great prophets. Generally speaking, we may say of all pagan peoples that they worshipped their deities long in advance of conceiving them, as few have ever come to conceive them, to be responsible for the existence of the world and of men.

It is, however, well known, that the most influential of the post-Aristotelian schools of philosophy, namely the Stoic, developed an entirely different line of explanation of the presence among all peoples of ideas concerning gods and the divine realm in general. Through the opening-up of the barbarian world that had meanwhile resulted from the conquests of Alexander they knew now much more than Aristotle and his predecessors had ever done of the religious beliefs of other nations; and they found that these had everywhere much in common. They explained the existence of these common notions (κοιναὶ ἔννοιαι), as they called them, by saying that they were native to the human mind as such—not anything injected into it at a later time but part of its very substance from the beginning. They did not doubt the validity of Plato's and Aristotle's syllogistic proofs and they would frequently be found repeating them, but they preferred to place their reliance on something prior to all proofs and syllogisms, namely the intuited knowledge already present in their minds as in the minds of all men everywhere. What was thus given *a priori* did not really need the further fortification of *a posteriori* considerations, however valid these might be. The common notions were what Zeno, the founder of the school, called 'cataleptic', or gripping perceptions (φαντασίαι καταληπτικαί) of a distinctness (ἐνάργεια) and intensity (τόνος) that 'seized men by the hair and dragged them to assent (συνκατάθεσις)'. The belief that God exists is such a common notion, and thus cannot be denied unless through some confusion of thought. 'People quarrel', says the Stoic in Cicero's dialogue *De Natura Deorum*, 'about what God is like, but that He exists nobody denies'.[1] He does not mean, however, that the common notion of God extends to *nothing* beyond his bare existence, for he says a little later on: 'Since we preconceive by an indubitable notion what kind of being God is, first that He is a living being, and second that there is nothing in all nature superior to Him, I do not see that anything can be more consistent with this preconception and notion of ours than to attribute life and divinity to the universe, than which nothing can be more excellent.'[2] So also Sextus Empiricus informs us that the Stoics understood the common preconception about God (κοινὴ πρόληψις περὶ Θεοῦ) to be 'that He is a living being, blessed, immortal, perfect in happiness and free from all evil'.[3] And Plutarch tells us that the Stoic Antipater of Tarsus began his book concerning the Gods with the following words: 'We shall begin what we have to say by briefly stating the distinct preconception which we have concerning God. We conceive Him as a living being, blessed, immortal and well disposed towards men.'[4]

What the Stoic teachers sought to do was thus not to *prove* the existence of God or his possession of such attributes, but to convince men that they already believed these things. Many men believe without knowing that they believe, but the Stoic always knows what he believes. He recognizes each cataleptic perception of truth for what it is, nor does he ever mistake for a cataleptic perception any belief which in reality does not possess that character. It is recorded by Diogenes Laertius that the Stoic Sphaerus was once at the court of King Ptolemy of Alexandria and was boasting that a Stoic never gave his assent to anything but a cataleptic perception. The king immediately bade one of the waiters serve Sphaerus with some pomegranates made of wax and, when the latter tried to

---

[1] Op. cit., II, 5.   [2] Ibid., II, 17.
[3] *Adversus Mathematicos*, IX, 33.   [4] *De Stoic. Repugn.*, 38.

eat one, shouted with delight that he had given his assent to a false perception. 'No', replied Sphaerus, 'I did not give my assent to the proposition that they were pomegranates, but only to the proposition that they were probably pomegranates [doubtless because they looked like pomegranates and had been offered to him by a king]. *That* proposition was true, and therefore I was not deceived.'

It is probable that Zeno and his immediate successors (of whom Sphaerus was one) were content to place their sole reliance upon the self-evidencing character of the common notions. They are true because they are cataleptic, because they cannot be doubted by those who clearly know what they themselves believe. But unfortunately the later Stoics were inclined to find a further buttress for their convictions in the argument that because they are universally held they must be true. In doing this they seem to have committed the fallacy which the logicians describe as the simple conversion of an A-proposition. Certainly all innate ideas must, as being part of the very substance of human intelligence, be universally held, but it is far from being the case that all universally held ideas are innate. At all events, it was thus that there came into being the argument *e consensu gentium*, which found sufficient proof of the existence of God in the fact that men of every race believed in him. One cannot help feeling that we have here a declension from the true Stoic position.

This position differs radically from that of Plato and Aristotle in that it relies upon an *a priori* knowledge of God as distinct from a knowledge of him gained from the excogitation of *a posteriori* proofs. Here, then, we have two quite different types of natural theology. The Stoic type had considerable influence in the early Middle Ages, in Erigena and the Victorines, and as late as the thirteenth century in St Bonaventure and some of his fellow Franciscans. But by that century the Aristotelian type had become dominant under Dominican influence. St Thomas Aquinas will have no traffic with innate ideas or with any *a priori* knowledge of God, placing his whole reliance, apart from the Christian revelation, on inferences drawn by the discursive reason from sense-observation of the corporeal world. It was only after the close of the Middle Ages, particularly in the seventeenth and eighteenth centuries, that the Stoic natural theology was to come into its own again, as for instance in Lord Herbert of Cherbury's *De Veritate* and *De Religione Gentilium*, among the Deists, and in Spinoza's *Tractatus Theologico-Politicus*.

But it is evident that this Stoic type of natural theology, instead of providing men with new knowledge, amounted to no more than a clarification and careful codification of knowledge they already securely possessed. Thus the important distinction is not really between two natural theologies, so much as between what is properly called natural theology and what we shall provisionally call natural religion; between what has been offered to men by the philosophic theologian and what men already believe before philosophic theology had begun its chosen task. My contention then is that, if we do speak of a natural knowledge of God or a knowledge gained by 'the light of nature', we should be clear which of these two very disparate things we have in mind. Only thus can confusion be avoided.

§ 38

Leaving aside what I have called natural theology, let us now consider the epistemological status of what I have, very provisionally, allowed myself to call natural religion. Are the adherents of pagan religions in possession of any true knowledge of God and the things divine?

The question has been much debated of recent years by theologians standing within the Reformed or Calvinist tradition, and therefore I find it convenient to begin what I have to say by summarizing Calvin's own views as found in the opening chapters of his *Institutes*. He sets out from the assumption, which he takes to be 'beyond controversy', that some sense of divinity, and indeed by a natural instinct, inheres in the human mind. It is present in the minds of even the dullest and least civilized races and of those who in other respects appear to differ least from the beasts. It is, he says, a common preconception, a *communis praesumptio*, inscribed on every human heart (and here we note that this Latin term was that universally used by the Roman Stoics to translate the Greek original κοινὴ πρόληψις περὶ Θεοῦ). Certainly many fabrications have been introduced into religion in order to persuade men to obedience or to terrify them into subjection, but it is absurd to say, as some do, that their belief in a divine being resulted from such a fabrication (and here we note the correspondence with the Stoic distinction between the common innate notions and those which have afterwards been added by various legislators and are different in different lands). 'It must therefore always be clear to those of sound judgement that a sense of divinity is engraved on human minds such as can never be deleted'; a sense that is 'natural and congenital, inherent as it were in the very marrow of our bones'.[1] Furthermore, however, 'God has not only implanted in men's minds that seed of religion of which we have spoken, but has so manifested Himself in the whole working of the universe, daily offering Himself to our view, that we cannot open our eyes without being compelled to behold Him.' 'There are innumerable proofs both in the heavens and in the earth which testify to His marvellous wisdom, and not only those more recondite which astronomy, medicine and the whole of physical science reveal to closer observation, but those also which force themselves on the notice of the most uncultivated of men. . . .'[2]

Yet, Calvin continues, it was in vain that God provided us with these witnesses of himself. 'In spite of the great clarity with which God exhibits both himself and His immortal Kingdom, such is our insensibility, and so dulled do we become in the presence of these transparent evidences, that they pass us by without profit.' The divinely implanted and divinely evidenced knowledge has been radically and hopelessly corrupted. 'Hence that flood of errors with which the whole world is

---

[1] Op. cit., Lib. I, Cap. III.   [2] Cap. V.

crammed.' Instead of acknowledging the true God the nations
have invented innumerable gods of their own. 'An immense
crowd of gods has issued from the minds of men', but all such
are 'only dreams and phantoms of their own brains'. To
acknowledge and worship them, far from bringing any profit,
is a grievous sin—the sin of idolatry against which the Bible
has so much to say. 'Those who adulterate pure religion, as all
must necessarily do who put forward opinions of their own devis-
ing, make a departure from the one true God. No doubt they
will say that such was not their intention, but it little matters
what their intention was or what they told themselves. . . . Any
opinion concerning the heavenly mysteries which has been
formed by men themselves . . . is the mother of error. . . . It
is no inconsiderable sin to worship God by guesswork (*fortuito*).'[1]
Only through God's own revelation can fallen man reach any
true knowledge of him. Only on the Church will the divine
light arise, and all without it are left in blindness and darkness.
'It is indeed a home thrust that is aimed at our human
capacities when [as so often in the Bible] all the thoughts
proceeding from them are derided as foolish, frivolous, insane
and perverse.'[2]

Calvin's answer to our question, then, is that though a
sense of God is so indelibly imprinted on the human mind that
it can never be totally effaced, and though the testimony of
nature is suited to provide further fortification for this sense,
nevertheless it is so defaced by sin that the only service it can
now render to men is to show them that, as St Paul says, they
cannot plead the excuse of having been left in ignorance. No
true knowledge of God can now be recovered by any save
those who have received the Christian revelation. The pagan
religions, though it was the innate sense of God that prompted
their conception, can do nothing but mislead. The pagans, it
seems, would be better without them, since by their adherence
to them they do but increase their guilt. To their sinful failure
to worship the true God they do but add the further sin of
idolatry.

[1] Lib. I, Cap. V.   [2] Lib. II, Cap. III, 1.

§ 39

Many Calvinist theologians of later generations are even more explicit than Calvin himself in declaring that it would be better for pagans to have no religion than to have those they profess. Does the great Calvinist theologian of our time, Dr Barth, say this too? It appears that he does, but with the very important difference that he includes the religion of Christians under the same judgement. 'Barth', wrote Dietrich Bonhoeffer in words that have recently attracted widespread attention, 'was the first theologian to begin the criticism of religion— and that remains his really great merit.'[1] 'He called the God of Jesus Christ into the lists against religion, *pneuma* against *sarx*. That was and is his greatest service.'[2] And when Bonhoeffer says 'against religion', he too has in mind the Christian religion as well as others, for it will be remembered how much he has to say about the necessity of understanding Christian truth 'in a non-religious sense'.

But let us hear Dr Barth himself. His fullest treatment of the matter is in the section entitled 'The Revelation of God as the Abolition of Religion' in the so-called second half-volume of his great *Church Dogmatics*. It contains over fifty thousand words. It is turgid and repetitive in style yet undeniably impressive. I hope you will bear with me if I try to compress the substance of it into two thousand words, mainly the author's own, and I hope equally that too much injustice will not be done to the original by such severe compression.

Dr Barth begins by defining human religion as 'the realm of man's attempts to justify and to sanctify himself before a capricious and arbitrary conception of God'. Yet, he goes on, the revelation of God in Christ, since it is a revelation to man, has also its human side in what we call Christianity or the Christian religion, and in this aspect it appears as 'only a particular instance of the universal which is called religion',

---

[1] *Letters and Papers from Prison* (Eng. trans. of *Widerstand und Ergebung*, 1951), p. 126.   [2] Ibid., p. 148.

a species within a genus which includes many other species—Judaism, Islam, Buddhism, Shintoism, animism, totemism and many more. 'It is difficult to find any time or place when it was not thought that the voice of God had been heard.' Every culture seems 'to have been determined or partly determined by a reverence for something ostensibly more than man, for some Other or Wholly Other, for a supreme relative or even an Absolute'. Nor can we claim that 'the Christian religion is the true religion fundamentally superior to all other religions', for the revelation of God in Christ judges and condemns all religions, including the Christian. Dr Barth quotes Luther as having said, 'The heathen have committed far greater sin by their worshipping sun and moon, which they have regarded as the true worship of God, than they have with any other sins. Therefore the piety of man is vain blasphemy and the greatest of all the sins which he commits . . . Whoso will not obtain grace by the blood of God, for him it is better that he should never come before God. For he but enrages the Majesty more and more thereby.' What Dr Barth adds to this is that it 'does not affect only other men with their religion. Above all it affects ourselves also as adherents of the Christian religion.' *All* religion is an attempt to reach God from our standpoint and to justify and sanctify ourselves in his sight by our own piety, but what revelation does is to teach us that only God can justify and sanctify us, and that he does this, not because of our religion, but in spite of it. He justifies us while we are yet sinners, and our having religion is a chief part of our sin. Dr Barth's statement at this point is so unqualified that I am reminded of having somewhere read that the perfection of exquisite good manners in China is to refer to one's own religion as 'the wretched superstition to which I happen to be addicted'! Revelation, he goes on, 'reaches us as religious men; i.e. it reaches us in the attempt to know God from our standpoint', but such an attempt is sinful, sharing in the sinfulness of all human activities. 'We need to see that in the view of God all our activity is in vain even in the best life; i.e. that of ourselves we are not in a position to apprehend the truth. . . .

We need to renounce all attempts even to try to apprehend this Truth.' We must put aside all reliance on anything we ourselves do, and rather acknowledge that in sending his Son God has already done everything for us. 'If a man tries to grasp at truth of himself . . . he does not do what he has to do when the truth comes to him. He does not believe. If he did, he would listen; but in religion he talks. If he did, he would accept a gift; but in religion he takes something for himself. . . . In religion man bolts and bars himself against revelation by providing a substitute, by taking away in advance the very thing which has to be given by God.'

Accordingly Dr Barth entitles a long sub-section 'Religion as Unbelief'. 'Sin', he writes, 'is always unbelief. And unbelief is always man's faith in himself. . . . It is this faith which is religion.' Revelation is indeed not alone in thus condemning all religion, since atheism does this too. But atheism does not condemn it as effectively, since it itself battens upon religion and, since its task is only one of negation, would be out of work if it succeeded in destroying it completely. This is why atheism has usually come in the end to 'a kind of toleration of religion'. 'But', concludes Dr Barth, 'the abrogation which is a genuine and dangerous attack on religion is to be found in another book', i.e. the Bible, beside which the atheistic books 'can only be described as completely harmless.' It does indeed behove Christians to be markedly tolerant towards all religions. But such tolerance is very different from the patronizing toleration of the atheist or sceptic; and again it is very different from the tolerance of those believers who have 'told themselves or been told that theirs is not the only faith, that fanaticism is a bad thing, that love must always have the first and the last word'. 'Tolerance in the sense of moderation or superior knowledge or scepticism is actually the worst form of intolerance.' The right kind of tolerance is rather 'informed by the forbearance of Christ, which derives therefore from the knowledge that by grace God has reconciled to Himself godless man and his religion'. It 'is possible only for those who are ready to abase themselves and their religion . . . knowing that they first, and their religion, have need of tolerance, a strong forbearing tolerance'.

After all this it comes as something of a surprise to the reader to find the final sub-section of Dr Barth's discussion entitled 'True Religion', though indeed they had already been given incidental hints that something of the kind was to come. That his repeated insistence on the falsity of all religion should be followed by an equally lengthy disquisition on true religion is, however, an example of that 'dialectical' mode of thought and exposition with which his readers have so long been familiar, and which is reminiscent of, while at the same time being subtly different from, the Roman practice of first stating a principle in unqualified form and afterwards proceeding to qualify it.

He now explains that we can speak of true religion only in the sense in which we speak of a justified sinner, who is *simul justus et peccator*. He goes on as follows:

Religion is never true in itself and as such. The revelation of God denies that any religion is true, i.e. that it is in truth the knowledge and worship of God and the reconciliation of man with God. . . . If by the concept of a 'true religion' we mean truth which belongs to religion itself and as such . . . no religion is true. It can become true only in the way in which man is justified—from without . . . The abolishing of religion by revelation need not mean only its negation—the judgement that religion is unbelief. Religion can just as well be exalted by revelation, even though the judgement still stands. There is a true religion: just as there are justified sinners. If we abide by that analogy, . . . we need have no hesitation in saying that the Christian religion is the true religion.

In our discussion of religion as unbelief, we did not consider the distinction between Christian and non-Christian religion. Our intention was that whatever was said about the other religions affected the Christian similarly . . . Therefore the discussion cannot be understood as a preliminary polemic against the non-Christian religions with a view to the ultimate assertion that the Christian religion is the true religion. . . . This religion too stands under the judgement that religion is unbelief, and that it is not acquitted by any inward worthiness, but only by the grace of God. . . .

The fate that has overtaken the religion of Israel, Dr Barth goes on, should be a warning to us in this regard.

Once it was the human answer to the divine revelation as demanded and ordered by God Himself. In its exercise it was accused and condemned of unbelief, but always re-adopted into grace. But now —the example had to be recorded—it is a rejected and emptied religion. . . . It is the Jewish religion from which God has turned away His face. It is one amongst other religions and no more than they. Its only advantage is the terrible one that once it was more than they, but only once. . . . If it rejects grace, and therewith its unmerited acquittal, it can never be anything more than false religion, unbelief, idolatry and self-righteousness.

But the same fate will overtake the Christian religion if it should even in the least degree rely on any virtue or superiority in itself, instead of casting itself without reserve upon the divine forgiveness of its sins. No doubt Christianity may be able to give a good account of itself as being *per se* better than they, but 'if it does this, it has renounced its birthright. It has renounced the unique power which it has as the religion of revelation. This power dwells only in weakness. And it does not really operate . . . unless Christianity has first humbled instead of exalting itself.'

But are there no non-Christian religions that also speak of grace, placing their whole reliance upon a God who justifies sinners? Dr Barth thinks there are, and he regards this as 'a wholly providential disposition' of things, teaching us a necessary further lesson. The Yodoism of Japan is very notably a religion of grace as also, less notably, is the Bhakti religion of India. Therefore

the Christian-Protestant religion of grace is not the true religion because it is a religion of grace. If that were the case, then . . . we could quite reasonably say the same of Yodoism and, with a rather more blunted sensibility, of the Bhakti religion. Indeed, why should we not say it of a whole range of other religions, for which grace in different names and contexts is not a wholly foreign entity. Only one thing is really decisive for the distinction of truth and error. And we call the existence of Yodoism a providential disposition because with what is relatively the greatest possible force it makes it so clear that only one thing is decisive. That one thing is the name of Jesus Christ. . . . The truth of the Christian religion is in fact enclosed in the one name of Jesus Christ and nothing else.

The heathen can in their own way rely upon divine grace, 'yet that does not mean that they are any the less heathen, poor and utterly lost'. 'Christians are what they are, and their religion is the true religion . . . not in virtue of their religion of grace, but in virtue of the fact that God has graciously intervened for them, in virtue of His mercy in spite of their apparent but equivocal religion of grace, in virtue of the good pleasure which He has in them, in virtue of His free election of which this good pleasure is the only motive. . . . But we can see the concrete significance of this, we can see how different it is from any higher principle, which might be used in the assessment of all human religion, only when we are clear that "by the grace of God" means exactly the same as "through the name of Jesus Christ".' 'If we try to look away from the name of Jesus Christ even momentarily, the Christian Church loses the substance in virtue of which it can assert itself in and against the state and society as an entity of a special order.' But 'in the relationship between the name of Jesus Christ and the Christian religion we have to do with an act of divine election . . . It is election, and only election, which makes the Christian religion the true religion . . . For the Christian religion is true because it has pleased God, who alone can be the judge in this matter, to affirm it to be the true religion. What is truth, if it is not this divine affirmation?'[1]

§ 40

Such, then, is Dr Barth's teaching. What are we to say about it? That it provides a much-needed corrective to certain errors into which we had been lately inclined to fall, I cannot doubt; but it administers this medicine in so brusque and defiant a way, and in such merciless over-doses, that in the end I find myself not only refusing to swallow it but at the same time suspecting that something is wrong with the prescription.

Dr Barth always writes, not merely from the standpoint of

[1] All the above quotations from Dr Barth are from pp. 280–361 of the Eng. trans., *Church Dogmatics*, 2nd half-vol. § 17.

Protestant Christianity, but from a standpoint which represents Protestantism, and especially the Protestant doctrines of justification by faith alone and of election, in what Catholics, both Roman and Greek, would regard as its most uncompromisingly one-sided form. He is quite explicit about this. 'Christian Protestantism', he declares, 'is the true religion to the extent that the Reformation was a reminder of grace and truth determined in this name [the name of Jesus Christ]. . . . Out of the reminder there sprang the doctrines of justification and election.'[1] His interest in Japanese Yodoism is that it yields the nearest, though still quite superficial, parallel 'not to Roman or Greek Catholicism, but to Reformed Christianity'.[2] The result is that he is led to regard world religion *only* as matter for divine forgiveness and *not at all* as a positive response to God's own gracious approach to men or as evidence of his gracious working in their hearts.

This latter was the criticism developed by Dr Hendrik Kraemer in the volume which he prepared for the World Missionary Conference at Tambaram in 1938. With much that Dr Barth writes he showed himself to be in full accord; so much so indeed that most of the English-speaking delegates came away regarding him as a pure Barthian, though he has since protested that this was 'especially because in Anglo-Saxon countries there arises easily the fearful suspicion of being manoeuvered into Barthianism'.[3] Like Dr Barth he insists that 'Christianity as a historical religious body is thoroughly human, that is, a combination of sublime and abject and tolerable elements', so that 'to speak glibly of the superiority of Christianity is offensive'. Its only superiority lies in the fact that 'radical self-criticism is one of its chief characteristics, because the revelation of Christ to which it testifies erects the absolute authority of God's holy will and judgement over all life, historical Christianity included . . . In the light of the Christian revelation, it is impossible and unnatural to think of achievement, whether ethical or religious: for the heart of the Gospel

[1] Loc. cit., p. 343.   [2] Loc. cit., p. 340.
[3] *Religion and the Christian Faith* (1956), p. 232.

is that we live by divine grace and forgiveness. . . .'[1] Thus the only relevant emphasis is not on the superiority of Christianity but on the uniqueness of what God has done for us in Christ.

Yet when Dr Kraemer comes to face the question: 'Does God —and if so, how and where does God—reveal Himself in the religious life as present in the non-Christian religions?'[2] he finds Dr Barth's uncompromising answer much too simple and unrealistic. Dr Barth, he says,

does not deny that there must exist something common between God and man, which makes it possible for man 'to hear God's Word'. However, to avoid the danger of making human religious experience and effort a preamble of faith, which would imply making the realm of revelation and grace continuous with human effort, he refuses to move one inch further. . . . He will not and cannot deny *that* God works and has worked in man outside the Biblical sphere of revelation, but *how* this has happened he refuses to discuss. . . .

This, it seems, savours too much of theological and logical consistency and breathes not the free atmosphere of Biblical realism. . . . Whosoever by God's grace has some moderate understanding of the all-inclusive compassion of God and of Christ rejoices over every evidence of divine working and revelation that may yet be found in the non-Christian world. No man, and certainly no Christian, can claim the power or the right to limit God's revelatory working.[3]

Incidentally, I wonder whether Dr Kraemer does not allow too much to Dr Barth in saying that the latter does not deny the existence of something common to God and man which makes it possible for man to hear God's Word. On the contrary, the thesis of the little brochure *Nein!* was that there is nothing in the nature of man which makes him a suitable recipient of divine revelation or enables him to hear it when it is given; the capacity to hear being given only in and with the Word itself, and given only to those to whom God has elected to speak it.

In his later book *Religion and the Christian Faith*, published

[1] *The Christian Message in a Non-Christian World* (1938), p. 108 f.
[2] Ibid., p. 111.
[3] Ibid., pp. 120–122.

eighteen years after the earlier one, Dr Kraemer goes still farther. He reproaches himself for having in the earlier book dealt with the non-Christian religions 'too unilaterally as purely human products', acknowledging the divine activity in them 'only in short parentheses'. He was, he confesses, 'too ambiguous' in his answer to 'the crucial question of whether or not there is revelation to be found' in these religions.[1] He regrets especially having said that it is 'not feasible to try to point out where the spots of this divine activity are',[2] and he now proceeds to make amends by specifying a number of such 'spots', as he quaintly calls them, concluding his list, interestingly if a little surprisingly, with the Aeschylean tragedies about which he asks, 'Has one no right to say that here was a meeting with the light- and life-giving Logos?'[3] He therefore puts to Dr Barth the pointed question, 'Has this whole business of religion anything to do with God, or has God anything to do with it?'[4] On a later page he gives his own answer:

If Barth says—and he does—that the Bible knows no other mode of revelation than Christ, he has the Bible against him. If he says that all modes of revelation find their source, their meaning and contention in Jesus Christ, and that the revelation of God's righteousness in Christ is the Truth, the *only* Truth, without whom no man comes to the Father—then he is quite right. . . .[5]

Some reference should perhaps also be made to the difficult but undeniably impressive works of the Swiss philosopher, M. Frithjof Schuon, three of which have appeared in English translation. He is reminiscent of Dr Kraemer when he begins the latest of these with the words:

Religions are cut off from one another by barriers of mutual incomprehension; one of the principal causes of this appears to be that the sense of the absolute stands on a different plane in each of them, so that what would seem to be points of comparison often prove not to be. Elements resembling one another in form appear in such diverse contexts that their function and nature too changes, at any rate to some extent.[6]

---

[1] Op. cit., p. 316 f.   [2] Ibid., p. 8.   [3] Ibid., p. 333.   [4] Ibid., p. 193.
[5] Ibid., p. 359.
[6] *Gnosis* (1957), Eng. trans. (1959), p. 11. Compare *Transcendent Unity of Religions*, Eng. trans. 1953.

He therefore believes that each of the great religions must faithfully abide by its own characteristic approach to the divine, and he deprecates any attempt to fuse them into one, whether by an eclectic fitting together of parts from each or by resting content with some vaguer religiosity that may be thought to be common to them all. Yet divine truth itself is one; for it is necessary, he says, 'not to confuse the phenomenal or cosmic with the spiritual reality; it is the latter which is one, and it is the former which is diverse'.[1] 'The uncreated Word shatters created speech, whilst at the same time directing it towards concrete and saving truth.'[2] It will be seen that we have here a different combination of positions from any that we have hitherto considered.

§ 41

If we now compare with one another the views of Calvin, Dr Barth and Dr Kraemer, it will be seen that all three insist with equal emphasis on the universality of religion among all races at all times. Everywhere and always men have looked up to and bowed down before a power or powers greater than themselves. But if we further inquire into the origin of this universal phenomenon, Calvin and Dr Kraemer answer that it derives from the *sensus divinitatis* implanted in human nature by God himself, whereas it would appear that Dr Barth will not allow this answer. He writes as if the knowledge so imparted was from the beginning so wholly destroyed by human sin that every pious impulse arising in men's hearts prior to and apart from the revelation of God in Jesus Christ was and is conceived in sin, having nothing at all in it which is of God or from God.

It is against this position that Dr Emil Brunner entered so emphatic a protest in his brochure on *Nature and Grace* and in his later book on *Revelation and Reason*; and, says Dr Kraemer, 'Brunner's protest is justified'.[3] Here the traditional distinction

---

[1] *Gnosis*, p. 14. [2] Ibid., p. 21.
[3] *The Christian Message in a Non-Christian World*, p. 133.

between natural and revealed religion is surrendered in favour of the distinction between general and special revelation. The substitution was of course not an original one on Dr Brunner's part, since it had already accomplished itself in the minds of numerous earlier theologians; but I, for my part, have no doubt that it is at least a change in the right direction. As a synonym for general revelation Dr Brunner uses the phrase 'revelation in creation',[1] and within this he includes both what St Paul calls 'the law written in the hearts'[2] of the Gentiles and what the same apostle calls God's manifestation of his invisible nature to them 'through the things that he made'.[3]

There has, however, been a tendency among those who have thus spoken to regard God's revelatory activity within the minds of the pagan nations as having been completed when he implanted the original seed of divine knowledge in their minds and at the same time left evidences of his handiwork in the external world. They have spoken as if, having provided this initial endowment, God had left the nations outside Israel to make the best they could of it, there being no continuing divine guidance of their minds throughout their later history. It is against this view that I am particularly anxious to enter a protest, so that I am glad to find Dr Kraemer acknowledging that 'God is continuously occupying Himself and wrestling with man, in all ages and with all peoples',[4] and that 'while the religious and moral life of man is man's achievement', it is 'also God's wrestling with him'.[5] If there is any measure of true insight into things divine, however limited, within the great ethnic systems of religious thought; if there is any element of truth, mixed with however much error, in the thinking of Gautama Buddha, the *Bhagavadgita*, Lao-tse, the Greek tragedians, Socrates, or Epictetus; it came through no 'unaided' exercise of human wit but from the working of the Holy Spirit of God. What is true in any religious system is from God; what is false is of our own imagining. Man can know

---

[1] *Offenbarung und Vernunft* (1941), I, § IIA (p. 58 ff. Eng. trans.).   [2] Rom. 2. 14.
[3] Rom. 1. 20.   [4] *The Christian Message in a Non-Christian World*, p. 125.
[5] Ibid., p. 126.

nothing of God except as God himself reveals himself to him. No man can by searching find out God, except as God himself takes the initiative both in prompting the searching and in directing the finding. Thus it is not only to Israel that God revealed himself through their successive historical experiences, but also to other peoples through theirs; though how far each people responded to what God was thus minded to teach them, and how far they mingled such response as they made with corrupt notions and practices of their own is, of course, another question.

Hence, while greatly preferring the distinction between a general and a special revelation to the traditional one between a natural and a revealed knowledge, I cannot find it wholly satisfactory. Not all the light that God has imparted to the various pagan peoples in the course of their historical experiences is general to them all; there is something that is special to each. It is for these reasons that I feel, like not a few of my predecessors, somewhat baffled by Lord Gifford's wish that his lectures should proceed 'without reference to or reliance upon any supposed special, exceptional, or so-called miraculous revelation'.

CHAPTER X

Salvation in a Name

§ 42

I wish now to revert to the decisive part played in Dr Barth's account by 'the name of Jesus Christ', and at the risk of repetitiveness I must remind you what this part was. Having insisted that all religion, including the Christian, is false and sinful and the very essence of unbelief, he then paradoxically (or should we rather say dialectically?) went on to speak of the Christian religion as the true religion. This, however, is not because of any superiority which the latter has in itself, but because God has chosen it from among the other religions to be the recipient of his forgiveness, accepting it and adopting it in spite of its own inherent unworthiness. Thus the Christian believes that he is saved by free and unmerited grace and by that only. But, said Dr Barth, he is not alone in believing this. There are other religions of grace; and most notably of all Yodoism, which likewise teaches that our salvation does not depend on any merit of our own gained 'by the execution of so-called good works and religious practices', but wholly upon the gracious willingness of Amida-Buddha, the Yodo deity, to grant it even to the greatest sinners if, calling upon his name, they pin their faith to him alone; while this faith itself is also acknowledged to be 'ultimately a gift of God'. Hence, Dr Barth went on, nobody who knows anything of Yodoism and of 'a whole range of other religions' which teach something not entirely dissimilar, can say that Christianity is the true religion because it is a religion of grace. It is the true religion because, and only because, while Yodoism calls on the name of Amida, and other religions of grace on the name of their own deities, the Christian calls on the name of Jesus Christ. 'Only one thing is decisive for the distinction of truth and error. . . . That one thing is the name of Jesus Christ. The truth of the Christian religion is enclosed in the one name of Jesus Christ and nothing else. It is actually enclosed in all the formal simplicity of this name as the very heart of the divine reality of revelation.' That the heathen nations call upon other names and put their trust in the grace conveyed through them 'does not mean that they are any the less heathen, poor and utterly lost'. Christians are what they are, and their religion is the true religion, not in virtue of their religion of grace, but 'in virtue of the fact that God has graciously intervened for them . . . in virtue of His free election'. There follow in Dr Barth's account many pages in which he rings the changes on this single theme— that of his own good pleasure and from no other motive God has elected the name of Jesus Christ to be the name which constitutes the truth of religion. 'For the Christian religion is true, because it has pleased God, who alone can be the judge in this matter, to affirm it to be the true religion. What is truth, if it be not this divine affirmation?'[1]

If, in spite of the decisive significance which we ourselves shall presently be found attaching to the name of Jesus Christ, we find Dr Barth's statement of it perplexing, I believe this is due to the almost parrot-like manner in which throughout many pages he repeats the phrase 'the name of Jesus Christ', understanding that name 'in all the formal simplicity' of it, without enlarging even in the least degree on its concrete content or indicating what it stands for. He makes no reference to what Jesus Christ was like as he appeared in the flesh. If he does this in other parts of his many-volumed work, he makes no appeal to it here, but merely affirms that God has affirmed that, from among the many names on which men have relied for their salvation, he has chosen the name of Jesus Christ to be the only true name. He does not tell us how he knows that God has done this, but is content to affirm that he has in fact done it. Here as always he eschews any sort of apologetic in

---

[1] All the passages and phrases enclosed within inverted commas, most of which I have already quoted in the previous chapter, are from pp. 340–350 of the English translation, *Church Dogmatics*, the second half-volume.

favour of dogmatic assertion. He passes too easily from the certainty necessarily attaching to whatever the all-knowing God has affirmed to the certainty of his own judgement as to what in fact God has affirmed. One is reminded in spite of oneself of the story told about A. K. H. Boyd and a friend who, when walking in the country, started a wild-fowl. 'That's a woodcock,' said Boyd. 'It's not my idea of a woodcock,' said the friend. 'Perhaps not,' retorted Boyd, 'but it's God's idea of one.' Probably it *was* a woodcock. Judging from what one knows about Boyd, it is likely he was right as regards the facts. Perhaps also his friend did not know enough about birds to entitle him to a judgement in the matter, so that the rebuke was not undeserved. But in theological debate it is surely arrogant to assume such incompetence on the part of one's fellow disputant. This is what Bonhoeffer had in mind in making it his chief ground of complaint against Dr Barth that he had set up a positivist doctrine of revelation which says in effect 'Take it or leave it'.[1] Dr Barth would surely not say *simpliciter* (as some others might) that we know the name of Jesus Christ to be the only saving name because the Bible says it is; for since we should have at once to add that only through faith in Jesus Christ can we become convinced of the authority of the Biblical witness, we should then be involved in a circular argument such as would get us no further. There is clearly no escape from this impasse except by acknowledging, as all good Calvinists do, the 'inward testimony of the Holy Spirit' to the truth of the Biblical affirmation, but this inward testimony can find nothing to feed upon if we are presented with a bare name and not at the same time told anything about the Person whose name it is. One is tempted to say that this would be like asking us to accept the teaching of the Epistles about the significance of Jesus Christ while withholding from us all that the Gospels tell us about what manner of Person he was, what he did and

---

[1] This is how the phrase is rendered in the English translation (*Letters and Papers from Prison*, p. 126) of the Bonhoeffer collection *Widerstand und Ergebung*. But the German original (p. 184) is '*Friss, Vogel, oder stirb*'—'Eat, bird, or die'; a phrase borrowed from Goethe.

what he said; though in fact our case would be even worse, since the Epistles themselves are not all that silent about these things.

But further: when Dr Barth contends that only those who call upon the name of Jesus Christ 'in all the formal simplicity of this name' can attain either to truth or to peace with God, many will want to ask, what then about the saints of the Old Testament period? Whatever else these knew, they did not know the name of Jesus Christ. From about the middle of the eighth century onwards they did indeed know the name 'Christ', i.e. in their own language 'Messiah'.[1] But they did not know the name of Jesus, and moreover their conception of the Messiah was for the most part ironically different from him who came. Were they therefore without any true knowledge of God and strangers to his salvation? I remember how Wilhelm Herrmann of Marburg, at whose feet both Dr Barth and I sat half a century ago, seemed always to find this question peculiarly difficult to answer. He would not for a moment deny that God had worked both revealingly and savingly in the minds of the Israelites prior to our Lord's advent, and indeed not in their minds alone but in those also of other peoples; but he professed not to know how this could be. Some of us Scots used to think this profession of ignorance strained and exaggerated on his part, and we would say that the difficulty was one he made for himself through his particular version of Christocentrism in which everything was made to turn on the 'inner life' of the historical Jesus. Yet Baron von Hugel went too far when he wrote that:

There is an insufferable defiance to history, and to the affinities and genius of Christianity itself, in the restriction (so emphatic in Herrmann's scheme) of every degree of genuine religion, of all true prayer, to those who explicitly know and formally acknowledge the historic Jesus' earthly life. Here even the Spanish Inquisitors were larger and more truly Christian.[2]

---

[1] 'It is with Isaiah that we find the beginning of that conception which later ripened into a full Messianic doctrine'—Oesterly and Robinson, *Hebrew Religion: Its Origin and Development* (1930), p. 209.

[2] *Eternal Life* (1912), p. 331 f.

Herrmann's real view is well expressed in the following sentences from his best-known book, *The Communion of the Christian with God:*

We by no means wish to assert, even for a moment, that the savages of New Holland have no knowledge of God, no pulsations of true religion, and therefore no communion with God. But we do not know through what medium such knowledge and such communion reach them. We cannot enter fully into the religious life even of a pious Israelite, for the facts which worked upon them as revelations of God have no longer this force for us.[1]

Our own answer was, as mine still is, that on which we had been brought up, namely, that such knowledge of God and such acceptance with him as was enjoyed by the men of the Old Testament were mediated through the eternal Son of God, though he had not yet been made flesh and none could yet call upon his name. Here I may quote the statement of the Confession on which we had been reared:

Although the work of redemption was not actually wrought by Christ till after his incarnation, yet the virtue, efficacy and benefits thereof were communicated unto the elect in all ages successively from the beginning of the world, in and by those promises, types, and sacrifices, wherein he was revealed and signified to be the Seed of the woman, which should bruise the serpent's head, and the Lamb slain from the beginning of the world, being yesterday and today the same, and for ever.[2]

But some of us at least were inclined to ask why, if this be indeed the true answer, we should not apply it also to adherents of other religions than that of Israel—perhaps even with Herrmann to 'the savages of New Holland'—and say that some of these, instead of remaining as 'poor and utterly lost' as Dr Barth affirms them to have been, may likewise have found acceptance with God through the mediation of One whose name it was not given them to know. Such an extension of the principle, though allowed by the Roman Church, was indeed condemned in the most violent possible language by our own Confession. We read in Cardinal Gasparri's Catholic

[1] Op. cit., Eng. trans. (1909), p. 62.
[2] *Westminster Confession of Faith*, VIII, § 6.

Catechism that 'God, who wishes all men to be saved, grants to all the graces they need for obtaining eternal life', and that God has accordingly made exceptional provision whereby one who has not had the opportunity of being baptized into the Christian faith may nevertheless obtain eternal life 'if through the operation of God's light and grace, he is—despite his invincible ignorance of the true religion—prepared to obey God and has been careful to keep the natural law';[1] while it is at the same time taught that this grace operates, not through the merit of such obedience, but through the efficacy of the sacrificial atonement that was to be made by the incarnate Christ.[2] Thus M. Jacques Maritain is able to write, with the closest and even verbal relevance to our present point at issue, that 'Under many names, names which are not that of God, in ways only known to God, the interior act of a soul's thought can be directed towards a reality which in fact truly may be God.'[3] It was, however, in pointed opposition to this Roman teaching that the Westminster Confession declared:

. . . much less can men not professing the Christian religion be saved in any other way whatsoever, be they ever so diligent to frame their lives according to the light of nature and the law of that religion they do profess; and to assert and maintain that they may, is very pernicious and to be detested.[4]

Fortunately, however, we of the Church of Scotland also have in our standards two later so-called Declaratory Acts, dating from 1879 and 1892 respectively, which lay it down:

That while none are saved except through the mediation of Christ, and by the grace of His Holy Spirit, who worketh when and where and how it pleaseth Him; while the duty of sending the Gospel to the heathen, who are sunk in ignorance, sin, and misery, is clear and imperative; and while the outward and ordinary means of salvation for those capable of being called by the Word are the ordinances of the Gospel: in accepting the standards it is not

---

[1] Op. cit., auth. Eng. trans. (1932); *Catechism for Adults*, Questions 288, 162.

[2] See e.g. Denzinger-Bannwart, *Enchiridion Symbolorum*, Index Systematicus, lx b and c and the refs. there given.

[3] *True Humanism* (Eng. trans. of *L'Humanisme Integral*, 1936), p. 56.

[4] Chap. X, § 4.

required to be believed that . . . God may not extend His grace to any who are without the pale of ordinary means, as it may seem good in His sight.[1]

Just, then, as Christians speak of the eternal Son of God, so also they must speak of an eternal atonement; and here I shall allow myself to quote some words of my late brother Donald:

To reduce the importance of the historical event would be contrary to every instinct of the Christian faith; and yet it seems impossible to say that the divine sin-bearing was confined to that moment of time, or is anything less than eternal . . . As God was incarnate in Jesus, so we may say that the divine Atonement was incarnate in the passion of Jesus. And if we then go on to speak of an eternal Atonement in the very life and being of God, it is not by way of reducing the significance of the historical moment of the Incarnation, but by way of realizing the relation of the living God to every historical moment. God's reconciling work cannot be confined to any one moment of history. We cannot say that God was unforgiving until Christ came and died on Calvary; nor can we forget that God's work of reconciliation still goes on in every age in the lives of sinful men, whose sins He still bears.[2]

Only in the sense provided by these considerations can we find justification for Dr Barth's declaration that 'in the New Testament faith is always faith in Jesus Christ'.[3] Only in that sense can we possibly say, for example, that the faith by which, according to the Epistle to the Hebrews, Rahab the harlot did not perish was faith in Jesus Christ;[4] and only so can we understand the same Epistle's contention that when by faith Moses refused to be called the son of Pharaoh's daughter, it was because he considered abuse suffered for *the Christ* to be greater wealth than all the treasures of Egypt.[5]

§ 43

It is reported by St Luke in the Acts of the Apostles that, speaking of the significance of Jesus before the Jewish supreme

---

[1] The quotation is from § 4 of the 1879 Act; but the Act of 1892 reads quite similarly.　　　　　　　　　　　　　[2] *God was in Christ* (1948), p. 190 f.
[3] Loc. cit., p. 313.　　　　　[4] Heb. 11. 31.　　　　　[5] Heb. 11. 24–26.

court within a few weeks or months after his death, St Peter declared, 'He is the stone . . . which is become the corner headstone. Neither is there salvation in any other: for there is none other name[1] under heaven among men, whereby we must be saved.'[2] After what has been said it is very necessary that we should face up squarely to the full import of this declaration.

The first thing to do is to ask what exactly is meant by salvation or being saved? It is to be feared that many will return the simple answer that it means going to heaven when we die. But that is certainly not what the Bible means by salvation. Clearly it is not what the Old Testament, the prophets and the psalmists, mean by it when they speak about it as often as they do; for these had no idea that anybody went to heaven when he died. But neither is it what the New Testament means by salvation, though it consistently teaches that those who are saved will continue to enjoy the blessings of salvation in an eternal life beyond the grave.

Rather I should like to begin by quoting the opening words of a little book written in 1920 by the philosopher Bernard Bosanquet, a former Gifford Lecturer who was not himself a professing Christian:

'What must I do to be saved?' The old monosyllable, which since the coming of Christ has sounded so clearly the S.O.S. call of humanity, utters, it would seem, an ultimate need. And yet what is it? Saved from what? The old word does not say; and this, I think, is very significant. We are to understand without telling, and I suppose we do.[3]

Yes, I suppose we do. The Latin word *salus*, from which our English word 'salvation' is derived, yields also such other English words as 'salutary', 'salubrious', 'eye-salve', etc.; and is cognate with the Greek word *holos*, with our English words 'whole', 'hale', 'health', and with the German word '*Heil*'— which does duty for both our English words 'health' and 'salvation'. The Greek word *sōtēria* used by St Peter is from a different root, but Souter's *Pocket Greek Lexicon to the Greek New Testament* has it that, while in extra-Biblical usage it 'has a

---

[1] Or 'no second name'.   [2] Acts 4. 11 f.   [3] *What Religion Is* (1920), p. 3.

reference generally to *bodily health*, *welfare*, especially as recovered after illness, but also as *deliverance* from every calamity,
victory over enemies, . . . in purely Christian terminology [it is]
far fuller in content, including complete *recovery of health* from
the disease of sin, release from captivity to it'.

Thus we do no violence to the term if we say that salvation
means wholeness, health, well-being. And it means well-being
of the whole man, body, soul and spirit. The New Testament
makes no such separation of body and soul as we have inherited
from Greek philosophy, but thinks of a man, as we have
recently learned again to do, as an essentially single psycho-
somatic organism. It is significant that it was in answer to a
question about the healing of a cripple that St Peter spoke
the words we are now considering. The Jewish high priest and
his party had asked, 'By what power and in what name have
you done this?' St Peter replied, 'If we are being asked . . . by
what means this man has been healed (*or* saved, σέσωσται),
(let it be known unto you . . . that by the name of Jesus Christ
the Nazarene . . . he now stands before you healthy (ὑγιής) . . .
Neither is there healing (*or* salvation, σωτηρία) in any other;
for there is no other (*or* no second) name under heaven given
among men whereby we must be healed (*or* saved, σωθῆναι).'[1]
It is significant also that the evangelists record Jesus as having
on four different occasions spoken the same identical words—
to a woman whose haemorrhage he had stanched,[2] to a blind
man whose sight he had restored,[3] to a leper whom he had
cured,[4] and to a woman of the streets whose only recorded
disease was that of sin;[5] and the words were 'Thy faith hath
healed (*or* saved, σέσωκεν) thee'. The difficulty of knowing
whether, if we are to be consistent in our choice of the English
equivalent of the Greek verb, we should say 'healed thee' or
'saved thee' has been overcome by many translators through
the rendering 'made thee whole'.

It will further have been noted that St Peter in his reply
used also another Greek word for 'whole' or 'healthy'—the

[1] Acts 4. 7–12.   [2] Matt. 9. 22; Mark 5. 34; Luke 8. 48.
[3] Mark 10. 52.   [4] Luke 17. 19.   [5] Luke 7. 50.

word *hygiēs* which yields our English word 'hygienic'. This adjective in its participial form is frequently applied in the pastoral Epistles to the accepted Christian doctrine, and our Authorized Version usually translates it as 'sound'[1] but once as 'wholesome'.[2] But if I were not to render the phrase 'sound doctrine' as 'hygienic teaching', I would be even closer to the original (ὑγιαινούσα διδασκαλία). It no doubt sounds very modern if I say that faith is the secret of spiritual hygiene, but in fact it is not modern at all—it is in the New Testament! I once heard a man say that the Gospel narratives are more redolent of the atmosphere of a hospital than of that of a meeting-house; and indeed Jesus seems to have spent as much time during his short ministry in healing diseases of the body as in healing the dis-ease of the soul. When John the Baptist sent two of his disciples to ask him whether he were indeed the expected Messiah, Jesus answered, 'Go and tell John the things you have seen and heard: the blind receive their sight, the lame walk, lepers are cleansed, and the deaf hear, the dead are raised up, the poor have Good News given to them.'[3]

We do then know what St Peter means by salvation, as Bernard Bosanquet said; and I think we also know that we need it. At least one phrase in the General Confession we can all make our own: 'There is no health in us.' We know that the world is sick and needs to be made whole. We know that the world is all wrong and needs to be put right. And you and I know that all is not well with our individual selves. Each of us stands in need of being made whole; though in acknowledging this we have lately preferred to use a somewhat more pedantic Latin word for 'whole', the word *integer*, and to say that our personalities are not properly integrated—perhaps it makes our condition sound a little more respectable. Those who have taken their lives seriously have at all times been aware of this need. The story of world religion in every age and every land is the story of an ardent and tireless and even desperate quest of salvation. We Christians cannot for a moment claim to have been more diligent than others in the quest. If we are

---

[1] 2 Tim. 1. 13: 4. 3; Titus 1. 9; 2. 1; 2. 8. [2] 2 Tim. 6. 3. [3] Luke 7. 22.

tempted so to think, a visit to the banks of the Ganges or to the shores of the Red Sea will swiftly disillusion us. And if we believe that in Jesus Christ we have found that which all men have sought, is it not rather that he has found us? If he should say to us 'I was found by them that sought me not', what is there that we could reply?

§ 44

But do I now believe with St Peter that this wholeness and well-being and health and salvation, whether individual or social, whether in time or in eternity, is to be found only in Jesus Christ? I am going to say that I do. I am going to say that I see no ultimate hope for our distraught and fevered world or for our distraught and fevered selves save as we follow the Way of Christ—save as we adjust ourselves to the new situation created by his advent and, as he himself began his preaching by saying, change our hearts and minds and put our trust in the Good News he brought us ($\mu\epsilon\tau\alpha\nu o\epsilon\hat{\iota}\tau\epsilon$, $\kappa\alpha\grave{\iota}$ $\pi\iota\sigma\tau\epsilon\acute{\upsilon}\epsilon\tau\epsilon$ $\dot{\epsilon}\nu$ $\tau\hat{\omega}$ $\epsilon\dot{\upsilon}\alpha\gamma\gamma\epsilon\lambda\acute{\iota}\omega$).[1]

As I have already argued, however, this does not mean that prior to the advent of Jesus Christ, and among those who did not yet know his name, God—Father, Son and Holy Spirit— was not already moving in the hearts of men for the healing of the nations, nor does it mean that even now he has ceased so to move. Therefore we must not say that in the pagan religions there is no apprehension of God's healing and saving power and no measure of trustful acceptance of it. The ardent seeking which is there manifested bears witness to minds that have already been invaded by the presence of God, whom none can seek unless he has first been seeking them or even, as Pascal said, unless they have in some measure found him.[2] Each one of the pagan religions has some light in it, but it has also much darkness—and how great is that darkness! There is something in each that makes for spiritual health, but there is much also that makes for spiritual disorder and sickness. I

---

[1] Mark 1. 15.   [2] *Pensées*, ed. Brunschvig, 555.

have already repudiated the view that the pagan peoples would be better without any religion than with those they profess, yet I cannot be blind to the havoc these religions have often wrought in the lives and societies of those who professed them. I have thus no hesitation in reaffirming my conviction that only by following the Way of Christ is there any hope for the ultimate salvation of mankind, and I make my own the words of Christina Rossetti:

> None other Lamb, none other Name,
>   None other Hope in heaven or earth or sea,
> None other Hiding-place from guilt and shame.
> None beside Thee.

It is often asked—and this is of course a separate question—whether the Christian whose hope is thus already fixed on Christ has himself anything at all to learn from what he knows of other religions than his own, from their sacred books, or from his observation of the piety of those whose lives are guided by them. It will be remembered that even Dr Barth declares that there is one thing he can learn: he regards it as providential that there should exist in the world other religions that speak of the free and unmerited grace of God shown to sinful men, since in this way we are warned against the mistake of supposing that Christianity, even in its Protestant form, is true because it is a religion of grace, instead of realizing that the only thing which 'is really decisive for the distinction between truth and error' is whether the name on which men call is or is not the name of Jesus Christ. The late Heinrich Frick of Marburg bases himself more broadly, and surely more wisely, on the declaration that 'The service which we ought to expect from other Faiths, in their encounter with us, is that they should shake up our Christianity and turn it into an authentic bearer of the Divine message';[1] so that 'It is from other Faiths that we learn how great is the gulf between our Christianity and the Gospel'. In this way alone, he writes, can 'we hear God speaking to us through the other Faiths'.[2] Thus nothing

[1] *The Gospel, Christianity, and Other Faiths*, Eng. trans. (1938), p. 63.
[2] Ibid., p. 54.

is added to the revelation of God in Christ by what we know of the partial revelations of himself which he vouchsafed in other ways to other peoples. The former is complete in itself and includes the latter within itself. Yet our encounter with the piety of those other peoples can do much to awaken us Christians to serious shortcomings both in our traditional understanding of the revelation of God in Christ and in our obedience to it. The difference between the two statements is that while the service which Dr Barth conceives to be rendered to Christian thinking by certain other religions is one which can be rendered in spite of there being no revelation and no truth-value in them, the service of which Dr Frick speaks is rendered by the presence in them of some 'general revelation' and some limited insight into the truth. I am sure the latter view is the right one, but I believe Dr Frick is also right in adding that only in the light of the fuller revelation are we able to recognize and assess the fragmentary apprehensions of truth in the non-Christian religions and distinguish them from the disastrous errors with which they are there intermingled. The explanation that the questing of all nations is a questing for Christ 'can be given only because the fulfilment has come. When we designate the non-Christian religions as general revelation, we are applying our knowledge of the Gospel.'[1] Dr Tillich expresses himself not dissimilarly, yet to my mind less judiciously, when he writes as follows:

If Christianity derives salvation from the appearance of Jesus as the Christ, it does not separate salvation through the Christ from the processes of salvation, i.e. of healing, which occur through all history. . . . What then is the peculiar character of the healing through the New Being in Jesus as the Christ? The answer cannot be that there is no saving power apart from him but that he is the ultimate criterion of every healing and saving process. . . . Therefore whenever there is saving power in mankind, it must be judged by the saving power in Jesus as the Christ.[2]

This is for the most part well said. Yet I should not myself care to speak of any saving power 'apart from Christ', but

[1] Op. cit., p. 58.   [2] *Systematic Theology*, Vol. II, p. 166 ff.

should rather insist that the Eternal Christ who was made *flesh* in Jesus of Nazareth, and the Eternal Atonement which was made *event* on Calvary, were and are the source of every 'saving process' which has at any time proved to be for the healing of the nations. In Jesus these found their only satisfying fulfilment. In him they are all summed up and brought to a head—as part of that ἀνακεφαλαιώσασθαι τὰ πάντα ἐν τῷ Χριστῷ of which the New Testament Epistle speaks.[1]

Yet there are those who would still give us contrary advice. The ancient Stoics advised us to extract as it were the Highest Common Factor from all the religions of the world and rest content with that—which would be a sort of Esperanto religion! The same prescription was widely adopted by the rationalist thought of the late seventeenth and eighteenth centuries, as in Herbert of Cherbury and Spinoza, and is not yet without its champions. But the truth is that, while such a common factor does indeed exist, it is far too exiguous and indeterminate to be of any use to anybody. It would leave out what has in fact been the effective strength and drawing-power of each of the positive religions from which it has been extracted. Hence from the beginning of the Romantic period another prescription has commonly taken its place—that of an eclectic syncretism. What appealed to the Romantics was the rich variety of religion rather than its distilled essence. Thus Hegel protested that there is no such thing as religion but only religions, just as one cannot eat fruit in general but only apples, pears, plums, etc.; and Schleiermacher that 'religion is real only in religions'.[2] There are accordingly still many among us who, believing that each one of the world's great religious traditions has been granted, in addition to what is common to them all, some characteristic insight of its own such as is hardly to be found elsewhere, hold that the way of enlightenment is to gather up these partial apprehensions into a single comprehensive outlook which they hope will be the religion of the future. This was the main argument of Dr Arnold Toynbee's Gifford Lectures, which he thus concluded:

---

[1] Eph. 1. 10.   [2] *Reden über die Religion*, V.

A time may come when the local heritages of the different historic nations, civilizations and religions will have coalesced into a common heritage of the whole human family . . . The missions of the higher religions are not competitive; they are complementary. We can believe in our own religion without having to feel that it is the sole repository of truth. We can love it without having to feel that it is the sole means of salvation.[1]

Well, I have already disclaimed the view that Christianity is the sole repository of truth or that no measure of healing and saving power is present in the teaching of other religions. But I have at the same time declared that what is true in the latter can be assimilated by the Christian only so far as he finds it also given in the Christian revelation, it being only in the light of that revelation that he is able to distinguish such fragmentary truth from the welter of error by which it is surrounded. Moreover it is surely difficult to think of (for example) Buddhism and Islam as complementing one another. Rather do they, as regards the most characteristic teaching of each, flatly contradict one another. Every one of the world's so-called 'higher religions' has its own special genius, if that word be allowed. Each is a logical whole by itself—a *Gestalt*, as the psychologists might say, with an internal self-consistency of its own. It is quite fanciful to suppose that you can take a piece of one, and then of another, and then of still a third, and glue them together. This again is something that we have most effectively learned from Dr Kraemer, from whom I cull the following further sentences:

Every religion is an indivisible, and not-to-be-divided, unity of existential apprehension . . . Every part of it—a dogma, a rite, a myth, an institution, a cult—is so vitally related to the whole that it can never be understood in its real function, significance and tendency, as these occur in the reality of life, without keeping constantly in mind the vast and living unity of existential apprehension in which this part moves and has its being . . . No element in a living system of religion or culture can ever be taken in isolation. . . .[2]

---

[1] *An Historian's Approach to Religion* (1956), p. 296 f.
[2] *The Christian Message in a Non-Christian World*, pp. 135–7.

§ 45

On the other hand we have to face the fact that the exclusive nature of the Christian claim—what German writers call the *Ausschliesslichkeitsanspruch*—is a very real stumbling-block for a large number of our contemporaries. The Greek word for stumbling-block is *skandalon*, and the feature of our Christian confession to which objection is here taken is very commonly spoken of as 'the scandal of particularity'. It is one aspect of the scandal of which Jesus himself spoke when he said to the disciples of John the Baptist 'Blessed is he who shall not be scandalized by me',[1] and which St Paul spoke of as 'the scandal of the Cross'.[2] It must at once be said, however, that the only exclusive claim which Christians are justified in making is not for what we call 'Christianity', not for their own brand of pious practice as empirically observable in the history or contemporary life of the Church, but in the revelation and 'unspeakable gift'[3] of God in Jesus Christ our Lord—a very necessary distinction which, as will be remembered, Dr Barth exaggerated into a complete disjunction.

More particularly, objection is taken to the Israelites' self-consciousness as being the Chosen People and to the claim of the early Christians to be the New Israel to whom this divine election has now passed. Dr Toynbee has the severest possible things to say against such a conception. He speaks of the evil 'that is inherent in the belief that there is a "Chosen People" and that I and my fellow-tribesmen are It'.[4] He also ventures on the prophecy that 'the spiritual struggle in the more exclusive-minded Judaic half of the world to cure ourselves of our family infirmity seems likely to be the most crucial episode in the next chapter of the history of mankind'.[5] Now, I do not doubt that there was a strong admixture of sinful national and racial pride in the minds of most Israelites when they thought and spoke of God's choice of their nation —a pride which manifested itself in their frequently shocking

---

[1] Matt. 11. 6.　　　[2] Gal. 5. 11.　　　[3] 2 Cor. 9. 15.
[4] Op. cit., p. 11.　　　　　　　　　　[5] Ibid., p. 283.

mistreatment of the surrounding nations; but on the other hand we must not forget that their great prophets, when they had finished their work, did not leave this pride a leg to stand on. They protested that it was not for any virtue or superiority in itself that Israel had been elected: 'It was not because you were greater than any other nation that the Lord set his heart on you and chose you; for ye were the least of all nations.'[1] Nor did the prophets ever tire of pressing the accusation that, as time went on, Israel proved more and more unworthy of its election, betraying the trust which God had reposed in it. Furthermore it is made clear that this election was not to any privilege such as could nourish self-esteem but to heavy responsibility and arduous service. The Second Isaiah, who perhaps dwells more than any other prophet on God's choice of Israel, declares that the service to which Israel has been called is the enlightenment of other nations: 'I the Lord have taken you by the hand, and kept you, and given you as a covenant to the people, to be a light to the Gentiles, to open blinded eyes.'[2] Dr Toynbee knows this, but still insists that the evil inherent in consciousness of being a Chosen People

is not exorcised by rising, as the prophets have risen, to a sublimely austere conception of the mission to which the 'Chosen People' have been called. They may accept the hard doctrine that they have been called, not to enjoy unique power, but to bear unique burdens and to suffer unique tribulations for the fulfilment of God's purposes: but, even then, their abiding belief in their own uniqueness still orients them towards a centre that lies in themselves and not in the God from whom their uniqueness derives.[3]

But, while I do indeed believe that to the very end there was a strong intermingling of self-regarding nationalistic pride in the Jewish self-consciousness, I am sure that Dr Toynbee here goes too far. If he believes in Providence at all, as he certainly does, how can he say that there is *inherent* evil in the conviction of an individual or people of being providentially called to a particular destiny, to a particular mission, and to the fulfilment of a particular office in the world of men? The truth

[1] Deut. 7. 7.   [2] Isa. 42. 6 f.   [3] Op. cit., p. 11.

rather is that the total disappearance of this kind of conviction from men's minds would itself be an evil of the most tragic kind. There can be no apprehension of the divine presence that is not at the same time a summons to a divinely-appointed task. 'Every revelation', says Dr Martin Buber, 'is a calling and a sending.'[1]

When the New Testament speaks of Israel as the people chosen of God, it thinks of it above all as the people whose divinely-guided history prepared the way for the gospel, the people who, when the time was ripe, gave birth to the Saviour of the World. It is this New Testament claim for the uniqueness and finality of Christ's mission and 'finished Work', which of course carries with it the claim for the unique calling of the Hebrew people, that is chiefly in men's minds today when they speak of 'the scandal of particularity'. We remember the much-quoted saying of the German philosopher of the *Aufklärung*, David Friedrich Strauss, that 'The Godhead loves not to pour its whole fulness into a single instance and to be niggardly towards all others (*Die Gottheit liebt es nicht ihre ganze Fülle in ein Exemplar auszuschütten und gegen alle andere zu geizen*)'. Why, it is asked, should things be ordered thus? Why should all men everywhere have to depend for their salvation on the occurrence of a single event or event-sequence? Why should God have chosen to reveal the fulness of his being and the fulness of his grace in only one historical figure, through only one people, and in only one age of the world's long history? And some would add, especially *that* people and *that* age?

> How odd
> Of God
> To choose
> The Jews.[2]

Why should he elect that little land of Palestine, that obscure backwater within the great Roman Empire? And that backward provincial people so little versed in the higher arts of civilization? And then from among them all a village carpenter's son?

[1] '*Alle Offenbarung ist Berufung und Sendung*'—*Ich und Du* (1933), p. 133.
[2] W. N. Ewer.

Well, there are two things I should like to say in answer. The first is that when we ask ourselves why these things should be, we have to answer simply that we do not know. But then, why should we expect to know? We have to take experience as we find it. We have to take history as we find it. Above all, we have to accept the action of God as we actually discover it to be. We cannot pretend to know in advance how God *ought* to act for the enlightenment and salvation of the human race. We are not in a position to lay down rules or conditions. The only question which—shall I say, as a good empiricist?—I have a right to ask is: Do I in fact find God coming to meet me in Jesus Christ as nowhere else, or do I not? Am I or am I not constrained, in spite of all my evasions and hedgings and reluctances, to regard this encounter as a 'paradigmatic experience' which must henceforth be the light of all my seeing? To this question the Christian can do no other than return an affirmative answer. So when the German philosopher, who was no empiricist but a Hegelian transcendentalist, tells me that 'The Godhead loves not to pour His whole fulness into a single instance', I cannot but wonder how he knew this. I have elsewhere[1] cited a letter of Rousseau to his friend de Beaumont in which he asked, 'Is it simple, is it natural that God should have gone and found Moses in order to speak to Jean Jacques Rousseau?' We must indeed allow that it is not simple, but what right have we to assume that truth is simple or that God governs his universe on a simple plan? And as to whether it is 'natural', have we any knowledge of what would be natural to such an encounter apart from the witness of the encounter itself? If we believe in God at all—and if we do not, *cadit quaestio*—we must allow him to bring us his enlightenment and salvation in ways of his own choosing, and it would indeed be surprising if these were not very different from anything that we, from our limited perspective and with our limited wisdom and intelligence, could have foreseen. The private soldier—and we are no more than private soldiers in God's battles—cannot expect

[1] *Our Knowledge of God* (1939), p. 185.

to have much insight into the strategy of a great campaign. It would be a weak enough strategy if he could, and one that the enemy could too easily anticipate and circumvent. Our Puritan forefathers used to say, and there is great wisdom in the saying, that God cheated our great enemy the devil by coming to us 'in the form of a servant'.

Thus when we ask ourselves why it should be ordained that there is only one Name by which all men everywhere must be saved, our first answer had to be that, if we do not know why, we do not need to know and could hardly expect to know. Nevertheless—and this is my second answer—we *are* able to say a little more than that. We could not be wise before the event, but perhaps we can be a little wiser after it. Perhaps the event itself has so enlightened us that we can now see something of the reason why things should stand thus. Is it not contained in Christ's own word, 'that they all may be one'— the word thrice repeated in his prayer to the Father before he crossed the brook Kedron into the Garden of Gethsemane on the eve of his crucifixion: 'that they all may be one; as thou, Father, art in me, and I in thee, that they may be one in us: that the world may believe that thou hast sent me. And the glory which thou gavest me I have given them; that they may be one, even as we are one: I in them, and thou in me, that they may be made perfect in one . . .'[1] For if it had been so that each could find God in his own way, each would be finding him without at the same time finding his brother. If the love of God were revealed to each in a different place, then we could all meet him without meeting one another in love. If the various tribes of mankind could find their ultimate enlightenment and salvation in different names, the human race would for ever remain divided. Men might still attempt to unite on the level of certain secondary and prudential interests, but are we not learning today from bitter experience how fragile and unstable this kind of association must always be, if in their ultimate concern, which is the concern for salvation, men remain apart and strangers to one another? Modern

[1] John 17. 21–23.

science has indeed given us a fine lead in its endeavour to transcend all barriers of race and nation and colour and language, so becoming international, but it becomes clearer every day that this will avail us little until we are of one mind about the ultimate good which our scientific skills should be made to serve.[1]

Was it not then a gracious ordering of things on God's part that there should be ultimate salvation for us all in only one Name; that we can meet with him only by meeting with one another; by betaking ourselves all together to one place—to one 'green hill far away'; by encountering there a single Figure to whom we offer our united allegiance; by listening to the self-same story; by reading in the same sacred book; by being baptized into the same fellowship; by eating and drinking at the same Holy Table; so that 'there is no difference between Jew and Greek, for the same Lord is Lord of all',[2] and 'here there is not Greek and Jew, circumcised and uncircumcised, barbarian, Scythian, slave, or free man, but Christ is all and in all'.[3] Is it not true that we cannot have real unity until we all have 'the same Lord'?

§ 46

By hindsight then, if not by foresight, we have been enabled to understand something of the reason why God has given us for our salvation only one Name. But by hindsight also we may know something of the reason why it should be just this Name and no other. Men had indeed long known that they needed a Saviour, but they did not know what kind of Saviour they needed until he came. H. G. Wells once said, when speaking of the universality of religion throughout the world, 'There seems to be a god-shaped gap in human nature.' Yes; but none of us really knew the shape of the gap until Christ came to fill it—and perhaps that is not the only case in which we do not know what we are seeking until we find it. It is Christ himself that has created the world's desire for him. The Wise Men of

[1] I have said something of this in my *Invitation to Pilgrimage* (1942), p. 122.
[2] Rom. 10. 12.   [3] Col. 3. 11.

the East did not know what kind of Saviour they were going to find when the star came to rest. The men of the Old Testament had long awaited the coming of Messiah but, as I have already said, when he came he was ironically different from all their preconceptions of him. Not just that a Saviour came, therefore, but the kind of Saviour he was—not just that God was incarnate in a man, but the kind of man in which he was incarnate, constitutes the essence of the Good News. A baby in a horse's stall, a village boy playing about a carpenter's bench, a wandering layman who had not where to lay his head, a condemned man hanging on a gallows-tree between two common thieves—these are the great archetypal images that have been given us by the event; and now by hindsight we have been given to understand why they should be so and not otherwise.

Consider here also another prayer of our Lord's, and the call to mankind with which he followed it:

I praise thee, Father, Lord of heaven and earth, that thou hast hidden these things from the wise and learned and revealed them to the untaught; yea, Father, that such was thy design. . . . Come unto me, all ye that labour and are heavy laden, and I will give you rest. Take my yoke upon you, and learn of me; for I am meek and lowly in heart: and ye shall find rest unto your souls.[1]

Consider with this St Paul's further interpretation: 'God chose what is foolish in the world to shame the wise, God chose what is weak in the world to shame the strong, God chose what is low and despised in the world, even the things that are not, to bring to nothing the things that are'; and notice that he is bold to give the reason for God's choice, which by hindsight he thinks he now knows—namely 'that no human being might boast in the presence of God'.[2] Thus nothing stands nearer to the centre of the Christian gospel than the lowliness of Christ, his humility and his humiliation. This it is that robs us of the last shred of justification of that human pride which is the very root of the disease from which we need to be made whole.

[1] Matt. 11. 25–29.　　　　[2] 1 Cor. 1. 27–30.

But finally, there are two complementary points that must be made with reference to our Lord's humility and humiliation. The Christian teaching is not simply that among the sons of men one Man was found who, being meek and lowly of heart, has left us the perfect pattern of humble demeanour. It is also, and more profoundly, that *God* humbled himself to be found in fashion as a man. It is that 'God was in Christ, reconciling the world to himself'.[1] This is not the lowliness of a man but the condescension of God.

Yet the two cannot be separated. In reality they are not two facts but a single fact; or they are two facts conjoined, as we theologians say, in 'hypostatic union'. St Paul cannot separate them. 'Christ Jesus', he says, 'though he was in the form of God, did not count equality with God a thing to be grasped, but emptied himself, taking the form of a servant, being born in the likeness of men [and there we have the condescension of the divine]. And being found in human form he humbled himself and became obedient unto death, even death on a cross [and there we have the lowliness of the human].'[2] The significance of this conjunction for our present argument is that, while the deepest truth of the gospel lies in the condescension of God, this latter would have remained, if not a meaningless, at least a problematic concept for us, if the Man in whom he condescended to become incarnate had not himself, and as a man, been a humble person—one whose every act and impulse and whole temper of mind showed that he had indeed come not to be served but to serve. If we speak only of God becoming man and do not at the same time speak of the kind of man he became, men will inevitably ask us why we believe that particularly *this* Name rather than some other should have been given us for our salvation. Nor can we then give them any satisfying answer, for we know that if we ourselves were ignorant of the narrative of the four Gospels, we should have found it impossible to accept the theology and Christology of the Epistles. The *faith* that through the death of Jesus God's love towards sinners was communicated and revealed, could

---

[1] 2 Cor. 5. 19. [2] Phil. 2. 5–8.

not have arisen apart from the *fact* of Jesus' own love for sinners or indeed from the fact that it was his love for sinners that led his enemies, the Scribes and Pharisees, to seek his death. Hence this fact and this faith are likewise conjoined in hypostatic union.[1]

[1] Compare D. M. Baillie, *God was in Christ*, pp. 180–184: 'And if we say, with the voice of the Christian ages, that Jesus died for sinners, it will be well for us to realize at the outset that this is profoundly true, not merely as a matter of theological interpretation, concerning the over-ruling purpose of God, but also in a purely historical sense, in respect of Jesus' personal relations with the sinners in ancient Galilee . . .

'Quite apart from . . . all subsequent theological interpretations, it is true in the plainest historical sense that Jesus died for sinners: it was His love for them that brought Him to the Cross . . .

'The crucifixion of Jesus set men thinking more than anything else that had ever happened in the life of the human race. And the most remarkable fact in the whole history of religious thought is this: that when the early Christians looked back and pondered on the dreadful thing that had happened, it made them think of the redeeming love of God.

'Not simply of the love of Jesus, but of the love of God.'

CHAPTER XI

Providence

§ 47

We have said that our sense of the presence of God is born of our encounter with certain occurrences or situations which provide the paradigm for our approach to, and profounder understanding of, all other occurrences and situations; and we quoted Whitehead's saying that the intuitions of religion, 'though derived primarily from special experiences, are yet of universal validity, to be applied by faith to the ordering of all experience', so that 'Rational religion appeals to the direct intuition of special occasions and to the elucidatory power of its concepts for all occasions.'[1]

Quite evidently there are many others who have encountered the very same occurrences as have been to us revelatory of the presence of God, but who have entirely failed to find in them any such deeper significance. Only a few of those who saw and heard all that transpired in Galilee and Jerusalem, only a few of those who witnessed our Lord's Crucifixion, were alive to the presence of God in these things. They were nothing to those who passed by. However cynical it may have been in intention, there is nothing extravagant in Anatole France's story of Pontius Pilate's meeting in his old age with a friend of his early days in Judaea, who asked him if he remembered a young man called Jesus, a native of Nazareth who was crucified for some crime or other, and of Pilate's knitting his brows for a few moments before replying, 'Jesus? Jesus of Nazareth? No, I don't remember.'[2]

This means that all those occurrences which to the eye of faith reveal the divine presence are capable of being explained

[1] See above, § 19.
[2] *Le Procurateur de Judée* in the volume entitled *L'Etui de Nacre.*

without apparent remainder in purely naturalistic terms. There
is no difficulty about fitting them all into what is called the
order of nature, for they belong to that order in the same sense
as do all other ccurrences. There is hardly another word in
our current speech that is patient of so many different meanings as the word 'nature', or any phrase whose coverage varies
so much as 'the order of nature'; but when philosophical
naturalism employs the phrase it is understood as relating to
the corporeal world such as can be described in terms of the
science of mechanics. Men of faith are accustomed to speak of
revelatory occurrences as miracles, and so indeed they are if
by miracles we mean mighty acts of God which call forth the
admiratio of those who recognize them to be such. But the Bible
never thinks of the 'signs and wonders' of which it has so much
to say as 'contravening the laws of nature'. The concepts, not
only of the laws of nature, but of nature itself, are wholly
absent from Biblical thought and could not indeed be expressed in the current language of the Biblical authors. The
later Greek philosophers, some of whose terms were familiar
to the New Testament writers, did certainly speak of the laws
of nature, but only with reference to the moral order of the
universe, and never with reference to the observed regularities
in the behaviour of the corporeal world: they were laws in the
proper sense of the word, legislative prescriptions that might
as often be honoured in the breach as in the observance. The
Hebrews were of course well aware of the regular sequences
of things in their external environment, of day and night,
seed-time and harvest, and the procession of the stars, but they
regarded these, not as forming a self-sustaining system or as
automatically or mechanically determined, but as gracious
ordinances provided and sustained by God for the benefit of
his creatures: their attitude being perfectly reflected in the
saying of Thomas Chalmers that 'the uniformity of nature is
but another name for the faithfulness of God'. Thus when
unexampled events occur, they are referred to the same divine
source as are more familiar happenings. They do not contra-
vene anything; they are not interventions save in the sense in

which all that comes to us from without is intervention. If they are supernatural, so also is the whole cosmic order supernatural. If the rest of the cosmic order is natural, so also are they natural. The office of those hitherto unexampled occurrences of which the Bible speaks as God's mighty acts is to reveal something of the purpose of God of which we had not previously been aware or else to startle us into obedient response to some part of his purpose already known but grievously disregarded —intimations which the more familiar round of things had failed to communicate. If we are to speak of miracles at all, then the essence of a miracle is that in it we are aware of being addressed by God. 'A miraculous event', writes Dr Farmer, 'always enters into the religious man's experience as a *revelation* of God. . . . Unless an event has this quality in some degree to someone it is not, in the religious sense of the term, a miracle.'[1]

It is, moreover, true in fact that those who find no revelatory significance in what men of faith speak of as God's mighty acts do refuse to accept their miraculous nature. They have no difficulty in explaining all they have heard or read about them in purely naturalist terms. Some of it they have no difficulty in dismissing as merely legendary material. Even the reports we possess from the hands of the Evangelists and St Paul of our Lord's Resurrection are certainly not such as to induce conviction in minds that are blind to its divine significance. If on the other hand these accept the historicity of the so-called miracles of healing and the like, they find it easy to naturalize them by referring them to 'laws of nature' that are not yet fully understood—the influence of mental attitudes on bodily conditions, telepathy and what not else. And who shall say that they are not so far right, or that God did not indeed accomplish these more striking manifestations of his purpose, as he accomplishes the more familiar, through the agency of created things? Who shall say that even the most exalted final causes, as well as the humbler ones, are not served by the operation of efficient causes? Whatever happens in the phenomenal world becomes part of nature as soon as

[1] *The World and God* (1935), p. 110.

it happens, however far it carries us beyond what we had previously known about nature.

There is, then, a justified naturalism. In earlier chapters I have spoken much against what I called a *reductive* naturalism but was always careful to include the adjective. The contention of the reductive naturalists is that the naturalist account of our experience exhausts the whole meaning of it, that there are no final but only efficient causes, that there is no purpose in the disposition of things but only mechanical determination, that nothing is real but body. The truth is, however, that the corporeal is only one aspect of our experience, which can equally be viewed under quite a different aspect. It is an aspect of our experience, not a section of it. The other aspect, which in different contexts we speak of as mental, spiritual, valuational, teleological, etc., is not apprehended through the gaps of a naturalistic explanation, but by adopting a wholly different approach to the whole. For example, in a broadcast lecture about the two different accounts that may be given of ordinary human action Dr Donald Mackay, an authority on physics and cybernetics, suggested the following helpful, though admittedly imperfect, analogy:

What the scientist is trying to do is to give us as complete an account of human behaviour as possible, from the standpoint of an observer, using a language whose terms presuppose that standpoint. He does not deny for a moment the validity of an account, in quite different terms, presupposing the standpoint of the actor himself. But it would be simply a logical error to mix terms that presuppose one standpoint with terms that presuppose another, and he doesn't do it. To treat a description in the language of the observer as if it were a rival of a description in the language of an actor is rather as if someone who did not understand algebra were to try to 'debunk' a printed algebra problem by proving that there was 'nothing but ink' on the page. Of course he would be telling the truth. There is nothing but ink there. But the algebra problem is not a ghost inhabiting one of the ink-patches. He will never find it as *something left over* after making an inventory of all the ink on the page. He will find it only by a different approach to the *very same data*.[1]

---

[1] Published in *Science and Faith To-Day* (Lutterworth Press, 1953), p. 34 f.

The account given by natural science of organic nature is thus, as its name implies, quite as naturalistic as that which it gives of inorganic nature, but both will be saved from being reductively naturalist if they recognize the right and validity of another and complementary account.

But furthermore it is well known that physical science now recognizes the necessity of offering two complementary accounts of certain phenomena within its own purview, of which the most familiar are the two accounts offered of the nature of light as consisting of waves and as consisting of particles. It was to meet this situation that Professor Niels Bohr first formulated his principle of Complementarity, but he has since advocated an analogous extension of it to the explanation of the relation in which the whole mechanistic aspect of our experience stands to its mental or spiritual aspects, suggesting its application to the mind-brain problem and likewise to the problems of the relation of human freedom to divine grace and of physical causation to divine providence.[1] It was by hinting at the possibilities thus opened that he concluded his Gifford Lectures in 1949, and I remember his saying to me at that time, 'I think you theologians should make much more use than you are doing of the principle of Complementarity.' But in fact not a few theologians had already been employing what is essentially the same principle, even if not quite under that name. This was notably true of Dr Karl Heim who in 1931 published the first volume[2] of his work *Die Evangelische Glaube und das Denken der Gegenwart*, and there expounded his principle of dimensionality. The concept of dimension is of course most familiar to us in reference to the tri-dimensional character of our experience of space. Each of the three dimensions can be indefinitely extended without meeting a boundary; but if we suppose the existence of a being whose apprehension of the world was only bi-dimensional, who lived in what an imaginative

---

[1] 'I believe that when Niels Bohr introduced this principle of complementarity into physics, and then extended it to apply more widely, he was opening a new chapter in our understanding of the universe we live in'—C. A. Coulson, *Science and Christian Belief* (1955), p. 93.

[2] Eng. trans. *God Transcendent* (1935).

writer has called Flatland, then nothing in his experience
could possibly suggest to him the existence of a third dimension
—that of depth. In something of the same way it is true that a
being whose apprehension was limited to what can be perceived by the bodily senses would meet with nothing in his
experience that could suggest to him the existence of a divine
dimension of things. He would have to say as Laplace said to
Napoleon, 'Sire, I had no need of that hypothesis', or with
Kepler, 'I searched the heavens with my telescope and found
no God.' Only to that mode of apprehension which is faith is
the presence of God revealed. In the fifth volume of his work,
published in 1951 under the title of *The Transformation of the
Scientific World-View*,[1] Dr Heim was now able to make full use
of the concept of Complementarity under that name. The
same is true of an interesting American book to which I shall
presently be making fuller reference, Dr William G. Pollard's
Chance and Providence.[2]

§ 48

We must, however, beware of speaking as if we had here to do
with two different worlds each of which complements the other.
What are complementary are two different attitudes to the
one world which we familiarly know, two different modes of
our apprehension of it, two different accounts that may be
given of it. This is of course true of the complementarity of
which natural science speaks—it does not speak of two kinds
of light but of two complementary ways of regarding one and
the same light; but it is also true of the wider fields of discourse to which, on the analogy of its use in natural science,
we have been encouraged to apply the term. Faith can neither
make over to science all interest in the external world nor deny
to science all interest in the spiritual life of mankind. Not a
little of what I believe about the world of nature I know only
from the Christian revelation, and not a little of what I believe
about the soul's response to God I have learned only from the

---

[1] Eng. trans., 1953.   [2] Scribners, New York (1958).

scientific approach to it—through the application to our religious experience of the purely empirical, observational, inductive and even statistical methods on which science relies, and of which psycho-pathology is only one example.

I have contended that the two accounts do not contradict but rather complement one another, each being true in its own kind, but neither saying all that may truly be said. At the same time and on the other hand, it cannot be claimed that this happy relationship could be maintained between all the accounts that have ever been rendered in the name of faith and all those that have been rendered in the name of science. Many Christians in the past have understood their Christian commitment in such a way as to lead them to reject what seem the most assured results of physics and astronomy, or of biology and genetics. Perhaps even in our own day there were some who refused to believe that the earth was a sphere, and not the flat surface which the Biblical documents presuppose, until we were able to encircle it with a satellite of our own making! But no less have many scientists rendered such an account of the course of nature as could not possibly be squared with the Christian view of God's active presence in and control over his world. They have defended a rigidly determinist view of efficient causation which conceived every event in nature and human history throughout the whole course of time, past and future, as being predetermined by natural necessity, as that all that happens *has* to happen precisely as it does, there never being at any point open alternatives either one of which the course of things may follow. This would quite evidently mean that the whole later sequence of events, every turn taken by human history, and any no matter how trifling incident within it, were already latent in, and inflexibly predetermined by the earliest form of existent being, whether conceived as a vast gaseous nebula or as an active electrical field or as what you will. It will be remembered how Laplace contended that if what he called a Perfect Calculator could be made acquainted with (a) the exact state of things either at the first moment of time or at any given later moment, and (b) the immutable laws of nature, he could work out with complete certainty and in minutest detail the exact state of things either at any past or at any future moment of history. As lately as my own student days there were not a few who still preached that doctrine, and I think there are some even now. Such a doctrine clearly excludes the possibility of any divine control over, or providential guidance of, the historical sequence of events, while at the same time it as clearly excludes any freedom of action on man's part. At the best God could then be conceived as the original framer of the laws of nature and at the same time the original creator of the primeval nebula or electrical field or subatomic units of being, but as afterwards leaving things to look after themselves in his absence—or in his presence only as a spectator; and similarly man could at best be regarded as a being who had no power to modify, but was only passively conscious of, what was happening to him. Perhaps, indeed, there was an occasional theologian who was not too much disturbed by this result, finding it not very dissimilar to his own version of the Christian doctrine of predestination, which denied all liberty to the human will and conceived all that has happened or will happen in history as having been immutably ordained and planned by God 'before the foundation of the world'.

Fortunately, however, it is a very different picture of things which the scientists are now presenting to us. A way of escape from the awkward corner into which the old classical mechanics seemed to be shepherding us has been provided by the advent of the new quantum mechanics. When Arthur Stanley Eddington delivered his Gifford Lectures in the University of Edinburgh in 1927 on *The Nature of the Physical World*, the account he gave of it was startlingly different from what had been offered to me in these same halls some fifteen or twenty years before, and when the lectures appeared in book form in 1928, the first chapter bore the title 'The Downfall of Classical Physics'. We were now introduced to what he called the 'random element' in nature, it being explained that the observable uniformities represent only averages taken over vast numbers of instances, there being no evidence of a similar uniformity in the behaviour of the individual entities which contribute to that average. The familiar laws of nature are thus of a statistical kind and, like other statistics, yield no more than probable results. Our city registrar can present us with an uncannily accurate forecast of the number of citizens who will marry in the course of next year, but (a) each individual citizen believes himself quite free to marry or not as he chooses and we can discover no law of nature to indicate that his belief is illusory, and (b) the registrar's estimate of the gross number of marriages can never be more than approximate. Similarly, if we pour white sand into one section of a container and red sand into another and then, after removing the partition, shake the whole well together, we can count on soon obtaining a fairly equal distribution, it being highly unlikely that the original clear division will ever again be restored after no matter how many further shakings, while obviously the larger the amount of sand with which we are dealing, the more unlikely does this chance become. That means that even if the movements of the individual grains of sand are controlled by no uniform law of nature but are quite random, we can still count for most practical purposes on the uniformity of the result. Eddington indeed writes that 'when numbers are large, chance is the best warrant of certainty',[1] yet on his own showing he should have written 'probability', not 'certainty'. Of course when we are dealing, not with relatively macrocosmic entities like grains of sand, but with the microcosmic ultimate constituents of nature such as electrons, we have to do with such unimaginably vast numbers that the chance of the expected or predicted result being disappointed, though it cannot be theoretically excluded, is virtually zero.

When Eddington began the delivery of his lectures, there were still many physicists (and I understand there still remain a few) who were convinced that although no principle of uniformity has yet been discovered which regulates the behaviour of sub-atomic entities, such a principle does exist

[1] *The Nature of the Physical World* (1928), p. 72.

and may one day come to light. They had no empirical justification for such a conviction, but it was to them a matter of
what might be called scientific faith. Yet in that same year of
1927, and before the last lecture was delivered, Heisenberg
enunciated his celebrated 'principle of indeterminacy', the
effect of which, if it were accepted as true, was to shatter that
faith. It was at once so accepted by Eddington, and in one of
the last of his lectures, as in his published volume, he states
the gist of it in the brief formula: 'A particle may have position
or it may have velocity but it cannot in any exact sense have
both.'[1] That is to say, the more accurately we are able to
determine the precise position of a particle, the less accurately
can we determine its momentum; and if we could reduce the
error in either computation to zero, the error in the other
computation would be infinitely large. Thus the indeterminacy
does not arise from our ignorance and lack of information, but
is, in Eddington's words 'a symbol for causal failure—an indeterminacy of behaviour which is part of the atom itself';[2]
and just because the future behaviour of the microcosmic
constituents of nature are thus unpredictable, not merely in
practice but in theory, no more than probable predictions
could conceivably be made of the future course of macroscopic
nature. As Dr Pollard, who is both an Anglican priest and
Executive Director of the Oak Ridge Institute of Nuclear
Studies, has written in his book already referred to:

Thus Laplace's demon, no matter how clever he might have been,
could not even have begun his calculations. If we gave him the
exact position of every particle in the universe at a given moment,
neither he nor we could have any information at all about their
velocities, and vice versa. The Heisenberg indeterminacy principle
strikes at the very root of the determinism of classical mechanics
and undermines its very foundations.[3]

Eddington in his lectures expressed this in the following way. It
might seem, he said, that if we could accurately determine the successive positions of a particle in two successive moments, we could
then accurately compute the velocity at which it was travelling.

---

[1] Op. cit., p. 220.   [2] Ibid., p. 306.   [3] *Chance and Providence*, p. 53.

This velocity, however, is of no use for prediction, because in making the second accurate determination of position we have rough-handled the particle so much that it is no longer the velocity we calculated. *It is a purely retrospective velocity.* The velocity does not exist in the present tense but in the future perfect; it never exists, it never will exist, but a time may come when it *will have existed.* . . . The velocity which we attribute to a particle now can be regarded as an anticipation of its future positions. To say that it is unknowable (except with a certain degree of inaccuracy) is to say that the future *cannot* be anticipated. Immediately the future is accomplished, the velocity becomes knowable.

The classical view that a particle has a definite (but not necessarily knowable) velocity now, amounts to disguising a piece of the unknown future as an unknowable element of the present. Classical physics foists a deterministic scheme on us by a trick; it smuggles the unknown future into the present, trusting that we shall not press an inquiry as to whether it has become any more knowable that way.[1]

The reason why, for my layman's account of the changed picture of the natural world which began to be offered us by the physicists so soon after my own student days, I have followed the argument of Eddington's lectures, in spite of a generation having passed since they were delivered, is that it was from these and from other books, of a semi-popular kind but written for our instruction by equally distinguished physicists, that I myself found escape from the determinism by which my student days were haunted. But of course I would not have so followed them, were it not that, so far as I can gather from more recent works of like authority, the parts of Eddington's argument on which I have relied would still find acceptance among the vast majority of his successors in the present generation who would, I think, agree that the future course of events is indeterminate. It is indeterminate until it has happened, when of course it will no longer be future but past. It is the past alone that is immutable, but occurrences that are now past were not immutable while they still lay in the future. They did not need to happen as they did, but we now know that they happened just so and not otherwise, and to a retrospective

[1] Op. cit., p. 307 f.

vision it may often be clear *why* they did so. We can often, with a reasonable degree of confidence, assign their causes, for the old principle that 'every event has a cause' still holds good in the realm of macrocosmic events—the world of gross reality and large numbers—however much the physicists may have to say about the non-caused character of the microcosmic field; but when these events still lay in the future there were alternative causes that might have produced different events in their stead. The choice between the alternatives—if I may for the moment speak of choice without insisting on giving it more than a metaphorical meaning—was an open one until it was made.

§ 49

Needless to say, this new scientific conception of the physical universe offers no more positive evidence of the presence of God in the world or of his providential ordering of it than did the older one. What it does do is to leave more room for these things, if they can be established on other grounds. I found myself quite unable to escape from the sense of God's presence with me in mercy and judgement even in those days when I could see as little escape from the deterministic strait-jacket within which the scientists were then trying to constrict me, but I could not then conceive how the two could possibly be harmoniously entertained within a single total outlook, and I suffered much from the resulting intellectual schism. All that the new physics has done for me is to relieve me of this particular distress. Contradiction has been turned into complementarity, it being on the basis of the Heisenberg principle of indeterminacy that the further principle of Complementarity was first formulated by Professor Bohr.

Providence literally means foresight. It was a technical term of the Stoic philosophy, a translation into Latin of the original Greek word πρόνοια (which rather means foreknowledge, but the meaning is the same). The Stoics, however, always used the word in the fuller sense of what Plato had already spoken of as the *care* (ἐπιμέλεια) exercised by God over the world and its inhabitants, and it is thus that it has ever since been understood. It is not itself a Biblical term, but the thought it represents, namely God's love and care for his people, dominates the Bible in every part. It is probably a pity that so impersonal-sounding a word has been frequently used in Christian circles as a proper name (as indeed it had been used by the Greeks for the goddess Athene); for this has sometimes led to its being vulgarly conceived as an impersonal power in some sense distinct from God, as by the farmer who, when annoyed by the bad weather, was heard to exclaim, 'It's that there dratted providence once again, but there's One above as'll see justice done.'

The Christian doctrine of providence teaches that the whole of history stands under an ultimate divine control. This does not mean that the Christian is able to trace the working of God's hand in it all, but that he can trace it in some events which have become what we have called paradigmatic for him, having what Whitehead called an 'elucidatory power' which casts light on all the rest. Nor does it mean that all that happens is the result of God's direct ruling, so that no room would be left for the free action of his creatures, but rather that he can and does so 'over-rule' these as to make them subservient to his own ultimate purpose.

> Oh yet we hope that somehow good
> Will be the final goal of ill.[1]

As Joseph said to his brethren, 'As for you, you thought evil against me; but God meant it for good, to bring to pass, as it is this day, to save much people alive.'[2] Or even, as the Church has been bold enough to sing in its office for Easter Eve, '*O felix culpa, quae tantum et talem meruit habere Redemptorem!*' If God 'maketh the wrath of man to praise him',[3] it is not by ruling it but by overruling it. God has something to do with all that is done in his world, though assuredly much is done that is not in accord with his will. This may sound to some mysterious

---

[1] Tennyson, *In Memoriam*, Canto liii.   [2] Gen. 50. 20.   [3] See Psalm 76. 10.

doctrine, yet if things did not stand thus, it is difficult to see how God could be in ultimate control of any event, since even his most cherished designs might be frustrated by some one thing in his universe that was wholly outside his control.

It is thus in the measure of indeterminacy now confessed by the physicists to be characteristic of the world of nature that we have found room, without too difficult an intellectual schism, for our belief in the operation of divine providence. We can now believe, without developing a bad scientific conscience, that not everything is ruled by natural necessity but that there is an element of chance or of 'random action' in the natural world. Chance sounds like the precise opposite of providence. I remember being told in my early youth—it was a favourite saying of my mother's—that 'Luck, fortune and chance are the devil's trinity', and I was frequently reproved for uttering such words. I was ready to accept the reproof, and I still believe that for the eye of faith there is no such thing as chance; yet, paradoxically enough, I find this faith made easier for me when I am allowed to believe that there is such a thing as chance for the eye of physical science. What science, from its limited point of view, rightly regards as 'random events' which might not have happened as they did, and which could not be predicted in advance except as possibilities or probabilities, faith regards as under either the ordering or the overruling of God's providence, believing with Alexander Pope that:

> All nature is but art unknown to thee.
> All chance direction which thou canst not see.[1]

Chance and Providence is the title of Dr Pollard's book, and from it I now quote the following:

The Christian sees the chances and accidents of history as the very warp and woof of the fabric of providence which God is ever weaving.[2]

Let us start with the Biblical idea of providence in all its fulness and inquire into what kind of a world we must have and what conditions must be satisfied in order to make this idea valid. When

---

[1] *An Essay on Man*, Epistle i, ll. 284 f.   [2] Op. cit., p. 71.

the question is put in this way, we see immediately that it must be a world which is so constituted that its history has at any moment many possibilities open to it. Only in such a world could the course of events be continuously responsible to the will of its Creator.[1]

There are two primary sources of indeterminacy in history. One of these is chance. When we speak of chance as a factor in history, we have in mind the experience, as a typical feature of natural processes, of alternative responses to a given act of causative influences for which the laws of nature specify only the relative probabilities. Insofar as alternatives are typical of all rational processes, chance becomes a universal ingredient of history. But there is another equally important source of indeterminism in history. This is accident. The accidental as used here in connection with the nature of history refers to situations in which two or more chains of events which have no causal connection with each other coincide in such a way as to decide the course of events. The accidental does not depend on the presence of choice and alternative in natural phenomena. Two chains of events could each be rigorously determined within themselves and yet be such that their accidental convergence would decisively modify the course of history. . . . Accident and chance are similar in their effects on history, but they are nevertheless independent and quite separate factors.[2]

I doubt, however, whether the two are so entirely separate as is here implied. A strict determinist would say that a coincidence of two events is no more accidental or indeterminate or theoretically unpredictable than the occurrence of each event separately regarded, since both alike follow necessarily from the same primordial state of the material world. But I am glad that Dr Pollard has drawn our attention to the coincidental element in the course of nature, as indeed Eddington had done when he wrote that 'There are such things as chance coincidences; that is to say, chance can deceive us by bringing about conditions that look very unlike chance. In particular chance might imitate organization, whereas we have taken chance to be the antithesis of organization or, as we have called it, the "random element".'[3] For I should hold that, while from the necessarily and justifiably restricted perspective of natural

[1] Ibid., p. 72 f. [2] Ibid., p. 73 f.
[3] *The Nature of the Physical World*, p. 71.

science chance seems to *imitate* organization, it will be apprehended from faith's wider perspective as being *in fact* organization—part of the organization of divine providence. I have already said that, if we believe in providence at all, we must think of it as extending to even the most apparently trivial occurrences, and in an earlier section I quoted Plato's remark that he would be a bad pilot who gave thought only to the big rocks and not at all to the small ones. The Christian view of the matter is quite clear. 'Are not two sparrows sold for a farthing? And one of them shall not fall to the ground without your Father. But the very hairs of your head are all numbered. Fear ye not therefore, ye are of more value than many sparrows.'[1]

Coincidence is defined in the Concise Oxford Dictionary as the 'notable concurrence of events or circumstances without apparent causal connexion'. Men often speak of such concurrences as 'mere' coincidences, implying that they refuse to regard them in any other light than that of chance, and therefore dismissing them from their minds as of no serious significance. But just as the Christian will not regard any event as 'mere' chance, so he will be on his guard against regarding any concurrence of events as 'mere' coincidence, and often he will find himself saying, 'This is the Lord's doing: it is marvellous in our eyes.'[2]

I shall offer two examples which I select just because the occurrences to which they refer are of the kind which would commonly be dismissed as trivial.

I am a bridge-player, and one winter when I played fairly regularly, I grew so keen to win that I allowed my equanimity to be disturbed, and sometimes even my temper to be frayed, when the cards were against me. Then I had a long run of what would be called quite phenomenal bad luck, so extreme and so persistent over many months that I was tempted to say the devil was in it. Will it surprise you to hear that suddenly it came to me that God was in it? That run of bad luck was good for me. I learned something from it, and I hope that by

---

[1] Matt. 10. 29–31.   [2] Psalm 118. 23.

God's grace I was thereby enabled in some measure to amend my ways in this little matter. But if I learned my lesson, it was because God meant me to learn it, because it was a lesson he was minded to teach me. If the hairs of my head are all numbered, then why not also the cards in my hand?

My other example is of a London business man who lived in a suburb but travelled into the city by the same early train every week-day morning. He was in the habit of saying his prayers before breakfast, and one morning his prayer was that God would grant him certain much-needed graces and very particularly the grace of patience. Unfortunately he lingered a little too long over his breakfast, or else his train was running a little ahead of schedule, so that when he reached the suburban station it was only to see the red tail-light disappearing at the far end of the platform. He turned round in disgust and occupied the ten minutes before the arrival of the next train by stamping angrily up and down the platform to the no small annoyance of more than one other prospective passenger with whom he forcibly collided. Then just as the second train came in, he realized that his enforced wait had been God's answer to his prayer: for how should God teach him patience unless by providing him with some opportunity of exercising it? But he had frittered away his opportunity and had not learned his lesson.

Trivial, we may say; but in God's eyes nothing is trivial. Moreover, the principle is the same as we should have to apply to the great events which determine the destinies of nations, some of which have turned, as the historians are fond of telling us, even upon a freak of the weather, such as the southerly gale that blew up the English Channel on August 9, 1588 bringing to an end the long dominance of Spain. Or we may take from the same period as the Armada another example of a 'lucky' conjunction of circumstances in the following passage from Professor G. M. Trevelyan's *English Social History*:

To remote posterity the memorable fact about Elizabethan England will be that it produced the plays of Shakespeare. It is not merely that the greatest of mankind happened to be born in that age. His work would never have been produced in any other period than these late Elizabethan and early Jacobean times in which it was his luck to live. He could not have written as he did if the men and women among whom his days were passed, had been other than they were in habits of thought, life and speech, or if the London Theatre in the years just after the Armada had not reached a certain stage of development, ready to his shaping hand.[1]

Thus we are again reminded of Plato's argument that it would be impossible to think of God as controlling the large-scale march of history if we believed him to be neglectful of even the pettiest happenings (τὰ μικρότατα) in his world.[2]

[1] Op. cit., p. 201 f.   [2] Laws, X, 901.

CHAPTER XII

Grace and Gratitude

§ 50

We have spoken of faith as our human response to God's approach, but now something more falls to be said both about the manner of the approach and about the manner of the response. God comes to us both in judgement and in mercy, and this double approach evokes in us the double response of fear and love. 'There is', we are told, 'no fear in love; but perfect love casteth out fear. . . . He that feareth is not made perfect in love.'[1] Yet we being what we are, there cannot be love unless there has first been fear. As men who 'have sinned and come short of the glory of God',[2] we cannot know him as mercy until we have first known him as judgement, nor as love until we have first known him as wrath. Yet this does not mean that God himself is first wrathful and then loving. Rather in the words of our Scottish paraphrase:

> He lov'd us from the first of time,
> He loves us to the last.[3]

The Bible can say 'God is love',[4] but it could not say 'God is wrath.' For his wrath is but the shadow cast by his love when his love is rejected, and his judgement but the misery men make for themselves when his mercy is refused. Thus our Lord according to the Fourth Gospel could say 'For judgement I am come into this world',[5] but at the same time 'God sent not his Son to judge the world; but that the world through him might be saved',[6] and again, 'I came not to judge the world but to save the world.'[7] Furthermore he could say, 'The

---

[1] 1 John 4. 18; Compare 2 Tim. 1. 7, 'For God has not given us a spirit of fear, but of power and love and good judgement.'

[2] Rom. 3. 23.   [3] Paraphrase 48.   [4] 1 John 4. 8, 16.

[5] John 9. 39.   [6] John 3. 17.   [7] John 12. 47.

Father judges no man but has committed all judgement to the Son'[1]; yet at the same time, 'I judge no man.'[2] We may ask, whence then does judgement come? But we have the answer, 'This is the judgement, that light is come into the world, and men loved darkness rather than light, because their deeds were evil.'[3] There is a sense, then, in which men judge themselves. 'He that believeth not is judged already';[4] and on this passage Archbishop William Temple comments, 'They loved darkness rather than light. That is their choice; there is nothing worse that can be done to them after that.'[5] Such is the solemn situation in which men have been placed by the love of God. He did not need to hate them in order that they should stand in fear before him; it was enough that he should love them, and *so* love them as to send his Son into their world to die for their sakes.

It would seem that fear of the gods is a universal element in all religions. Yet this is not because the gods were thought oj either as evil or as ill-disposed towards men. As Lewis Farnell declared in his Gifford Lectures on *The Attributes of God*,

It is difficult to sum up the multifarious evidence concerning the savage mind; but generally it is near to the truth to say that for the most savage communities the belief is attested in a good or kindly God or spirit . . .

And further,

It is a fact of great significance that the history of religions nowhere presents us with the phenomena of a High God conceived as malevolent and definitely accepted by the worshipper as such.[6]

The ground of fear lay rather in men's consciousness of their own guilt by which they had offended their gods, who would therefore withhold the blessings at their disposal and visit men instead by fearful punishments. Thus in their worship there was less adoration and thanksgiving for benefits received than of petition accompanied by propitiatory offerings. The

[1] John 5. 22.   [2] John 7. 15.   [3] John 3. 19.   [4] John 3. 18.
[5] *Readings in St. John's Gospel*, First Series, p. 51.
[6] Op. cit., p. 164 f.

propitiation of the gods may indeed be said to be the *Leitmotiv* of world religion. That fine scholar and my former teacher, the late Professor A. W. Mair, has written that, if we leave out of account 'some rare and sporadic utterances of the more enlightened thinkers and confine ourselves to the typical Greek conception of worship', we find that

Man worships his god or gods not because he has any lively feeling of gratitude for blessings experienced, still less because he desires to live a better life, but because he has an overwhelming conviction of his dependence on his god or gods for all temporal blessings.[1]

Again, in another article,

It would not be true to say that the Greek prayer was never a prayer of thanksgiving. . . . But it is undoubtedly true that prayer in general, as we find it in the Greek authors, is essentially a petition for blessings of a utilitarian kind—health and wealth, children, success in business and in battle.[2]

When we pass to the religion of the Bible, we find that the Old Testament is full of petitions for these same temporal blessings, but by far the greater weight of supplication now falls upon the desire for spiritual blessings—upon prayers for divine forgiveness following upon confession of sin, prayers for the restoration of an affectionate relationship between God and man, prayers for moral renewal by God's cleansing of the heart. But above all Israelite worship, as we know it from the Book of Psalms, is dominated by the note of praise and thanksgiving. 'O give thanks unto the Lord, for he is good: for his mercy endureth forever. . . . Oh that men would praise the Lord for his goodness, and for his wonderful works to the children of men!'[3] The note of fear remains, as it must do while man himself remains a sinner in the presence of the all-holy God, but because the worshipper approaches God in penitence and knows that God is ready to forgive, not rewarding him according to his iniquities, such fear is transfigured by its never-failing accompaniment of love and praise. As one psalm

[1] *Encyclopaedia of Religion and Ethics* Article 'Worship (Greek)'.
[2] Ibid., Article 'Prayer (Greek)'.
[3] Psalm 107. 1, 8.

has it, 'The fear of the Lord is the beginning of wisdom', but 'his praise endureth for ever'.[1] And if this should seem to contradict the New Testament declaration that there is no fear in love, we need only remind ourselves that when the Old Testament speaks of the fear of the Lord, the emotion referred to is almost always awe or reverence rather than terror.

In the New Testament also we are encouraged to pray for temporal blessings. Jesus 'spake a parable unto them to this end, that men ought always to pray, and not to lose heart'.[2] And St Paul wrote to the Philippians, 'Have no anxiety about anything, but in everything by prayer and supplication with thanksgiving let your requests be made known unto God.'[3] We must keep nothing back from God, but must share all our desires with him, and if we *are* troubled by the lack of food or drink or raiment, we must share these troubles with him too. But in the first place our Lord enjoins us not to be troubled about these things, but to set our minds rather upon our spiritual needs and the provision of spiritual blessings, and leave the rest to God.

Therefore take no thought, saying, What shall we eat? or, What shall we drink? or, Wherewithal shall we be clothed? (For after all these things do the Gentiles ask:) for your heavenly Father knoweth that ye have need of all these things. But seek ye first the Kingdom of God and his righteousness; and all these things shall be added unto you.[4]

And in the second place, there is in the New Testament the constant implication that our desire for material well-being should always be in the service of our desire for spiritual well-being. This indeed is something on which Socrates had already strongly insisted. 'For the sake of the soul' ($\tau \hat{\eta} s \ \psi v \chi \hat{\eta} s \ \check{\epsilon} \nu \epsilon \kappa a$) was his constant watchword. In his speech of defence at his trial, as written up afterwards by Plato, he declares that his only offence was his habit of confronting everyone he met with the question whether, by caring so much for riches and honours and reputation and so little for wisdom and truth and the bettering of their souls, they were not in fact placing the higher

---

[1] Psalm 111. 10.   [2] Luke 18. 1.   [3] Phil. 4. 6. R.S.V.   [4] Matt. 6. 31–33.

value on what is of less account and lower value on the most important things of all. But, he goes on,

I am convinced that God has commissioned me to do this very thing, and I believe that no better piece of fortune has ever befallen you in Athens than this my enlistment in the service of God. I have indeed no other business in life than to go about persuading you all, young and old, to care less for your bodies and your possessions and to make the protection of your souls your chief concern; and telling you that goodness does not come from possessions, but that goodness alone makes possessions or anything else worth having, whether in public or in private life.[1]

And in the *Republic* Plato makes Socrates say that even the practice of gymnastics should be ultimately 'for the sake of the soul'.[2] All this is nobly spoken, but in the New Testament there is the further thought that God will provide for those who are called to serve him in the world *just such lesser necessities as they require for the faithful fulfilment of their calling.* He will care for our wants if we are intent on doing his will. 'Seek ye first the Kingdom of God and his righteousness; and all these things shall be added unto you.'[3]

In the Bible the two concepts of worship and service are a single concept. The Greek words for service (*latreia* or *leitourgia*) are also the Greek words for worship. When we speak of worship nowadays we think first of going to church, and when we speak of service we think first of going out into action in God's world. But that this dichotomy is a modern one is still evidenced among us by the fact that we at the same time retain from the older tradition the habit of speaking of our acts of worship as 'divine service', 'morning and evening service', *Gottesdienst* and so on; as well as by the fact that we speak of the form of our worship as the liturgy (*leitourgia*). This word was originally applied to any form of public service or office in the State; St Paul himself speaks of the rulers of the State as 'God's liturgists' ($\lambda\epsilon\iota\tau\text{o}\upsilon\rho\gamma\text{o}\grave{\iota}$ $\theta\epsilon\text{o}\hat{\upsilon}$),[4] and he uses the word also for works of Christian beneficence and charity.[5] Hence, if we do persist in our differentiated modern

[1] Plato, *Apology*, 30.　　[2] *Republic*, 410.　　[3] Matt. 6. 33.　　[4] Rom. 13. 6.
[5] 2 Cor. 9. 12; Phil. 2. 17, 30.

usage, we must at the same time remind ourselves that our worship of God is part of his service and our service of his worship.

§ 51

I have felt these few explanations and reminders to be a necessary preamble to the point I am principally desirous of making, namely, that gratitude is not only the dominant note in Christian piety but equally the dominant motive of Christian action in the world. Such gratitude is for the grace that has been shown us by God, and again it is significant that gratitude and grace are hardly more than two forms of the same Latin word. Very often when I am present at a luncheon or dinner party, and especially when I am the only ordained minister of religion in the company, I am given a certain duty to perform, but in calling upon me my hosts do not always use the same words. Sometimes it is 'Will you say grace?', sometimes 'Will you return thanks?', and sometimes 'Will you ask a blessing?' This variation of phrase, usually with little or no variation of intended meaning, indicates the close relationship between the three concepts of thankfulness, grace and blessing.

In classical Latin there is of course no such word as *gratitude*, the simple *gratia* having to do duty for thankfulness as well as for grace; and in the Greek of the New Testament there is only the one word *charis* which in our English versions has to be rendered in some contexts as 'grace' and in others as 'thanks'. This may seem confusing, and indeed our translators frequently disagree as to which word to use in a particular passage;[1] but in fact it is illuminating as pointing to the close connexion between the two meanings—between the spring of God's action towards us and the spring of our response to him. Again our words 'thank' and 'bless' very often translate the same word in the Hebrew of the Old Testament (*barak*). And when Psalms 103 and 104 have 'Bless the Lord, O my soul', and the three

---

[1] E.g., Heb. 12. 28, where the A.V. has 'let us have grace', and the R.S.V. 'let us be grateful'.

following have 'O give thanks unto the Lord', the meaning is the same, though in the latter cases another word is used (*yadah*).

But though the single word *charis* has to do duty not only for grace but also for thanks, there is another New Testament word formed from the same root but slightly different in meaning and usage, so that it appears in our English versions as 'thanksgiving' rather than 'thanks'. This is the word *eucharistia*, so familiar to us as the name of the central act of Christian worship, the Eucharist. 'The Lord Jesus the same night in which he was betrayed took bread: and when he had given thanks, he brake it . . .'[1] Here the phrase 'when he had given thanks' represents only a single word in the Greek original, the word *eucharistēsas*. Thus the central rite of the Christian liturgy is a rite of gratitude. It is also a rite and liturgy of remembrance, for our Lord went on to say, 'This do in remembrance of me.'[2] But we remember in order to give thanks, as is already made plain in the Old Testament where it is in psalms of thanksgiving that we come upon such declarations as 'I will remember the works of the Lord.' And what is thus true of the Christian worship is also true of the whole Christian life. It is a life of remembrance which issues in thanksgiving. A true Christian is a man who never for a moment forgets what God has done for him in Christ, and whose whole comportment and whole activity have their root in the sentiment of gratitude.

There is nothing of which I am more firmly persuaded than that this is the right attitude to life. It is precisely in regard to such a conviction as this that I feel able to speak of certitude, and to do so without the least scruple or diffidence. Our natural tendency is to take the good things of life for granted, but to grumble when things do not fall out as we would wish. That is because we set out from a complacent view of our own worthiness, our own deserts. But the beginning of wisdom is to realize that such a view is without any foundation in reality. I am reminded of a conversation which I had many years ago

[1] 1 Cor. 11. 23.   [2] 1 Cor. 11. 24.

with a certain excellent lady in America who came to see me to say that she had entirely lost the Christian faith in which she had been brought up. She could, she said, no longer accept any of the comforting beliefs on which Christians so confidently leaned; and then I remember the very words that followed: 'It seems to me that we mortals have no claim on the universe. We have no right to expect anything. We cannot say that we deserve anything.' Well, I thought how exactly right she was. To think like that is not yet to be a Christian, but it is to have a mind open to Christian truth. To have surrendered our own claim to a good thing is to be ready to recognize it as a free gift if and when it comes.

If we did but keep steadily in mind what surely in the bottom of our hearts we all know to be true, that we deserve nothing at all, perhaps we should never grumble again but, as time went on, find more and more for which to be thankful. 'If I look rightly into myself', says Thomas à Kempis, 'I cannot say that any creature hath ever done me wrong, and therefore I cannot justly complain before Thee.'[1] Perhaps we would even find cause for gratitude in *everything* that happens to us, so obeying the apostolic injunction, 'In everything give thanks (ἐν παντὶ εὐχαριστεῖτε): for this is the will of God in Christ Jesus.'[2] The perfection of Christian saintliness is that we should be enabled to thank God even for the worst troubles that come to us, including death, realizing that their ultimate purpose is to bring us closer to himself, and that without them we cannot be made perfect. 'Praised be my Lord', said St Francis, 'for our sister, the death of the body.' I believe that nothing more reveals our shortcoming in this matter than the fact that our prayers of petition always outnumber our prayers of thanksgiving: and here I am thinking not of the prayers we say in church, when the liturgy we use preserves the proper balance for us, but of all the unformulated impulses of petition that rise up in our minds in the course of daily life. If ever, for example, I have any serious fears for my health or for the health of someone dear to me, if I am confronted with some sudden

---

[1] *Imitatio* Bk. III, ch. XLI.   [2] I Thess. 5. 18.

danger, as of accident, or if some long-cherished plan looks like miscarrying, such an impulse always declares itself. Indeed a familiar rhyme goes so far as to say that

> When the devil was ill, the devil a saint would be;
> When the devil was well, the devil a saint was he.

But however that may be, I wonder whether something like this is not an almost universal experience among us humans, so that Arthur Hugh Clough was not going too far when he wrote that

> . . . Almost every one when age,
> Disease or sorrows strike him,
> Inclines to think there is a God,
> Or something very like Him.[1]

Yet I know that in my own case, if the imagined danger disappears, as it usually has done (or I would not be here today), I incline only to think how absurd were my fears and to banish the whole little episode from my mind with a shrug of relief. How often I forget to follow up my petition with thanksgiving! Nine times out of ten do I forget; thus justifying Christ's question, 'Were there not ten cleansed? but where are the nine?'[2]

In this as in other things our Lord himself has given us the perfect paradigm. His whole demeanour was one of thanksgiving to the Father, just as before partaking of the last meal he ate on earth, εὐχαριστήσεν—he gave thanks. Here he was following the invariable and prescribed custom of his own Jewish people, but at the same time foreshadowing the solemn Christian rite. The tract *Berakoth* (blessings) in The Talmud says, 'It is forbidden to taste of this world without saying a blessing: only the unfaithful do so.' No less full of thanksgiving are the letters of St Paul, who sometimes finds the most surprising occasions for it. Canon T. R. Milford, for instance, has drawn our attention to the fact that the Apostle can hardly

---

[1] *Dipsychus.*

[2] Luke 17. 17. Compare Karl Barth, *Church Dogmatics*, Vol. IV, Part I, Eng. trans., pp. 139–141. 'Man's sin is not merely one of disobedience to law, but one of ingratitude to grace . . . Radically and basically all sin is simply ingratitude.'

begin a letter without thanking God for his correspondents. The exceptions are Galatians and Second Corinthians, and 'To receive a letter from St Paul which did not somewhere near the beginning thank God for your existence, your conversion and your faith was a sure sign that you were in disgrace.'[1]

When, following our Lord's example, we give thanks before the breaking of the bread at the Eucharist, we are in the first place giving thanks for the bread itself. Like him we are saying a grace before meat, for it is likely that the words he used were those on which he had been brought up. 'Blessed be thou, Lord God, eternal King, who bringest forth bread from the earth.' Here I am reminded, though quite incidentally, of having in my student days listened to a sermon by that prince of Scottish preachers who was then Principal of my own college, Dr Alexander Whyte, in which he declared that there was no more significant difference between a man and a brute beast than that, while dogs and pigs attacked the food presented to them with greedy and unreflecting taste, human beings will often be observed to bend their heads for a moment before setting to, and that in that little inhibition, that moment of pause, our sole human dignity resided.

But of course in the prayer of thanksgiving before the Fraction in our service of Holy Communion, we are expressing our gratitude not only for the food God provides for our bodily needs, but above all for the Bread of Life here symbolized and betokened, for the great salvation that has come to us all through the breaking of the Bread that was our Lord's Body. All other blessings are seen in the context of this supreme blessing, and all other thanksgivings are contained in this central eucharistic action; as in the words of our General Thanksgiving, 'We bless Thee for our creation, preservation, and all the blessings of this life: but above all, for Thine inestimable love in the redemption of the world through our Lord Jesus Christ.' Nor must it be forgotten that our prayer

---

[1] *Foolishness to the Greeks* (1953), p. 97; a little book from which I have borrowed more than this.

is said in the full realization that Christ is there with us as we pray. It is an act of grateful recognition of his real and personal presence in our midst.

§ 52

I have now sufficiently insisted that gratitude is the dominant emotion in the heart of a right-minded man in measure as he realizes that grace has been shown him, as in our Lord's words, 'To whom little is forgiven, the same loveth little';[1] and that this emotion is the dominant one in all true Christian worship. But now I wish to dwell on the further point that it is likewise the dominant emotion inspiring Christian action in the world. Emotion that exhausts itself in mere feeling and contains no impulse to overt doing is not only sterile but ultimately insincere. As we read in the First Epistle of John, 'My dear children, let us put our *agapē* not into words or into talk but into deeds, and make it real.'[2]

Such deeds, however, must not for a moment be understood as an attempt to repay God for what we owe to him. Rather must we remember our Lord's words, 'When ye shall have done all these things which are commanded you, say, We are unprofitable servants.'[3] Our best service is no more than a token, and even then it is not a token repayment, but only a token of gratitude. We must never try by anything we do to put ourselves right with God. 'It is God who puts us right',[4] says St Paul—for I think that is the best current English for his θεὸς ὁ δικαιῶν. We are, he says, 'put right gratis by his grace';[5] and it is out of the confidence that we are thus already right with him that our sense of gratitude is born. The Apostle has sometimes been misunderstood as disparaging 'works', but the truth is that he is continually urging us to their performance, while at the same time warning us against supposing that by performing them we can put ourselves right with God, justifying ourselves in his sight.

[1] Luke 7. 47.   [2] 1 John 3. 18: Moffatt's trans.   [3] Luke 17. 10.   [4] Rom. 8. 33.
[5] Rom. 3. 24: *gratis* being the exact (post-classical) Latin equivalent of St Paul's δωρεάν: compare Vulgate.

Two things the New Testament says with equal emphasis. The first is that men are not made saints (or, as we would say, Christians) by anything they themselves do. But the second is that it is nevertheless by what they do that Christians are recognized. 'Ye shall know them by their fruits', said Jesus with impressive reiteration, '. . . every sound tree bringeth forth good fruit: but a rotten tree bringeth forth bad fruit. A sound tree cannot bring forth bad fruit, neither can a rotten tree bring forth good fruit . . . Wherefore by their fruits ye shall know them.'[1] 'By this', writes St John, 'it may be seen who are the children of God, and who are the children of the devil: whoever does not do right is not of God, nor he who does not love his brother . . . We know that we have passed out of death into life, because we love the brethren.'[2] On the other hand, the good fruit by which the children of God are known, and which St John here identifies with *agapē*, extends to the motive as well as to the intention. It includes, as *agapē* always does in the New Testament, not only the overt action, but also the emotive impulse behind it. So St Paul says, 'If I distribute all that I possess, if I deliver my body to be burned, but have not *agapē*, it profits me not at all.'[3] The loveless deed has in it no healing power but rather increases the soul's sickness. Men can by their own efforts produce what overt actions they please, they may be led by a great variety of motives to imitate the deeds of love, but they cannot by their own efforts produce love in themselves; for, as St John again says, 'love is of God, and he who loves is born of God and knows God'.[4]

Thus we are led back to the first of the two emphases we distinguished in the New Testament, namely that we are saved, not by anything we ourselves can do, but only by the grace of God. 'By grace are ye saved through faith, and that not of yourselves: not of works, lest any man should boast. For we are his workmanship. . . .'[5] Salvation, we have said, means healing; and how often has the sick soul tried to heal

---

[1] Matt. 7. 16–20; Compare Matt. 12. 33.
[2] I John 3. 10, 14.
[3] I Cor. 13. 3.
[4] I John 4. 7.
[5] Eph. 2. 8–10.

itself by a feverish resort to action! To what desperate extremes have men gone, in all ages and in all parts of the world, to cure their spiritual sickness by deeds of self-denial, self-immolation, self-flagellation, as well as by almsgiving and deeds of munificence. Yet, psychologically regarded, no procedure could be more futile, since as our clinical psychologists so well understand, it leads not to healing but to a dangerous masking of the symptoms of the disease. It tackles the problem from the wrong end. The only authentic altruism is one that flows spontaneously from the heart that is already at peace with itself, and then only in the profounder sense in which being at peace with oneself is to be at peace with God. Acts of *askēsis* or of beneficence which spring from spiritual unease or (what is the same thing) from spiritual dis-ease, and which are performed with a view to self-relief and self-release, are necessarily tainted with that egocentricity—that state of being, in Martin Luther's oft-repeated phrase, *incurvatus in se*—which lies at the root of the very trouble from which we need to be delivered. Professor Tillich expresses this in his own more abstract way:

The principle that being precedes acting implies a basic criticism of the history of religion, as far as it is the history of man's attempts and failures to save himself . . . (Such religion) distorts what it has received and fails in what it tries to achieve. . . . Man, seeing what he ought to be, driven by the anxiety of losing himself, believing in his strength to actualize his essential being, disregarding the bondage of the will, tries to regain again what he has lost. But this situation of estrangement, in which the law becomes commandment, is just the situation in which the law cannot be fulfilled. . . .

As an element in the processes of life, asceticism is necessary; as an attempt at self-salvation, asceticism is a dangerous distortion and a failure.[1]

§ 53

Not only, however, does gratitude impel the Christian to act, but it at the same time provides guidance as to the particular course of action to be followed. What can we do for God in

[1] *Systematic Theology*, Vol. II (1957), pp. 80–83.

acknowledgement, still less in return, for what he has done for us? He stands in need of nothing that we can give. Nothing we can do can enhance his glory or add anything to his fulness, just as nothing we fail to do can diminish these. 'God doth not need, either man's work or His own gifts . . . His state is kingly.'[1] They were therefore natural enough questions that were put to the King by those on his right hand in Jesus' parable:

Lord, when did we see you hungry and fed you? Or thirsty and gave you drink? When did we see you a stranger and give you hospitality? Or naked and clothed you? When did we see you sick or in prison and visit you?[2]

The answer expected by a flat common sense could only be 'Never', but the King's answer was 'Inasmuch as you did it to one of the least of these my brethren, you did it to me.'[3] No more beautiful words have ever been spoken, nor have any others given us clearer direction as to what we are to do with ourselves in our passage through the world. They tell us that only in our service of our needy human brethren can our loving gratitude to God find outlet in action. God has, as it were, nominated these as his proxy, and what I would fain have given to him had he needed it, I must now give to them. It will be remembered that when in 1925 George Bernard Shaw was offered the Nobel Prize of some £8,000 in recognition of his literary eminence, he replied at once that while gratefully accepting the compliment he had no need of the money and would like it to be applied rather for the encouragement of other and younger writers who had not yet made their name and did need the money badly. It was as if he had said, 'Inasmuch as you give it to the least of these my literary brethren, you give it to me.' He nominated a definite class as his proxy, and Jesus did no less; but his nominations were (a) those who lack food or drink (b) those who are insufficiently clad, (c) strangers (or, as we might say today, displaced persons and refugees), (d) those who are sick (and there is no

---

[1] Milton, *On his Blindness.*   [2] Matt. 25. 37–39.   [3] Matt. 25. 40.

more authentically and originally Christian way of employing our time than going to see people when they are sick), (e) those who are in prison (and for us that would include the inmates of concentration camps). Elsewhere he adds (f) little children— 'Whosoever receives one such little child in my name, receives me.'[1] Nor does he allow any distinction between what is thus done to him the Son and what is done to God the Father: 'He who receives me receives him who sent me.'[2]

Thus nothing could be clearer than the intimate nature of the interconnexion between the two great injunctions in which our Lord summed up the whole duty of man—to love God with all our heart and mind and strength and to love our neighbours as ourselves. Without this interconnexion the Christian's love of God would be an exceedingly abstract and elusive thing. Many honest souls have been greatly troubled by asking themselves, 'Can I really say that I love God?' Spiritual counsellors are very familiar with this kind of distress, and the best of them will be found to say the same two things about it. We must, they say, tell ourselves first that it is not upon our feeling for God that our salvation depends but—and we may allow ourselves the expression—upon his feeling for us. I shall quote only one such counsellor, but a good one, the Abbé Henri de Tourville, who writes in one of his *Letters of Direction:*

You want to compete with His affection before you have understood it; that is your mistake. . . . Come then! show a little more deference to our Lord and allow Him to go first. Let Him love you a great deal before you have succeeded in loving Him even a little as you would wish to love Him. That is all I ask of you, and all that our Lord asks of you.[3]

But they say, second, that if we love our needy human brethren, we are *thereby already* loving God, even if, like those on the King's right hand, we do not know that we are doing so. Are the two things then the same thing? Had St Paul in mind to reduce the two great commandments to a single commandment when he wrote, 'Through love be servants to one another;

---

[1] Matt. 18. 5.   [2] Matt. 10. 40; John 13. 20.
[3] Op. cit., Eng. trans. by Lucy Menzies (1939), p. 78 ff.

for the whole law is fulfilled in one word—thou shalt love thy neighbour as thyself.'[1] I can perhaps, if I so desire, escape from so surprising a conclusion by contending that here he is thinking only of the law that governs interhuman relationships. Yet the writer of the article on *agapē* in Kittel's *Word Book of the New Testament*, than which it would be difficult to mention a more nearly unbiassed scholarly work of our time, says without hesitation that for St Paul 'the purpose of divine love is not that we should return love to God; . . . it is that he who is called should put himself in love and freedom at the service of his neighbour. . . . His main interest is in brotherly love'; and of St John he declares that in his mind, 'love to God or Christ takes second place after love to the brethren.' But no! I cannot allow the phrase 'takes second place after'; but would rather say that love to God and Christ *means in practice* love to the brethren, that only there can its reality and sincerity be tested; and this at least is much emphasized by the Johannine writings. The Gospel of John reports Jesus as having said:

By this shall all men know that you are my disciples, if you have love one to another.[2]

It is the same Gospel that gives us the incident in which Peter three times protested to Jesus, 'Lord, you know I love you', and three times Jesus would return no answer but 'Feed my lambs', 'Tend my sheep', 'Feed my sheep'.[3] The First Epistle of John makes the point with impressive reiteration:

If a man say, I love God, and hates his brother, he is a liar; for how can he who does not love his brother whom he has seen, love God whom he has not seen?[4]

Beloved, let us love one another . . . he that does not love does not know God.[5]

Nobody has ever seen God (but) if we love one another, God dwells within us, and his love is perfected in us.[6]

To these references we may add the declaration of the First Epistle to Timothy:

[1] Gal. 5. 13 f.   [2] John 13. 35.   [3] John 21. 15 ff.
[4] 1 John 4. 20.   [5] 1 John 4. 7.   [6] 1 John 4. 12.

If anyone does not provide for his relatives, he has disowned the faith and is worse than an unbeliever.[1]

And as to this last, perhaps there has never been a period in which there have been more Christians than there are now who show more love and considerateness for those who are far away than for those nearest to them—more, as we might say, to their far-boors than to their closest *nigh-boors* or neighbours.

'By this shall all men know that you are my disciples.' But likewise by this shall we ourselves know. Assurance of salvation, certainty of being right with God (of being δικαιωθείς) has been the object of much distressful heart-searching throughout Christian history—a fact as well known to clinical psychologists as to pastoral counsellors. Many different things have been said about it. There has been wide variation in the doctrines of assurance current in the various Christian communions and theological schools. But St John has his own clear word about it:

He who loves his brother lives in the light, and there is nothing in him to stumble at: but he who hates his brother is in darkness and walks in the dark.[2]

And we may complete a quotation already given in part, using in this case Moffatt's excellent rendering:

But whoever possesses this world's goods, and notices his brother in need, and shuts his heart against him, how can love to God remain in him? My dear children, let us put our love not into words or talk but into deeds and make it real. Thus it is that we may be sure we belong to the truth and reassure ourselves whenever our heart condemns us; for God is greater than the heart, and he knows all.[3]

One final point: The direction given by our sense of gratitude towards the particular source of action which the Christian is to follow is in one respect even more profoundly based than this. For it instructs and compels him to take God's conduct towards him as the specific paradigm of his own conduct towards his fellow men. And this not only in principle but also

---

[1] 1 Tim. 5. 8.   [2] 1 John 2. 10.   [3] 1 John 3. 17–20: Moffatt's trans.

in detail, the grace he has received reproducing itself in the grace he bestows.

Whoever claims to dwell in him should himself walk just as he walked.[1]
Freely ye have received, freely give.[2]
If I, your Lord and Master, have washed your feet, you should wash one another's feet; for I have given you this example, so that you should do just as I have done to you.[3]
Should you not show compassion to your fellow servants, just as I have had pity on you?[4]
Walk in love, just as Christ loved us and gave himself for us.[5]
Be kind to one another, tender-hearted, forgiving one another, just as God for Christ's sake has forgiven you.[6]

Such is the *imitatio Christi*.

§ 54

I have already said that the sentiment of gratitude towards deity is not a leading motive in world religion as a whole, its place being taken rather by efforts at propitiation; but it has certainly not been absent. I quoted A. W. Mair as saying that while ancient Greek worship betrayed little 'lively feeling of gratitude for blessings experienced', yet 'it would not be true to say that the Greek prayer was never a prayer of thanksgiving'. We remember also Dr Barth's appreciation of Amida-Buddhism as a religion of grace which dispenses with all attempts to propitiate the deity by good works or ritual observances, so that, as he says, 'calling on Amida loses the last remnant of the character of an achievement or a magical act. It becomes simply a sign of our thankfulness.'[7] In his book on *Religions of Mankind* the Roman Catholic Dr Otto Karrer quotes the following prayer from the circle of the Shantung monastery:

My heart is full of thanksgiving that it has been given me to learn the way of deliverance which Buddha has taught us. . . . 'Vouchsafe that my understanding may awake under thine enlightenment, that

---

[1] 1 John 2. 16.　　[2] Matt. 10. 8.　　[3] John 13. 14 f.　　[4] Matt. 18. 33.
[5] Eph. 5. 1.　　[6] Eph. 4. 32.　　[7] *Church Dogmatics*, II/2, Eng. trans., p. 341.

I may grow in spiritual insight and knowledge . . . that I may shew myself thankful for all the mercy shewn me. . . .'[1]

He quotes also the following from the confession of faith of one of the Japanese sects of Amida worshippers:

All other methods and works and every thought that I am able to help myself I reject, and with my entire heart I place my trust in this alone, that Amida Nyorai will vouchsafe me his aid for the life to come. . . . Convinced that even the first stirring of this confidence is a guarantee of his help in my daily needs I rejoice in the thought that henceforward my prayer will be rather a thanksgiving for his loving kindness. . . . Therefore will I also observe the commandments which he hath ordained all my life long.[2]

Dr Barth, as we saw, welcomes such sporadic professions of belief in divine grace and resultant human gratitude, but only as a warning to Christians that it is not these things as such that matter, but only the grace of God in Christ and our gratitude for that as manifest in the Christian's use of the name of Christ. I have sufficiently indicated that I cannot for a moment accept so strange and so grudging a view, preferring to believe that wherever men have been grateful for divine grace received, it is the fruit of the hidden working in their hearts and lives of the Holy Spirit of God in Christ, whose name they do not know.

Similarly, I should say that many of our own contemporaries in the Western lands who believe themselves to have wholly surrendered all their former or ancestral Christian convictions, are nevertheless left with some impulse or feeling of gratitude for the blessings they have enjoyed, though they are now without any means of making this articulate; and this is not the least of the vestigial forms of faith of which I have already spoken. More than twenty years ago I offered two examples of this: Katherine Mansfield's exclamation, when speaking of her delight in a lovely spot in the Alps, 'If only one could make some small grasshoppery sound of praise to some one, of thanks to some one—but to who?'; and a 'prayer' I once heard offered by a humanist preacher in America who claimed not to believe

[1] Op. cit. (1936), p. 97.   [2] Ibid., p. 98.

in God, and who, instead of beginning each phrase with the words 'We thank thee', satisfied some inward urge by saying simply 'We are thankful.'[1] But of course we cannot be thankful except to a person. If the preacher had said 'We rejoice', he would indeed be leaving God out; but by saying what he did, he was unwittingly acknowledging God's presence (though instead of reproaching him for inconsistency and wishing he had the courage of his humanist convictions, I confess I was glad that, if I may so put it, he had the conviction of his courage, in however unconscious and repressed a form). So much at least Katherine Mansfield clearly understood. There afterwards came to my attention another virtually identical remark made by Sir Leslie Stephen on the occasion of the death of his first wife in 1871 in a letter to James Russell Lowell —and indeed it is the most apt of the three cases since I have always regarded John Stuart Mill, Karl Marx and Leslie Stephen as in one sense the farthest from belief of all unbelievers in that their chief point was not that religion was nonsense (though that they certainly believed) but that it was the most harmful of all nonsenses; 'I thank—something—that I loved her as heartily as I know how to love, that I would have died for her with pleasure, and that (still more) I scarcely ever saw a cloud upon her bright face.'[2]

[1] *Our Knowledge of God* (1939), p. 248 f.
[2] F. W. Maitland, *The Life and Letters of Sir Leslie Stephen* (1906), p. 256.

CHAPTER XIII

Retrospect

With the fore-going chapter I have really finished my argument but some kind of epilogue seems to be required, and I do not know what form to give it except a series of retrospective comments on the way we have travelled. In making these comments I propose to 'let myself go' and 'give myself away' to an extent to which I have not hitherto done, being more outspoken in my impatience with some of the schools of thought and the individual writers in my discussion of whom I have always tried to mingle a due deference with my criticism.

*   *   *

In the early chapters I argued at considerable length with the school of logical or conceptual analysis which has recently dominated the philosophical thinking of Oxford and Cambridge, has spread to the provincial English Universities, and is increasingly invading the American Universities and Colleges. I have made many concessions to this school, have accepted no small part of what it puts forward, and have learned much from it. But when I am asked to swallow it whole, I become angry, and the more of the recent books I read by its representatives, the angrier I become. I therefore ask permission to read to you rather a long passage from the chapter entitled 'A Crisis in my Mental History' in John Stuart Mill's *Autobiography*:

For now I saw, or thought I saw, what I had always before received with incredulity—that the habit of analysis has a tendency to wear away the feelings: as indeed it has, when no other mental element is cultivated, and the analysing spirit remains without its natural complements and correctives. The very excellence of analysis (I argued) is that it tends to weaken and undermine whatever is the result of prejudice; that it enables us mentally to separate ideas which have only casually clung together: and no associations whatever could ultimately resist this dissolving force, were it not that we owe to analysis our clearest knowledge of the permanent sequences in nature; the real connexions between Things not dependent on our will and feelings; natural laws, by virtue of which, in many cases, one thing is inseparable from another in fact; which laws, in proportion as they are clearly perceived and imaginatively realized, cause our ideas of things which are always joined together in Nature, to cohere more and more closely in our thoughts. Analytic habits may thus even strengthen the associations between causes and effects, means and ends, but tend altogether to weaken those which are, to speak familiarly, a *mere* matter of feeling. They are therefore (I thought) favourable to prudence and clear-sightedness, but a perpetual worm at the root both of the passions and of the virtues; and, above all, fearfully undermine all desires, and all pleasures, which are the effects of association, that is, according to the theory I held, all except the purely physical and organic; of the entire insufficiency to make life desirable, no one had a stronger conviction than I had.[1]

It is significant that the term 'analysis' was familiar to Mill, not only in the *Autobiography* (which was published only post-humously) but quite certainly also at the very early period in his life when 'the crisis in his mental history' overtook him; and that it was used, if not in precisely the same sense, at least in a sense bearing a very strong ancestral resemblance to the sense in which it has recently been used by the logical analysts. I agree with Mill, then, that the practice of analysis, when it stands alone as so many of its practitioners have insisted that it must, is 'a perpetual worm at the root both of the passions and of the virtues'.

*   *   *

My next remark is one which I do not at all wish to apply to any of the distinguished advocates of logical analysis against which I have argued. I have argued against their philosophy, but I believe in the men in spite of their philosophy, that is, I believe that in their 'passions and virtues' and in their general

[1] Op. cit., chap. V.

management of their lives and their relations to their neighbours, they manifest qualities of mind and heart to which their
philosophy, as such, does not seem to entitle them. But there
are some among those who listen to them, or who have imbibed
the outlook of a reductive naturalism from some quite different
and probably much older source (by means however indirect),
of whom I could not say the same. Not do I here speak of their
morals in any ordinary sense, for we are all miserable sinners,
but of a certain painful restriction of outlook, of interest, of
understanding and of sympathy which seems to leave them
as very incomplete human beings. I find this to be true of
some students of science, including not a few who are engaged
in scientific research or who occupy (perhaps junior?) teaching
posts in our Universities. So much do their minds travel along
one particular track that I find it difficult to establish any
contact with them. They are incomplete personalities.

On the other hand I know well that there are men and
women of the most active aesthetic, ethical or devoutly religious
outlook who are incomplete personalities also. I have known
artists, or students of one or other art, who seemed to be quite
imperceptive of any values in life beyond their own narrowly
restricted aesthetic field, knowing nothing but 'art for art's
sake'. But those whom I have chiefly in mind are the representatives of a type of piety that has never subjected itself to
any kind of logical or other analysis. They lack just what the
most myopic students of natural science possess, their own
myopia being of precisely the opposite kind. With these also I
find it very difficult to communicate. And here I should like
to quote a remarkable passage from one of Thomas Carlyle's
essays:

It is worthy of note that, in our little British Isle, the two grand
Antagonisms of Europe should have stood embodied, under their
very highest concentration, in two men produced simultaneously
among ourselves. Samuel Johnson and David Hume . . . were
children nearly of the same year; through life they were spectators
of the same Life-movement; often inhabitants of the same city.
Greater contrast, in all things, between two great men, could
not be. . . .

Through Life they did not meet; as contrasts, 'like in unlike', love each other, so might they too have loved, and communed kindly, had not the terrestrial dross and darkness that was in them withstood! One day their spirits, what Truth was in each, will be found working, living in harmony and free union, even here below. They were the two half-men of their time: whoso should combine the intrepid Candour and decisive scientific Clearness of Hume, with the Reverence, the Love and devout Humility of Johnson were the whole man of a new time. Till such whole man arrive for us, and the distracted time admit of such, might the Heavens but bless poor England with half-men worthy to tie the shoe-latchets of these, resembling these even from afar![1]

I have quoted this passage because it gives me the term for which I have been seeking, 'half-men'. In a general sense I accept Carlyle's verdict on the two half-men he instances. But I take leave to think that Johnson had the better half. 'Reverence, love and devout humility' are qualities more necessary to wholeness of outlook than 'decisive scientific clearness'. They engage us, and enable us to meet with one another, on a far deeper level. At all events, it is with the half-men who know nothing but analysis, and leave us with nothing but the reductive naturalism in which it issues, that my present argument has been concerned; and I confess that in my heart of hearts my impatience with them knows no bounds.

*   *   *

Next I would say something in further explanation of the respects in which I differ from Dr Karl Barth. I need not say that Dr Barth is a great man and a very great theologian, because everybody knows it. He has changed the face of Protestant theology far more radically than any other theologian during my life-time. He has also made more difference than anybody else to my own attempts at theologizing. Whatever the measure of our agreements or disagreements with him, we have all to reckon with him. I have often said that there can be no hopeful forward advance beyond his teaching,

---

[1] Thomas Carlyle, essay on Boswell's *Life of Johnson* (1832), ad fin.

as I fervently hope there will be, if we attempt to go *round* it instead of *through* it. There are already many signs of a reaction towards a more liberal outlook, but it must be a liberalism which, while regaining some of the lost pre-Barthian ground, has been much chastened by the many valuable things he has taught us.

I had of course always believed that there is no ultimate salvation for mankind save in Jesus Christ, but when I began to read Dr Barth's books, what struck me at once as unfamiliar was his insistence that mankind had no *knowledge* of God save in Jesus Christ. This is new teaching, and it is precisely what I have never been able to accept. I still believe, as I had always done, that at all times God 'left himself not without witness',[1] but has revealed something of his holy nature to men through creation, that is 'through the things that are made';[2] through 'their conscience also bearing witness, and their thoughts the meanwhile accusing or else excusing one another';[3] and above all through the law, whether this be the Torah of the Israelite people to whom 'were committed the oracles of God'[4] or the works of the law 'written in the hearts of the Gentiles':[5] and all this is knowledge which man possesses before he meets with Jesus Christ.

It is clear to me that this is the view which pervades the whole Bible. It has nowhere been more strongly re-affirmed, in cogent and indeed merciless refutation of Dr Barth, than in Dr Gustaf Wingren's book *Theology in Conflict*, and from it I give you the following brief passages:

The knowledge of God which man lacks he receives from Scripture, i.e. from Christ. This is the simplest formula in which Barth's theology can be expressed. And about this formula we must say that it is entirely unbiblical. There is no possibility of interpreting the biblical writings correctly from this point of view.[6]

That which disappears from our attention through the theological work of Barth in this generation is the living and active God of the Bible, this God who continually creates and gives.[7]

Barth has the ability to a very large degree of being able to employ

---

[1] Acts 14. 17.   [2] Rom. 1. 20.   [3] Rom. 2. 15.   [4] Rom. 3. 2.   [5] Rom. 2. 15.
[6] G. Wingren, *Theology in Conflict*, Eng. trans. (1958), p. 42.   [7] Ibid., p. 43.

the language of Scripture in a system that is totally foreign to the Bible.[1]

He has removed the law as a power that rules over man even before the preaching of the gospel appears.[2]

The gospel is a part, the more important part, in a history of salvation in which creation, the election of Israel, the covenants, etc., also belong. If it is separated from this context, it is no longer a 'gospel', nor a witness to that Agape of which the New Testament speaks. The gospel acquires its meaning through its connections forward and backward, to creation and to the consummation. The gospel itself presupposes that every man to whom it comes stands subjected to the conditions of God's acts even before he hears it. . . .[3]

All that is very uncompromisingly spoken, though not nearly so uncompromisingly as Dr Barth's attack on Dr Emil Brunner in his pamphlet called *Nein* with its 'Angry Introduction'.[4] I should probably not myself have been quite so outspoken as Dr Wingren, but I am in full agreement with him none the less.

* * *

Next, I propose to return to the topic with which I began, namely, certainty. My contention then was that, while indeed it seems impossible to enunciate any theoretical propositions concerning God and the unseen world about which we could be certain that they were true just as we enunciated them, nevertheless all our experience, in this realm as in others, is 'transfused with certitude' or, in Tillich's phrase, that certitude 'pulsates through all our thinking'. Our direct knowledge, I agreed, is not knowledge of truths but knowledge of realities, and it is out of our immediate contact with these realities that certitude is born.

At a later point I contended that the affirmations of faith are always practically orientated, providing us with a frame of reference within which our lives are to be lived rather than as adding to the sum of our theoretic, speculative, not to say

---

[1] Ibid., p. 125. [2] Ibid., p. 159.
[3] Ibid., p. 19. The first sentence of this quotation has already been given in a footnote to § 29 above.
[4] *Nein* (1934); Eng. trans. in *Natural Theology* (1946).

scientific, knowledge; and I ventured to use in description of them Kant's phrase 'practical and regulative', though not without pointing out my discontent with Kant's own use of it. Still elsewhere I remarked that there is nothing of which I am more firmly persuaded than that the right attitude to life is that of the man whose whole comportment and activity have their root in the sentiment of gratitude, and I added that 'it is precisely in regard to such a conviction as this that I feel able to speak of certitude, and to do so without the least scruple or diffidence'.

And now I shall ask your leave to quote another passage from Mill's *Autobiography*. Speaking in the chapter entitled 'My Most Valuable Friendship' of the remarkable influence exercised upon him by his wife, Mill writes as follows:

With those who, like all the best and wisest of mankind, are dissatisfied with life as it is, and whose feelings are wholly identified with its radical amendment, there are two main regions of thought. One is the region of ultimate aims; the constituent elements of the highest realizable ideal of human life. The other is that of the immediately useful and practically attainable. My own strength lay wholly in the uncertain and slippery intermediate region, that of theory or moral and political science: respecting the conclusions of which, in any of the forms in which I have received or originated them, whether as political economy, analytic psychology, logic, philosophy of history or anything else, it is not the least of my intellectual obligations to her that I have derived from her a wise scepticism, which, while it has not hindered me from following out the honest exercise of my own thinking faculties to whatever conclusions might result from it, has put me on my guard against holding or announcing these conclusions with a degree of confidence which the nature of such speculations does not warrant. . . .[1]

Surely Mill had learned something immensely valuable when his wife persuaded him that 'real certainty' lay not in the theoretical realm but in 'the region of ultimate aims; the constituent elements of the highest realizable ideal of human life'. And as to the other region which Mill mentions, 'that of the immediately useful and practically attainable', I should prefer to express myself in a less utilitarian fashion, and say that we

[1] Op. cit., chap. VI.

can often be certain of our immediate duty, even when the intermediate steps between it and 'our ultimate aims' are shrouded in darkness for us. Perhaps Mill's friend, Thomas Carlyle, was not after all so far wrong when he said, '*Do the Duty which lies nearest thee*; which thou knowest to be a Duty! Thy second Duty will already have become clearer.'[1]

I have contended throughout that Christian faith is essentially trust. It is placing our complete reliance on God—Father, Son and Holy Spirit, committing ourselves wholly to his care, nowise doubting that he will betray our commitment. I have always been careful to add that there are certain intellectual implicates latently contained in such trust. When I trust a man, I have grounds for trusting him. But it is often very difficult to say what they are; and when I try to express them in the form of propositions which I am prepared to make about him, I am never sure that I have got them quite right. The kind of assurance which attaches to my trust itself no longer attaches to the reasons I give, to the theoretical propositions I formulate. If we can say with the Reverend Thomas Brown of Whitehall in his version of Martial's epigram,

> I do not love you, Dr. Fell,
> But why I cannot tell;
> But this I know full well,
> I do not love you, Dr. Fell[2]

so surely we can say that we love and trust our friends, while finding it very difficult to tell why. The reasons Christians give for their trust in God stand, of course, on an altogether more secure basis, because they rest upon the accumulated wisdom and keen and tireless inquiry of the theologians of twenty centuries, beginning with the apostolic authors themselves. Nevertheless not one such theological proposition attracts to itself the full degree of assurance that attaches to the Christian's simple trust in God.

*　　*　　*

---

[1] *Sartor Resartus* (1833–34), Book II, chap. IX.
[2] Thomas Brown 1663–1704; Martial, *Epigrams*, i, 32.

This leads directly to the last topic over which I wish to cast a retrospective glance. I want to say something more in defence of the title which I have ventured to give to the lectures and to the book as a whole, and I shall begin by quoting some words of Dr John Hick. The Christian, he writes,

sees in his situation as a human being a significance to which the appropriate response is a religious trust and obedience. His interpretative leap carries him into a world which exists through the will of a holy, righteous and loving Being who is the creator and sustainer of all that is. Behind the world—to use an almost inevitable spatial metaphor—there is apprehended to be an omnipotent, personal Will, whose purpose toward mankind guarantees men's highest good and blessedness. The believer finds that he is at all times in the presence of this holy Will. . . .

Thus the primary religious perception, or basic act of religious interpretation, is not to be described as either a reasoned conclusion or an unreasoned hunch that there is a God. It is, putatively, an apprehension of the divine presence within the believer's human experience. It is not an inference to a general truth, but a 'divine-human encounter', a mediated meeting with the living God.[1]

It will be noted that although Dr Hick's book did not come into my hands, nor was it in fact published, until well after I had completed the draft of the relevant chapters of this book, he insists, as I have done, that faith is an act of perceiving rather than of conceiving, that he is not afraid to apply to it the language of vision, and that he speaks of the presence of God within the believer's human experience. Moreover, it is just because the divine presence is perceived by us, never in isolation from, but always in and through some familiar human experience that he speaks of it as a *mediated* meeting with the living God.

It has always seemed to me that much confusion has surrounded the frequently quoted Biblical saying that 'no man has seen God at any time.' The question is whether the word 'see' is here used in its primary sense of seeing with the eyes of flesh, or in its derivative and no doubt symbolic sense of seeing with what we may call the eyes of the spirit or, if you prefer it,

[1] John Hick, *Faith and Knowledge* (1957), p. 129.

the eyes of the mind. Now it is clear that for us today there can be no question about it. Nobody can see God with his corporeal eyes, because there is nothing there to see; God is not a corporeal being located in space, so that in no circumstances could he be seen in the primary sense of seeing. On the other hand it is equally clear that the early Hebrews did not know this. They thought of God as having a body, and according to the thirty-third chapter of Exodus Moses was permitted to see part of his body with his own bodily eyes, but not permitted to see God's face.

And the Lord said unto Moses . . . Thou canst not see my face: for there shall no man see me and live. And the Lord said, Behold, there is a place by me, and thou shalt stand upon a rock: and it shall come to pass, while my glory passeth by, that I will put thee in a clift of the rock, and will cover thee with my hand while I pass by: and I will take away mine hand, and thou shalt see my back parts: but my face shall not be seen.[1]

As time went on, the Israelites came more and more to understand the incorporeality of God, and of course in the New Testament it is everywhere taken for granted, but there the old phrase that 'no man has ever seen God' is never allowed to stand unqualified. It still remains true that the perception (or sense or vision) of God's presence is never vouchsafed save in the context of familiar experience, and is thus mediated by such experience. The chief of such contexts, which governs all the rest, is of course the Incarnation, that is, the appearance of God in the man Jesus. 'We have seen his glory',[2] says St John —and glory both in the later Old Testament and in the New is really only another word for presence. 'Nobody has ever seen God', but 'the only Son, who is in the bosom of the Father, he has made him plain (ἐκεῖνος ἐξηγήσατο).'[3] And again, 'He who has seen me has seen the Father.'[4] But a further context of the vision of God, a further mediation of the divine presence, is spoken of in the Johannine Epistles. 'Nobody has ever seen God', but, 'if we love one another God dwells in us and his love is perfected in us.'[5] 'He who does evil

---

[1] Exod. 33. 17–23. [2] John 1. 14. [3] John 1. 18. [4] John 14. 9. [5] 1 John 4. 12.

has not seen God.'[1] In the Beatitudes we read that 'Blessed are the pure in heart, for they shall see God'.[2] The Beatitudes are of course eschatological, pointing to a state of things that has not yet supervened, but I do not myself believe that the fulfilment our Lord had in mind was 'beyond history' and in another world, but rather on this familiar earth, after his own death and resurrection and the formation of the pentecostal community. This, however, is a large and still hotly debated issue, and I shall not press it further.

At all events my main contention throughout has been that we have to do, not with an absent God about whom we have a certain amount of information, but with a God whose living and active presence with us can be perceived by faith in a large variety of human contexts and situations. This is the true burden of Kierkegaard's—the only original—existentialism; the true meaning of his declaration that true Christianity is not doctrine but existence. As he says somewhere—and I regret that, though I once copied the words carefully, I cannot now find the reference, 'Truth is not an objective statement about certain relations of being, but a form of existence in which such relations are actualized.'

* * *

And now, I do not believe that Lord Gifford would object to my quoting in conclusion a prayer by Henry Vaughan, the last of our Caroline poets: 'Abide with us, O most blessed and merciful Saviour, for it is toward evening and the day is far spent. As long as Thou art present with us, we are in the light. When Thou art present, all is brightness, all is sweetness. We discourse with Thee, live with Thee and lie down with Thee. Abide then with us, O Thou whom our soul loveth; Thou Sun of righteousness with healing under Thy wings, arise in our hearts. Make Thy light then to shine in darkness, as a perfect day in the dead of night.'

[1] 3 John. 11.   [2] Matt. 5. 8.

Index

ρ